RETURN OF THE WHITE SERPENT

By

David Leesley

First published in 2012 by:

Penwith Press
Cornwall
UK
www.penwithpress.co.uk

ISBN 978 – 0 – 9533316 – 3 – 5

Printed by TJ International Ltd.
Trecerus Industrial Estate
Padstow, Cornwall
PL28 8RW

MIX
Paper from
responsible sources
FSC
www.fsc.org   FSC® C013056

ACKNOWLEDGMENTS

To May Harrison, Professor S R M Ellis, Margery White,
Captain Andrew Douglas, MHK, Catherine Bell,
Nicöla C Summers, Mo Colley,
Barbara Meiklejohn-Free, Paul Johnston,
Jill Moss and Thomas Egan

© David Leesley
Art work – Paul E Johnston

DEDICATION

This book is dedicated to Aaron Ross Leesley

May he stand firm as the next White Serpent

CONTENTS

Page

WORLD LOCATOR MAP

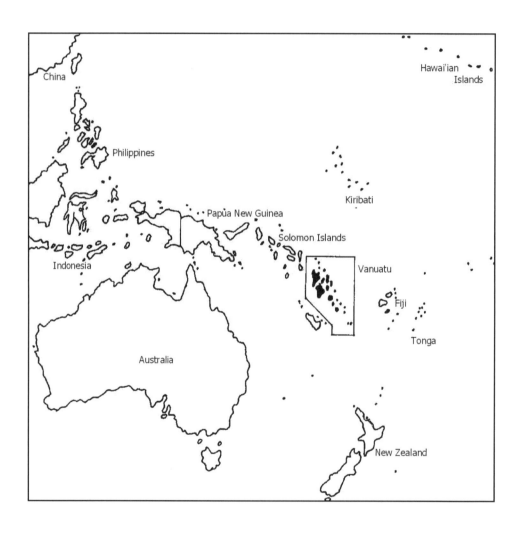

VANUATU

Torres Islands

Banks Islands

Espiritu
Santo

Ambae

Maewo

Pentecost

Malo

Ambrym

Malekula

Paama
Ulveah

Epi

Shepherd Islands

Efate

Port Vila

Erromango

Aniwa

Tanna

Futuna

Aneityum

Matthew and Hunter Islands

TANNA ISLAND

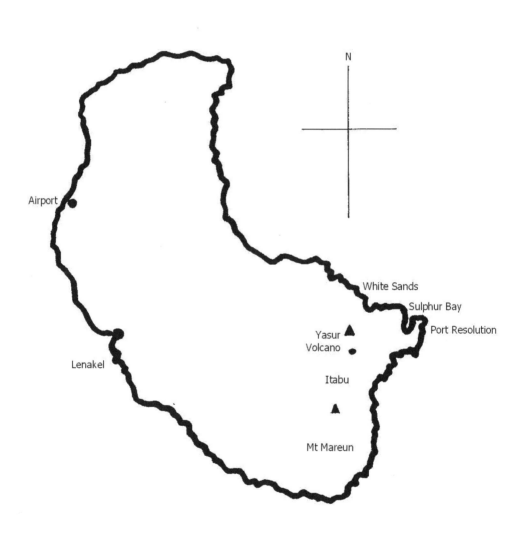

Airport

Lenakel

White Sands

Sulphur Bay

Port Resolution

Yasur ▲
Volcano ●

Itabu

▲

Mt Mareun

N

x

PREFACE

We are on the threshold of a new dawn of human enlightenment. Ancient physical rites of passage, now lost to us in the West, are returning at a higher level of consciousness to enable us to reach beyond the illusion of self (ego) into the metaphysical reality of our true potential – that of becoming God men and God women.

It is an exciting time to step out of familiar external belief systems and indoctrination of the mind to go deep within, to the place of our own truth – the heart.

We are in what is sometimes called "the end times" where, globally, ancient cultural and tribal myths are being fulfilled to enable humanity to ascend spiritually.

All of us have a vital role to play in this process, right NOW.

I have learnt that the greatest and most powerful thing we can do is simply to be ourselves, in other words, to become empowered from within, to find and acknowledge who we truly are as individuals by reconnecting to Spirit in the appropriate way. Once this occurs, our energy bodies will change their frequency and automatically we will have the power and potential to alter the probable outcomes of humanity and, therefore, our world, to one of peace, love and respect for all life.

Have courage to follow the calling of your own heart. Only then will you find your path of destiny, as I have done.

INTRODUCTION

This is the true story of a spiritual quest. Through a series of bizarre synchronicities, David found himself in a situation where he was reunited with his spiritual twin on a small tropical island in the South Pacific, where in a tribal legend there was a mythical link to the Isle of Man (British Isles). It is a story, recorded in his journal, of spiritual awakening, sacred ceremonies, initiations, tests and trials, tribal warfare and marriage. It is a unique and extraordinary account of an endangered way of life with all its joys and difficulties.

High Chief Wai Wai Rawi had asked David to tell their story to those in the West. The kastom (custom) people are highly intelligent but, on the whole, are uneducated to western standards so names are spelled phonetically and certain things could not be interpreted or explained. David always cross-referenced answers with a minimum of two people to get correlation. When a letter is written to the Chief, he has to find somebody who can read it to him, then somebody else who can write a reply on his behalf; this is providing he can find writing paper and an envelope! This process can take many weeks.

This story then is not meant to be an intellectual, anthropological work of mind-numbing boredom, but rather an account of a simple, magical journey of self-discovery, that culminates in the reuniting of the black and white serpent twins that the tribal storytellers spoke of for many generations around their naka-mal fires, and the secret reconnection to the Dragon Men. The first stage of the ancient legend is now fulfilled.

This story can now be told. Now that the serpents are reunited, how will the future unfold?

Subheadings of key words have been used to give the reader a "flavour" of each section.

PART 1

THE DRAGON SWORD

Destiny

The shockwave from the volcano startled me. It was an especially violent explosion this time that shook the whole valley like a swaying field of green barley, causing fine dust to fall from the thatch of my leaf hut, covering my naked body. I raised my eyes from where I knelt in prayer to the ancestors, as commanded by the High Chief, to see hundreds of large black fruit bats circling, like startled crows, from their day roosts high above the canopies of the huge banyan trees growing on the slopes at the bottom of the rugged cliff face of Mt. Mareun. White sulphurous smoke briefly engulfed my body and the hut, obscuring the valley, causing a small brown lizard with an iridescent blue stripe down the centre of its back to scuttle for cover into one of my discarded leather shoes, now green with mould from the constant heat and high humidity.

I felt as though I had somehow slipped through a portal into a lost moment of history, feeling, sensing with every fibre of my being as my ancient ancestors must have done at the dawn of humanity. My soul was lost in the place between time and space. I felt as though I had returned home to the land of my forefathers in a way that cannot be explained, yet only realised and understood in the deepest recesses of my heart. Salty tears stung my eyes falling down my cheeks on to the pandanus mats. Then I heard it! The sound I had been expecting, yet secretly dreading, the repetitive drumbeat, quickening, sending its echo of the call of sacred ceremony to the warriors in the distant villages hidden in green foliage, visible only by their blue fire smoke. They were coming for me now. I felt so alone and vulnerable, yet now was the time for courage. What did they intend to do to me? ……..

Let me now explain how I came to be in this situation. Several months earlier my mother had received a letter from her elderly friend, May, in Australia, saying that she was dying and would one of the twins escort her home to the Isle of Man as, for a variety of reasons, her family were unable to do this. May's husband, Tommy, had died some months earlier so she was persuaded to sell their home and move out to Australia in late 2002. It was now April 2003. My twin brother, Barry, was unable to get time off work at such short notice so, after speaking with my employer, I managed to get compassionate leave, but with loss of pay.

My mother telephoned May to say I could come when she wanted me to do so. May instructed us to go to a travel agent immediately to book return flights for her and myself in Business Class! When I had provisional bookings and costs, we contacted May who posted a cheque to us which arrived within the week. Initially I had refused to contemplate this idea, for, as a teenager, I had emigrated alone to Australia and spent several years out there. Now, aged 49, I didn't feel like facing another long-haul flight in "cattle class". The fact that I was travelling Business Class helped to change my mind, yet I still didn't want to go as I would lose my wages for three weeks and escorting a very elderly lady, I guessed, would be a nightmare.

Basically I was looking for any excuse why I couldn't or shouldn't go, even though my soul yearned to do so. Then I began to notice constant information about the area around the Solomon Islands coming to me from different sources. Inexplicably I knew I had to go there and that the trip to Australia was my passage "arranged" by Spirit. Why? I didn't know. So I kept rejecting my intuition and inner feelings and began to get sick, really sick. As a spiritual healer, I recognised the symptoms and realised there was a very important reason why Spirit wanted me to go to the Solomon Islands at this time. I still persisted in denying the obvious facts until one morning I could hardly move in my bed. I couldn't get up without severe pain in my chest. I thought I was having a heart attack. I was on my knees at the side of my bed after crawling to the toilet, when I opened my heart to Spirit and agreed fully with their plan, knowing secretly that this was the answer all along, but being too stubborn and fearful of the unknown to admit it. Luckily it was a weekend so I managed to crawl back into bed and fall asleep, waking two hours later totally pain free with a sensation of being energetically expanded, lighter and less dense. I knew that something very important was ahead of me and prepared myself for the task ahead fully and completely. I felt excited, exhilarated and at peace now that I had committed my heart. I also knew that, if Spirit wanted me to fulfil some plan, they would prepare the way.

Everything went smoothly from that day on. The airline tickets were confirmed, having been paid for with a financial adjustment, collected, and within a few days I left my home on the Isle of Man heading for the South Pacific, via the USA and New Zealand. I arrived in Brisbane, Australia at the end of April 2003, telephoning May from my hotel room to let her know I had arrived and that her tickets were now in the hotel safe. She was ecstatic over the phone. I had already informed her I had planned to spend almost two weeks in the Solomon Islands which I obviously was paying for myself. She agreed to this wholeheartedly and had already pencilled in the date and time of our departure back to the Isle of Man!

I had arrived at Brisbane in the morning so decided to ignore the jet lag and go to a travel agent near the hotel. I had been to Brisbane before, therefore had a rough idea of my way around. The travel agent could not schedule a flight to the Solomon Islands for the date I wanted for some reason, so suggested Vanuatu, the neighbouring archipelago. I had not heard of Vanuatu (pronounced van-WAH-too) but within my heart it felt right. The Solomon Islands no longer did!

When I was shown on the map of the South Pacific where Vanuatu is, I realised that I knew it by its former name, The New Hebrides. The travel agent insisted on booking me into a 5 Star hotel in the capital of Vanuatu, Port Vila, but I refused because I do not do "tourist" travel. I left feeling disheartened, exhausted, and I returned to the hotel. On the table was a free tourist periodical about Brisbane. When I turned the pages at random, I saw an advert for Air Vanuatu with their details so I immediately walked back into the city and to their office. I spoke to friendly staff who were very helpful and was shown a variety of brochures for tourist resorts which I dismissed. I asked if there was a remote place I could go to away from the bloated tourists where I could interact with the indigenous people. A small insignificant brochure was located at the back of a cabinet and on the front was a picture of the active volcano Mt Yasur on Tanna

Island. This was it! I had found my destination. My heart sang. I booked and paid for the flight to Port Vila, then the onward flight to Tanna Island. I also paid for accommodation and transport on Tanna, but I had to get this documentation from a travel office in Port Vila on my arrival, then return to the domestic terminal to catch the flight to Tanna Island. I was assured that the connections would be fine and all documentation ready for collection. I would fly out in two days' time which would enable me to get some shopping, Vanuatu currency, Vatu, and some rest.

2nd May 2003

Colonial oppression

I left on the early flight to Port Vila. It was exciting to look out of the window as we flew over New Caledonia and the Coral Sea. This was truly the South Pacific; it was amazing, the vastness of endless blue ocean from horizon to horizon.

We landed in Vila, as it is known locally, and, on disembarking from the aircraft, the hot steamy humid air enveloped me like a sauna. A man in native costume blew a conch shell on the tarmac near a large rain puddle to welcome us. Whilst going through immigration we were entertained by a colourful string band playing and singing local songs.

As soon as I emerged into the sunlight again I went to a taxi rank, my shirt stuck to my back. At first I thought that the vehicle that came to me was a refugee from a stock car race. The back door was opened and helping hands put my bags on to the rear seat which looked as though a demented terrier had shredded it. Stuffing and padding was stuck back in place with carpet tape. It was a left hand drive vehicle so I got into the front passenger seat which virtually collapsed. My window had dropped into the door panel and the door was held together with wire. None of the vehicles had tread on any of their tyres or had working indicators. One working headlight seemed to be a luxury. This was my kind of vehicle – exciting, dangerous and great fun! Thank God the health and safety brigade had not found this place to ruin self-expression and the joy of life.

The driver was friendly and jovial and spoke good English. We drove over potholed roads and through dilapidated commercial areas to the centre of Vila and located the travel office where I left the driver waiting in the car with my bags. I went to collect my documentation, which was not ready. I had to wait some time and when I eventually returned to the car, the driver had disappeared and the vehicle left abandoned with all of the windows down, simply because they couldn't be wound up, and my bags left on display to all the passing pedestrians. The bags were untouched and all of the local people appeared to be very honest. I asked a few people nearby where the taxi driver may be found and they directed me to a nearby boules match, a remnant of French Colonial rule. The driver seemed unable to comprehend my anxiety of getting back to the airport in time to catch my flight to Tanna Island but, after eventually extracting him from the match, we raced to the airport and I arrived just in time.

The domestic terminal was very basic. I was weighed, as well as my bags. It was a small aircraft flown by a company called Van Air and it was full. There were a few Australian tourists on board staying at a local resort. The plane was small with everything well worn and grubby. On my arrival at White Sands Airport in Tanna, I was met by a native woman with her driver who took me to their guest house, or "bungalow" as they are known, which was about twenty minutes away in Lenakel, the capital town of the island. My accommodation was a concrete brick building which was suffocatingly hot, even though Tanna Island was less humid than Efate Island which was where the capital was.

On the pillow of my single bed lay a red hibiscus flower which was a local tradition for all guests. The guest house was near the beach, which was rough white coral sand and pebbles leading down to a cobalt blue sea. White crested waves rolled over the black volcanic reefs which were so sharp they cut the soles of my hiking boots. The locals walked barefoot over them! Several men were fishing with rods and others were fishing in dug-out outrigger canoes at sea. I wandered over the reef astounded by the array of multi-coloured tropical fish caught in the clear rock pools between tides. Some pools were so deep they seemed bottomless. To prevent cutting my boots further I decided to walk along the shore amongst the mangroves and trees. Often I encountered posts with signs in Bislama (a form of pidgin English) saying "Private" or an animal skull on a post. I suddenly realised that these reefs were all private property and that, in essence, I was trespassing. I decided to return to the guest house after wandering around the market where I met the owner, a retired national government Member of Parliament representing Tanna in the Province of TAFEA. We spoke at length and he told me all about the problems they had with the Anglo-French Condominium Colonial rulers when the country was known as The New Hebrides, where certain parts of the country were governed by the English and others by the French. Not wanting to go to war with each other over a few "worthless" islands, the French and the English decided to share the country and the outcome was known locally as Pandemonium as both Colonial powers had their own courts, police forces, health services, education systems, prison systems and currencies. Depending on which area you lived in, you either spoke English or French. I wish to protect this man's identity for he explained to me his involvement in the uprisings for independence which finally occurred in 1980 with the new name of Vanuatu. This means "our land" and its native people are known as Ni-Vanuatu or Ni-Vans which means "of Vanuatu". The natives are classed as Melanesians.

We talked late into the evening and I asked him many questions about his country and customs. He lent me several books to look at the independence struggle and general information. What I found was, initially, Commander James Cook gave the country its name as the archipelago's rugged islands reminded him of the Hebrides of Scotland. Vanuatu has three official languages – Bislama, English and French – although the country has over one hundred distinct traditional languages still in use. Bislama, or Pidgin English, introduced by Colonials enabled the local islanders to communicate for the first time with each other. This is probably the only good thing that came out of Colonialism. The French still claim Vanuatu's two southerly islands of Matthew and Hunter to extend their ocean territory of New Caledonia.

Until recently it was official government policy to restrict tourism.

This has now changed and tourism is openly encouraged throughout the islands. The early peoples of Vanuatu came from Papua, New Guinea, and travelled between islands and, indeed, crossed oceans in long-range canoes carrying with them pigs, poultry, yams, taro, and so on. Some of the raiding parties carried fifty warriors in large ocean-going canoes. Tribal warfare was commonplace, along with cannibalism, with reprisal raids lasting for generations. The last officially recorded cannibal feast was in 1969 (see Appendix A).

The first European to visit the archipelago was Quirós in 1606, a Portuguese in service to the Spanish Crown, who claimed the islands for Spain. Later in 1766, Bougainville claimed the islands for France. Then in 1774, Cook claimed them for Britain. Trading ships that anchored soon cut down most of the sandalwood trees for the Chinese incense market. The payment for these was often captured men from enemy tribes who were then cooked and eaten. This eventually led on to "blackbirding", basically the exploitation of black slave labour taken to other Pacific islands and the Queensland sugar plantations.

Christian missionaries arrived in the 1800s. The early Polynesian missionaries sent by the church were killed and eaten. When the church found these expendable people were no longer being killed, they sent in white missionaries from Europe who systematically set about destroying the culture and way of life of the indigenous people. The missionaries often knowingly distributed diseased blankets to the local people to make them sick and weak or they contracted western diseases, such as cholera, smallpox, dysentery and influenza, to which they had no immunity. Thousands of people died.

Vanuatu is a Y-shaped chain of islands, about 83 of them inhabited, south of the Solomon Islands. The current population is approximately 206,000 people. Vanuatu lies on the top of the Pacific Rim of Fire which causes frequent volcanic eruptions and earthquakes. It has nine active volcanoes, seven on land and two under the sea. The national land area is approximately 12,300 square kilometres. Cyclones are a common phenomenon in Vanuatu between November and May, which is the wet season, and the name Tanna means earth or ground in the local dialect. The area of Tanna Island is 565 square kilometres compared to the Isle of Man which is 572 square kilometres. I found it fascinating that both islands are virtually the same size.

I talked with my host long into the night about kastom healing traditions; also, which fascinated me, about the spiritual aspects of the people of these local islands. He explained that his brother was a kastom healer and that one of the traditional techniques that he uses involves relieving pain by a cut to the bone to release the trapped evil spirits, which is then filled with magic leaves. Often the patient would die of infection so are sometimes now taken to the local hospital for medical intervention, which really annoys the local healers. Because of my early departure the next day, I was unable to meet his brother. I learnt much from this man about his country of which he was fiercely proud and rightly so.

4th May 2003
Interrogation   Kava ritual   Projectile vomiting
I woke early to the sound of the sea and laughing children. I dressed

and went for a stroll at 6 o'clock before breakfast and my departure at 8 o'clock for southeast Tanna. Blue smoke filtered through the thatches of the bakeries as fresh bread was being made. I was bitten several times during the night and early morning by mosquitoes which, as usual, turned into large, red, itchy weals. Even at this early hour people were about their business. Most of the women dressed in bright floral print dresses which had long ribbons hanging from their sleeves. These were a leftover relic from the prudish missionaries who, shocked at seeing the bare breasts of the local women, forced them to wear what became known as "Mother Hubbard dresses". This tradition persists even today.

I returned for a breakfast of fresh bread and tropical fruits followed by hot tea. By the time I had finished, a four-wheel drive pick-up truck was waiting to take me to Loanengo Village, a drive over rough roads taking about two hours. Pick-ups are the island's taxi and bus service. People from the outlying regions use them to bring their produce and animals to market to sell, then return with items they have bought, such as axes, machetes, or a cooking pot. Some of these trucks are covered by a tarpaulin over a metal frame; most just have planks in the back to sit on. When it rains, you get wet – very wet. I sat in the front with the driver. We chatted politely for a while; then I was glad to sit in silence and enjoy the breath-taking scenery of the island.

Shortly after leaving Lenakel, we drove over a rickety bridge and on to red dirt roads which, at this time of year, were dry and dusty. When a vehicle passed in the opposite direction, I wound up the windows until the cloud of red dust had dispersed over a few hundred yards. It was also very hot. The vegetation is lush and tropical and, in the cyclone season, roads are virtually impassable because of flooding and sticky mud. We met many local people walking along the road carrying their produce, all barefoot. The courteous drivers slowed down to avoid choking the pedestrians with the dust, while others seemed to speed up for the fun of it, which really upset the walkers.

We climbed up a steep road which had been concreted to avoid erosion, to the top of a mountain range. The views of the south of the island were stunning, especially the solitary volcano gushing black smoke across the ash plain; two of the neighbouring islands were clearly visible out at sea. Tropical flowers, birds and butterflies spilled colour along the road. We eventually crossed the ash plain which looked like a black desert. Sparkling glass-like fragments glittered everywhere – on trees, on the ground – like a blanket of diamond dust. At this point we came to a steep drop and at the bottom was a river. When we reached it we saw there were deep ruts in the mud so, after putting the vehicle in four-wheel drive, we crossed to the other side of the ash plain and continued through the coconut plantations to the village.

We pulled up at a group of wooden shacks with palm leaf thatches. My bags were taken out of the back of the pick-up and put on the grass. They were covered in red dust and black glitter. An old man strode over and shook my hand introducing himself as David Hosea. When he found that I too was called David, he said that this was significant and laughed. He spoke excellent English, which surprised me. He was a big, strong, powerful man and was much blacker than the rest of the locals gathered nearby. He looked different, as though he

7

were from a different tribe or race. Others were clearly afraid of him and kept their eyes lowered when he spoke. He wore a large cowboy-like hat, a torn black jacket and black trousers. The hat gave him status; nobody else wore one. He sat on the steps of one of the huts and explained that his father worked as a civil servant for the British Colonial Service so, because of this, he was well educated. Then he sat in silence for some time looking at me. I realised that he was actually scanning me and "reading" my aura in some way. I felt a little uncomfortable as I found this intrusive. Then his demeanour changed and he became more serious, dismissing all the others around us. He asked, 'Why are you here?'

I explained to David that I was here on Tanna Island to learn and to study the local customs, belief systems and culture; I was not here as a tourist. David looked at me further and scanned me deeper. I put up an energetic barrier around me. Then he stood, picked up my bags, put them inside the leaf hut and then he said to me, 'Would you like to see a sacred waterfall?'

I said, 'Yes.'

The walk through the rain forest became an interrogation exercise by David, who asked me question after question on seemingly unrelated topics to the point I was becoming rather annoyed. But I remained calm, pleasant, polite and answered his questions at length to the best of my ability. David's bearing was very powerful and he asked me to guess his age. I felt as though diplomacy would be the right thing here so I purposely guessed a lower age and he kept smiling. Suddenly he stopped, sunlight glinting in his eyes, and said he was seventy years old. I must add that he was a formidable seventy at that, strong, barefoot, walking over rough rocks, standing in the sun with a heavy jacket, trousers and hat and there was not one bead of sweat upon his brow. I was saturated in perspiration!

There was something about him which I was drawn to but strangely, a part of me was very wary of him. He was persistent in his questions, such as: how does a volcano work? We stopped and sat on the earth amongst the debris of a past flood in the dried up river bed and he said, 'Draw me a map in the sand and show me where the Holy Land is.' And then Egypt, followed by Syria, Pakistan, Australia and England. He asked me to explain about the United Kingdom, being particularly interested in the Royal Family, especially Prince Philip. He asked me to explain to him about Skylab. How does a bird fly? How do you understand the relationship between God and the earth? What is Spirit? What do you know about ancestors? How can I improve the sandy earth to grow more vegetables? We stood and continued our journey.

In between these general questions he would ask me an unrelated question of a personal nature. The following questions were asked in between the others and I knew he was testing me for my honesty and patience for some reason but did not know why.

'Do you believe in God?'

I answered, 'Yes.'

'Is your father alive?'

'No, he is dead.'

'Do you have brothers or sisters?'

'I have a twin brother called Barry.'

Then David became excited and he said, 'Who was the firstborn?'

So I said, 'I am the firstborn.'

Then he looked at my beard and he said, 'How long have you had your beard?'

I answered, 'I can't remember; possibly twenty years.'

'And why do you have a beard?'

'I have a beard because it feels right for me to have one at this time.'

The following question was asked in a very subtle manner. It was inviting an answer, not really a direct question.

David said, 'We are circumcised as boys. How about you?'

'Yes.' I answered, 'I am circumcised.'

Once David had got all the answers he wanted, we arrived coincidentally at the waterfall which, because it was in the dry season, wasn't very productive. It was more like a heavy dribble, but it was a beautiful place and I imagine that in full flow it would be very impressive. He said that this was a sacred waterfall where his ancestors had worshipped. We spent a little time there. It seemed as though it was important for him to bring me to this place for some reason.

Suddenly he said, 'We go back.' We returned through the jungle back to the hut and he disappeared leaving me with a young man whom he introduced to me as Philip, his nephew. I felt baffled at his interrogation and irritated by its persistence, but now I was able to enjoy my explorations with Philip. David obviously taught his family well for most of those whom I encountered spoke reasonable English or at least they understood what I said if I spoke slowly. They spoke amongst themselves in their local language or in Bislama when meeting other locals.

In the late afternoon I met Jerry who was to be my guide, interpreter and cook for my stay. Jerry was the firstborn son of David, who lived in Port Resolution. He looked very much like him, same shaped head and very dark. Yet he was much gentler in so many ways. His eyes were soft and he didn't appear to have a cruel streak as his father did. Everybody liked Jerry. When we went for a walk along the jungle trails everybody waved to him and smiled and shook his hand. Jerry introduced me and they shook my hand also. The people were very friendly.

Then we returned to my hut, known as a leaf house because of the banana leaf thatch on a wooden frame; Jerry said that he would prepare a meal for me which he would give me later that evening and that, when darkness fell, he would take me to the local nakamal, the men's sacred praying ground. I looked forward to this very much. As the setting sun slipped behind the mountains, the red glow from the volcano became brighter and more powerful. It almost seemed as though the explosions of the volcano became more gentle, softer in the evening sky.

Jerry and Philip called for me and, as we walked under a canopy of a clear starlit night, I could see and hear the huge fruit bats flying around overhead, the size of crows landing in the trees, squabbling, fighting to get their fruits. As we walked through the jungle trails, we met people carrying burning sticks and Jerry explained that these were known as fire sticks, wood from a type of banyan tree which, when lit, simply smoulders and glows; people carry these with them wherever they go so that they can light a fire at any time. But they also act as a very weak torch during the evening and people can find their footing in the darkness. Ahead of us and behind us were bobbing little red glowing sticks. It looked as though humanity had morphed into a myriad of fireflies.

We reached the nakamal, a huge round area cleared of all undergrowth, and at the ends were two huge banyan trees. At the base of one banyan tree was a fire. The place was already full of men and boys sitting around the edges waiting to drink kava, a local narcotic drink, to connect with the ancestors, to connect with the Great Spirit. Men greeted me as we entered and Jerry sat me down on a log near a man who sat in the shadows, out of view. In the moonlight I could see that he had a beard. He looked at me and nodded his head but remained silent. Jerry introduced this man to me as Chief Jack explaining that he was the kastom Chief, the man who dealt with all of the tribal ritual, ceremony and healing. This was the very man that I was hoping to meet! I shook his hand and he took from behind his ear a cigarette which he lit from a glowing stick from the fire. As he drew upon it, the light illuminated his face, a very interesting face, full of lines of wisdom and knowing. He offered me the cigarette and I drew upon it. It was pungent and bitter, very strong, and it made me feel a bit dizzy and sick. Jerry explained that they grew their own tobacco in this part of Tanna Island and it was known to be very strong. I handed the cigarette back to the Chief and he drew upon it himself. Those who sat around us nodded approvingly. Then the Chief, through the interpretation of Jerry, asked me a few questions. He wanted to know why I was in Tanna so I explained to him that I was not here as a tourist; I came to learn his way of life, his culture, his traditions. He understood. He nodded and smiled.

Jerry then explained to me the ritual of how the kava was prepared. He showed me a circle of gathered men and explained that only circumcised boys were allowed to prepare the kava. There were boys who were cleaning the kava root, which was very hard and woody, with coconut fibre to remove all the excess soil and sand. Other boys cut the kava root into small pieces with machetes or knives, along with other young men who were chewing these bits of roots with their very sharp, clean, white teeth. After they had chewed the root into a gooey pulp they spat the kava pulp out into leaves and then cleared their throats gutturally to remove the last vestiges of kava juice and saliva. Other boys carried these leaves full of masticated kava to two youths who sat on either side of a filthy looking plastic bowl. Both boys had a sieve, which was the leaf sheath of the palm tree, placing handfuls of this gooey mass into the sieve and, pouring water from a gourd, they sieved the masticated kava so that the liquid fell into the plastic bowl beneath. The half coconut shells were dipped into this as cups from which the men drank their kava.

Jerry explained that the kava was exceedingly important in their custom and ritual and that at every ceremony or ritual kava was drunk either during or after the process. At the nakamal in the evening the kava had to be drunk in a certain way and the last vestiges were then sprayed upon the earth to honour the Spirit of Place and to honour their ancestors. He explained further that their ranking system of chiefs and elders was very complex and that the first person to drink was the highest ranking male, which was usually the High Chief, followed by other chiefs and elders and men of higher grade. The last person to drink would be the newly circumcised boy.

When the kava had been prepared the Chief indicated that I was to drink first. This was a great honour for me. A youth came out of the darkness holding a half coconut shell full of kava and offered it to me. Jerry explained to me that this had to be drunk straight away in one go and the vestiges sprayed upon the earth, as he explained before. I couldn't see what was in the cup because it was too dark but the brew smelled as if it was from a stagnant pond, almost as if it was from a fish tank. I lifted it to my lips after Jerry had told me which direction to face and I drank deeply, quickly so that I wouldn't smell or taste it. I sprayed the last bit thankfully upon the earth. Immediately I felt sick and dizzy. My lips went dead and it felt as though they were swelling, as though I'd been to the dentist for several injections. My throat began to close. I could not feel my tongue. My eyes began to ache as though they were sticking out like snails horns. I became very confused and disorientated. I managed to find my way back to my log and sat down next to the Chief, hoping and praying that I wouldn't pass out or vomit.

Then the Chief stood and he took his drink of kava. Each man then followed in rank, spraying the kava on the earth to honour the ancestors, to honour the land. Then a very thin, bony elderly man with white hair stood and began to call in the ancestors. It was a type of song like a yodel; it was so haunting and so beautiful. The hair stood up on the back of my neck. My heart opened. I recognised this song; I recognised this place. In some dark recess of my heart I just knew that I had returned home. Suddenly I was distracted by the same youth, who was introduced to me as Samson. He offered me a second cup of kava. The Chief looked at me and I knew that Samson and some of the other young men had decided to have fun with the visiting white man. I instinctively understood that this was not the correct procedure. The Chief said nothing. He sat in silence, watching, listening. I did not want to make a fuss so I stood and went forward and took the coconut cup from Samson's hand and I drank it in one as instructed beforehand along with others around me who drank from their shells. Immediately I began to feel very ill and dizzy and the sensations of numbness in my throat and lips became worse. I staggered back to my log and, as I sat upon it next to the Chief, I simply fell backwards on to the earth, sprawling on my back into the undergrowth. All the young men laughed. The Chief remained silent, listening and watching. Jerry and Philip came to my aid and lifted me to my feet and, as they did so, I began to vomit – very impressive projectile vomiting. My belly was in cramps, I could not see, my eyes hurt. They lifted me and carried me towards my hut along the jungle tracks in the darkness. I apologised to them for letting them down and Jerry replied saying, 'This is good. This is our teacher plant, our medicine plant. Everybody who takes kava vomits at first. It cleans you out; it is good. Rest. I will bring your meal.' This was my first Rite of Passage.

I staggered into the little back room of my hut and fell on to my bed, a twisted wooden frame with a thin straw mattress. I pulled the mosquito net around me as best I could. I could hardly see. Everything was spinning. Everything connected with the hut seemed as though it was fluid. I couldn't focus and, even though I felt so very sick and dizzy, once I lay down I was unable to move. Then I heard Jerry arrive with my meal, placing it on a little wooden table on a very small, rickety verandah; he also brought with him a hurricane lamp – I heard it hissing. Jerry laughed and then he left. I tried to get up to have my meal but, as soon as I raised my head from my pillow, I had the sensation of wanting to vomit so I lay back down and tried to sleep, yet I was wide awake and remained so the entire night.

5th May 2003
Penis sheath   Secret initiation   Spirit Knights

I got up at 5 a.m. and walked across the grass to a little bamboo shed which was the toilet and wash area. The toilet was simply a hole in the ground and they had left me a bucket of water and a small bar of soap. This is the only means I had of washing myself so I had a quick body wash, which made me feel better. I returned to my hut and changed my clothes. My untouched evening meal was crawling with hungry, small, brown ants. I marvelled at how perfect nature is; nothing is wasted.

I went for a stroll in the early hours of the morning. It was silent. Even though I was still fighting nausea and dizziness, I marvelled at the absolute beauty of this place. The birds and butterflies were out and the tropical plants bloomed. Lemons hung in profusion on bushes. I walked along a track where I found a man sleeping in a little hut on four stilts and beneath this hut was a telephone. I found out later that the Vanuatu government had a programme of installing a public solar telephone in every major village. It was this man's job to sleep above the telephone and, whenever it rang, he was to find the person the call was meant for. He slept there day and night; this was his job.

I wandered through the plantations looking at the fallen coconuts in the undergrowth. The place smelled so fresh and clean. Every so often a thick pall of white sulphurous smoke enveloped me as the volcano exploded once more. Then I returned to my hut. Jerry arrived at about 6 o'clock bringing me some fresh pawpaw and other tropical fruits for my breakfast and some tea. As I ate, I invited Jerry to sit with me and we spoke at length about tribal customs and the different hierarchies. Jerry informed me that David Hosea was in fact known as Chief Kahi and that, since he was the firstborn son, he was eligible to take over as Chief when his father died. He also told me that further down the track lived his brother Kelson, the Chief's second born son, who he would introduce me to later that day. Another son lived elsewhere, I think in Port Vila. Jerry further explained that his father went by the name of David Hosea instead of Chief Kahi because he had now become a Seventh Day Adventist Minister or Pastor and he had built a small church not far from where I stayed and, because Jerry had refused to go over to the Christian way, choosing to remain with the kastom traditions, his father had ostracised him and placed Kelson in his place to become the next Chief when he died. David was not liked by the kastom people. Because his father was so formidable, when anybody needed a guide, or basically any sort of servant, Jerry was told to do this particular work where the other two brothers weren't. His father ridiculed Jerry for his kastom beliefs so Jerry felt very isolated and that is why he moved far away to Port Resolution to get away from him. Jerry was able to explain to me many things about the culture and the way of life of these wonderful people.

Jerry left me to finish my breakfast and, at about 10 o'clock in the morning, he came back to my little hut saying that Chief Jack wanted to see me and it was very urgent. We left immediately. We walked along the rain forest trails for about two miles to the nakamal of Itabu village, which seemed to be very similar to the one I went to the night before – a cleared large circular ceremonial place. At the west end was a huge banyan tree and through the centre of the tree the men had cut a tunnel – a complete hole right the way through. I was asked to sit down on the edge of the nakamal and then the Chief and a group of men and boys came through the hole in the banyan tree in a single file, the Chief at their head. They all wore the kastom attire. This was the nambas or penis sheath, made from hibiscus fibre, woven into a fine mat, rolled tightly and secured by vine around the waist. This gave the appearance of an erect phallus. The scrotum was covered by loose, hanging fibres. Chief Jack wore a headband and armbands which were made of sacred leaves, where the others just had nambas. The singing and dancing shook the ground. As they danced, they moved always in an anticlockwise fashion, stamping their feet and clapping their hands, and it was almost as though they were keeping in unison with the explosions of the volcano. I could feel the ground shaking beneath my feet. It was such an amazing sensation, especially when a pall of white sulphurous smoke engulfed the entire ceremony. I felt as though I had been transported back to my Neolithic ancestors again.

After the dancing and singing had taken place, I chatted to the children while Jerry spoke at length to the Chief. The Chief then called me over and, with the aid of Jerry interpreting, he began to speak. The Chief told me that, after he had met me last night, he had had a very powerful and vivid dream, where the ancestors had come to him and had insisted that he was to perform a sacred ceremony initiating me as a chief of the tribe. The Chief said that this dream was so powerful that he could not refuse to do their bidding. Afterwards when he awoke, he spoke to some of the other chiefs and elders first thing in the morning and some of them were very hostile about the idea of letting an outsider, especially a white man, into their sacred ceremony and ritual. So he said to me that, as he had no choice in performing this sacred ceremony, on no occasion was I to go off anywhere by myself without Jerry or somebody else with me as some of the elders or chiefs would try to harm or kill me because they did not want me knowing their secret ways. I had to agree to this rule, which I did.

The Chief then continued to explain that he would perform a ceremony to enable me to reconnect with my ancestors. This ceremony would initiate me as a chief of the tribe so that the ancestors would see that I was now a "Big Man" of high rank and they would then have to listen to my words.

'Spirit would recognise you more if you went through a sacred ceremony,' he said. 'This ceremony would end in me (that is the Chief) bestowing upon you my rank and the shared guardianship of this position that I hold.'

The Chief added that after the ceremony I must return home to my land and tell my people about his culture and tradition. He said that this was important. He invited me to return to Vanuatu and to his tribe to live with him for two years where he would teach me the basics of his culture, traditions and magic – his secret knowledge.

On the walk back to my hut Jerry explained that this was a privilege that had not been bestowed on anyone else before, especially a white man. Jerry said that I was to rest, bathe and pray for the remainder of the day until I was called for the ceremony. He said the Chief had commanded him to tell me to do this. Jerry wasn't sure what would take place later in the day but continued to explain that, after the ceremony, I would be called Chief. No women would be allowed in the sacred area as he informed me I would have to be naked to wear the nambas. It would be a secret ceremony.

'Remember,' Jerry said, 'that the kastom Chief is the same as a high ranking priest. Chief and priest are the same.'

I now began to understand the significance of this initiation. I was being initiated into an ancient culture of spirituality that began at the dawn of humanity. Jerry further explained that in the Chief's tribe the title of Chief was hereditary so, at my death, my firstborn son would inherit the title automatically or, in my case as I had no children, my nephew Aaron. Jerry went on to remind me that this was a great blessing for me and I must understand the important significance of the situation and that I had to obey the rules exactly, as the Chief commanded, this was for my safety apart from anything else.

I suddenly realised that it was almost midday, the highest point of the sun, and interestingly I also realised that, as today was the 5th of May, it was my ancestors' Celtic Fire Festival of Beltane. I was going to be initiated in a sacred ancient ceremony at the foot of an active volcano within the Pacific Rim of Fire. I felt thrilled at the absolute synchronicity of all these connections and so-called coincidences that Spirit had somehow enabled me to connect with these ancient people and their traditions at this time. I laughed out loud at the absurdity of everything that appeared around me and yet I marvelled at the absolute magic of it all.

I did as I was commanded. I went to the little bamboo hut and there waiting for me was a clean bucket of water and some fresh soap. I bathed myself from head to toe with the intent that I was cleansing myself physically and energetically for what would probably be the most important initiation of my life.

I returned to my hut and there, naked as instructed, I prayed to the ancestors in the way that I knew best, calling upon the Goddess of my ancestors and my culture and also to the Deity of the Chief's culture and to the Spirit of this place. I soon dropped into a meditative state praying that I would be guided and protected in what lay ahead and that I would be given the courage to face whatever would befall me. The volcano exploded and I was engulfed in white sulphurous fumes. The pressure wave from the explosion caused the dust from the thatch to fall on my naked body, now wet with sweat, and then I heard the drums beating quicker and quicker into a rhythm that called the warriors to sacred ceremony. A thrill rose within my heart but also a little bit of fear. Jerry came to the door calling softly to me. I dressed in clean clothes ready for sacred ceremony.

As we walked the two miles along the jungle trails to Itabu village, other men joined us to go to the ceremony. I remained silent, holding the thought and intent within my mind that this was going to be the most important experience of my life. Jerry chatted here and there about little things and I sensed that he was avoiding talking about the ceremony to ease my nervousness about the unknown. Jerry explained that kava had to be prepared and drunk at the ceremony to complete the rite. This was part of their culture. I looked at him and raised my eyes, hoping and praying that I would not vomit or pass out as I had the night before. He smiled at me. The only thing that I remember asking Jerry was: what was the kastom name for the Chief, his tribal name? Jerry told me that he was known as Chief Wai Wai Rawi (pronounced Way Why Rah wee).

We arrived at the nakamal. A fire was lit at the foot of the banyan tree. Jerry explained that the place of divinity was held by the energy of fire and this was placed at the base of the banyan tree, which represented the stability and the strength of the Chief, therefore all the ceremonies were conducted within the shadow of this tree. If the Chief needed to speak, he would stand at the foot of the banyan tree and talk to the men. Some of the men and boys were already preparing the kava ready for the ritual after the ceremony. Jerry pointed out the Chief's uncle, a very elderly, frail-looking man, and I was touched that this old man was prepared to participate in a ceremony on behalf of a white man, a total stranger, and also the Chief's firstborn son, who he introduced as Donald. When the Chief dies this young man will automatically become the next chief in his place. Donald wore a white feather plume in his hair. He was short, muscular and athletic.

I waited patiently at the base of the banyan tree listening to the noises of the jungle and the volcano. Jerry beckoned to me and told me to remove my boots and socks. It was time! I was then led through the banyan tree to a small clearing where there was a preparation site, a tiny hut. I entered the hut and inside were several men, who wore nambas. I was instructed to stand naked upon the earth. It felt strange, a little embarrassing even, that here I was standing naked – a white hairy man amongst all these black men, none of whom, especially the boys, had ever seen a naked white man before. The boys did their best not to stare at me but they couldn't help it. I heard suppressed giggles from one boy. I found out later that it was important that the Chief and the elders saw that I was actually circumcised. Had I not been, then I would not have been able to undertake the ceremony.

One of the elders then tied a pandanus belt around my waist and placed my penis in the nambas, tying it in position tightly and strapping the phallic end under the belt against my belly. Chief Wai Wai placed upon my right upper arm a pandanus palm leaf armband which was woven intricately and, inside this, he placed green leaves which were very aromatic and pungent reminding me of aniseed. These I found out later were the sacred herbs of their God Majikjiki. The Chief then gave me a large root of kava and he instructed me that I must hold it against my heart, as this was the tribal sacred medicine plant. Then, in procession, I followed him through the banyan tree and into the nakamal. I was instructed to stand still in the centre of the sacred circle while the Chief, elders and boys sang, danced and stamped their feet, clapping their hands around me, in an anticlockwise direction getting faster each time and stamping harder until the ground shook and the dust rose. Yasur volcano called and thundered in the background and the smoke from the sacred fire at the base of the banyan tree curled between our legs and wrapped itself around our bodies. I could feel the energy rising through my feet and legs and moving into my heart and into my head as it moved its way through me, serpent-like, opening my heart in such a way that I felt so emotional, so vulnerable and yet strangely strong. I felt myself slipstreaming through a veil of some sort into a parallel existence. A portal opened between realms, revealing to me an outer circle of Spirit Knights from my Celtic lands. Each held his sword in front, point into the earth, heads bowed. I felt confused. (This phenomenon will be explained later.)

After completion of the dancing and singing, all stood silent and still. Chief Wai Wai raised his right hand and brought it down upon my crown, speaking in his local dialect. He bestowed upon me the rank of Chief and the shared guardianship under his care, invoking Deity to bless me and to walk with me. We shook hands and embraced each other, a black man and a white man, joined together as brothers in sacred ceremony. As the boys chewed and prepared the kava, Jerry interpreted, explaining further what the Chief was saying at the point of placing his hand upon my head in blessing. Jerry said that I would be known as Chief Iarueri (pronounced ear-you-w eri) and that I was now guardian of the flying fox (and all bats), the banana plant and the nabanga (this was their tribal name for the banyan tree).

I was then called to assist in the preparation of the kava, a very important privilege. I held the end of the bark sieve with one boy and the Chief held the other with another boy, whilst an elder poured water from a dirty plastic bottle on to the chewed masticated mass of kava moving it through the sieve with his hand until the fluid flowed into half coconut shells placed underneath. The Chief stood, taking a cup and instructed me to drink first, offering it to me. I then passed the shell to him. We shared the shell together, drinking alternately as an act obviously acknowledging our equal status. Jerry also pointed out this fact to me later. After we had finished the shell of kava, Chief Wai Wai pronounced that 'we are now brothers'. We sprayed the dregs upon the earth together and I was really pleased to find that I didn't feel as ill as I had before. I asked Jerry to explain the significance and meaning of my name Iarueri and he asked the Chief. Through interpretation he told me that by tribal law the Chief and his son would take my name or my grandfather's name to be exact so his family line would now be known as "Rawi Leesley". Jerry said that his father David would explain the name better than himself.

I then felt the nausea, dizziness and numbness start to sweep over me after taking the kava. I returned back through the banyan tree where I was helped to undress and put my western clothes on. Chief Wai Wai said that now I had undertaken sacred ceremony he would make me a nambas and armbands that were genuine tribal artifacts and not tourist trophies, for myself only. These would be given to me in a few days time. The Chief said that I must tell my people about the ceremony so that I will be recognised as a "Big Man" (the local name for Chief is "Big Man" and also the local name for the Chief's wife, who technically is known as High Woman, is also "Big Woman").

When I sat by the fire at the base of the banyan tree Chief Wai Wai spoke to me at length. Jerry interpreted as required about the ceremony and their traditions. The Chief went on to say, 'I could see that you were no ordinary tourist and that you had returned to the place of your birth! England may be on the other side of the earth but we are now joined as brothers and, when I die, my son will take your grandfather's name Leesley as you have taken my grandfather's name Rawi. You are to find a wife or to marry locally and return to us, where she will be known as "Big Woman" and a tribal wedding ceremony will take place. You will be taught about our customs and traditions and way of life. The Church is separate from the kastom ways but our ways are traditional, they are the natural ways. Our God is Yasur volcano from whom all life is given and to where our ancestors return. This ceremony will not be fully completed until you have climbed up to the summit of Yasur (pronounced Yasoor) to meet our God and connect with our ancestors. Yasur means "Old Man". You must teach your friends, family and others about us and our way of life.'

The Chief pulled at his thick, black beard and said, 'You must continue to wear your beard as a symbol of your status. This represents maturity as a chief and in this part of the island the status of a chief is a thick beard. Only chiefs are permitted to have a beard. In other places on the island the chief's symbol is something else.'

More kava was drunk. Then Chief Wai Wai continued, 'The Church took away our tribal names and made us wear clothes so that we could no longer dress in our native way but now we are teaching our children about the ancestral ways and our culture. Every time you hear a bang you will remember Yasur volcano and your home. You must get a musket and fire it up into a tree as if you are hunting a bird, then Yasur will speak to you through our ancestors and you will remember us – your brothers. You are now Tannese! You have been searching all your life for your spiritual kastom. Now you have returned to your roots. You are home!'

Darkness had begun to fall so Jerry took a smouldering stick from the fire to light our way back to my hut along the jungle tracks. I felt a great peace within me that I had never experienced before. I spent the night sitting in silence watching the flocks of flying foxes silhouetted against the moon, shimmering its silver light across the jungle. I wondered with awe at the simple, yet deeply profound ceremony I had experienced. Tears fell from my eyes onto the dark earth and I offered my thanks to Spirit and to the Spirit Knights of the Golden Order of the Dragon Sword (a sub order of the Knights of Avalon) who were standing in a circle around the nakamal, the Dragon Sword itself halfway up the banyan tree, point downwards. It was a strange and mysterious feeling to be part of an ancient ceremony with its origins in the Stone Age, along with Celtic Knights from my ancestors participating in this ceremony. For some years, I had been meditating on the Arthurian Grail mysteries and the Knights of the Round Table, and, through these dreamings, was initiated into this Order as Knight.

To understand this bizarre connection I will take the reader back now to 31st October 1998. I had completed a year's training programme for shamanic practitioners in Avalon and, as we finalised the training and had our last evening meal together, I was suddenly and deeply overcome with an inner urgency that I must undertake an initiation that very night. This was extremely important, but I didn't know why. Also, I was to enlist the help of two of the shamankas (female shamans) on the course to help me in this process. I knew this was to be a ceremony working principally with the element of water but did not know how it would take place. I thought to myself that I couldn't possibly go to these two girls with such a bizarre request. They would think that I was seriously unbalanced. The more I convinced myself that I couldn't do it, the stronger the spiritual urge became and the more urgent the inner instructions until I couldn't stand it any longer. I had to follow my heart wisdom, not my head confusion. I took my courage into my hands and sought out the two girls. I found Elena and Julie sitting together away from the others. I related my story to them about how I felt urged from my heart to ask them to participate in a ceremony with me. They looked at each other and then said, 'We were expecting you to come to us to ask for such a thing. We wondered why it took you so long! Spirit had told us to prepare for you.'

I was absolutely amazed. Elena and Julie agreed without asking any questions. They said that, if they were acting as my handmaidens, they would see to everything for me and I was to go and prepare myself in meditation. As they walked away, Julie said, 'We will come for you just before midnight.' My heart sang and opened.

I now understood that Spirit had organised everything for me and that this ceremony, no matter how simple it may be, would be one of the most important experiences of my life. I showered and prepared myself mentally, emotionally and physically. I felt nervous. I thanked Spirit for giving me the courage to speak my truth.

Just before midnight, Elena and Julie came to where I slept alone in a small caravan. They slipped inside without being seen by the other members of the course who were still celebrating the end of an eventful year's training. No-one spoke. We all knew what was involved and required. I stood naked between Elena and Julie, my handmaidens and priestesses. Julie smudged me with aromatic sage smoke to cleanse my energy body, while Elena sang softly as she held me in the light with visualisation.

Then the three of us slipped into the icy blackness of the Samhain winter's night. It was almost a full moon. I saw the moonlight reflected magically upon the surface of the large pond, occasionally disappearing as another black hail-filled cloud sped across her shining face. Julie took off her robe and stood naked before me at the edge of the pond and waded in to her waist. I followed, the icy water taking my breath away, until I stood almost waist deep. Elena stood naked behind me upon the bank, arms raised to the Goddess, her eyes closed, a look of spiritual ecstasy upon her silver-lit face as she rhythmically shook the rattle calling in the spirits.

Julie stood before me. She was transformed somehow into the Goddess herself, her golden hair and slight figure highlighted in the silver moonlight. In preparation, Julie had placed an enamelled jug from the venue kitchen by the pond. Lifting her arms high in the traditional Goddess position of worship, she spoke gently to the Goddess, calling to Her to bear witness this night to the initiation of one of her neophytes.

My eyes flooded with tears as I became overwhelmed with the simple power of this experience – two priestesses, one with light skin and golden fair hair, one with dark skin and raven black hair, a symbol in itself of balance. I bent lower into the pond as Julie took the white jug and poured icy water over my head and down my spine. The shock took my breath away, yet I knew that this water, physically near freezing, was charged with silver moonlight, the Goddess light. I offered my love to the Goddess as I stood in the sacred waters of Avalon. It was magical. The three of us stood naked in a state of spiritual ecstasy before the Goddess, before the Dragon consciousness of Avalon and all of its history, myth and legend. We were now part of that legend, unrecorded in the annals of man, but recorded in Akasha (see Glossary).

We dressed and returned to the venue to get a hot drink. Julie said that she felt it important to have a glass each of red wine to represent the ancient rite of communion. I went to bed and during the night had a clear, lucid dream, which I remember still to this day in all detail such was the profound impact it had upon me on that night. I saw myself very clearly in the pond at Avalon which became larger until it became a lake with misty vapour rolling across its surface. The water was no longer cold but a pleasant temperature and it was daylight. Ahead of where I stood waist deep in the lake was a thicket of willow trees and reeds. Out of the mist there appeared a beautiful woman attired in a translucent garment of gossamer white held in at the waist, very similar to pictures of the garb ladies wore in medieval times. She had long golden hair tied loosely back and she wore a circlet of forget-me-not flowers around her brow. The strikingly beautiful blue flowers were most noticeable and full of symbolism for me. The Lady of the Lake, as I called her, stood before me. My heart filled with love to see her. In her hand she held a large golden sword and upon its hilt was an emerald green dragon. The Lady of the Lake held the golden sword horizontally, the handle in her left hand and the point in her right hand. She then offered the sword to me, speaking these words, which I shall never forget, 'Behold, a bearer of the Dragon Sword.'

The Lady of the Lake then presented me with the sword which I took with my right hand, tip in my left. I was amazed at how solid and heavy it initially felt. I held it high above my head, feeling its power and realising the responsibility that came with the use of such a powerful magical tool. The Dragon Sword felt ancient, beyond the spheres of time and space. Its energy awoke the dormant crystalline consciousness deep within my soul, heart and bones of a period beyond the rim of human memory from where this sword was first forged. It began an awakening of a desire that burnt within my breast like the eternal flame. I returned it to the Lady of the Lake who I sensed was also the Guardian of the Dragon Sword. The following morning I related this experience to Elena and Julie who also had similar experiences that night. They knew her as the Lady of Avalon. (I later realised that this experience was vital for the work to be achieved in Vanuatu.)

I spent the next few days alone in Glastonbury where, most of the time, I wept uncontrollably. Something deep within my soul had been released. I felt the Dragon consciousness moving through my veins. I felt the sword held in my hand. I felt like a Knight, bizarre as that may seem. Everywhere I looked I could see the form of the Dragon – in the clouds, in the water, in the trees. It rained very heavily at that time and, as I stood upon the Tor at Glastonbury, all the fields below were flooded. Once more this sacred land had become Avalon, a misty inland sea.

Later I was given an explanation about the Dragon Sword, its origin and meaning from Spirit. I was told not to reveal this information, because those who are ready must seek and find their own truth.

6th May 2003
Volcanoes   Guardian of the Element of Sulphur

Today Jerry, his young sons and I went up to Yasur volcano. It was a two hour's hike through the rain forest which enabled me to ask Jerry more questions regarding the ceremony yesterday and the position of his father regarding his status. Jerry said that Chief Kahi would be speaking to me later and went on to explain about the volcano.

'It is a dangerous active volcano so, when it explodes, you must not run initially but watch where the lava bombs are going to fall. Then you run. There have been fatalities and many injuries in the past.'

Looking down into the volcano crater was awesome, frightening and yet beautiful. I gave thanks to the God Yasur for calling me to Tanna and for the ceremony. I called upon the Guardian of the Element of Fire and then the Guardian of the Element of Sulphur who once severely reprimanded me for not showing respect at an active volcano in Zaire (Congo) in Africa. Lesson learnt.

Let me explain. In 1976, several of us went on a trans-African expedition from Johannesburg, South Africa to London which took five months. We had reached the Rwandan/Zaire border and directly across the border was a very active volcano called Mount Nyiragongo. It was 31st October 1976 and, for some reason, throughout my life, at the time of Samhain (or Hallowe'en) when the veil traditionally in the northern lands is at its thinnest to aid the communication with the ancestors, I have had the most profound, magical, spiritual experiences. This is my time of year – my power time.

I watched with incredulity as the darkness fell around the volcano. The night sky filled with an orange glow; the moon was almost full with a white ring around it. Horizontal white lightning circled the volcano as if it actually came out of the crater. It was so powerful. I could feel myself being drawn energetically to the volcano where I felt myself rising upwards and outwards with such speed that I left my body and became totally and utterly formless within the universe. I had no shape. I felt as though I was part of the universe itself. I felt as though I was eternal Spirit. Then I returned to my body, feeling disorientated and later realised that I had had an out of body experience and had received a traditional shamanic awakening. The Guardian of this volcano is now a Spirit Guide of mine.

When we crossed into Zaire the following morning, we immediately climbed up the volcano but, unknown to us, the expedition leader had signed a contract stating that we would not go into the crater itself. One of the African guides asked if we would like to go inside the crater. Half of us decided to do so. We climbed down a rope hanging over very loose pumice stone, which cut our hands and faces as it fell from one person to the other; eventually we arrived at the bottom of the crater. We jumped over sulphurous fissures, until we actually stood at the very rim of the lava lake. It was absolutely amazing, yet also frightening. I lost all of the hair on my arms and legs, I singed my beard and lost my eyebrows. We had to be careful, for the lava shot into the air like sparks from a raging bonfire landing in all directions, everywhere. A girl, who stood many yards behind me, had her hair set on fire, possibly by a piece of molten lava no larger than a pinhead. I started to feel sick with the sulphurous fumes and, as a young man, I started to show off and didn't treat the place with the respect it was due.

I had difficulty in climbing back up the rope because I felt nauseous and disorientated. The volcano erupted a few months later with great loss of life. Since that day I have never slept properly. I have prayed to Spirit many times for help with my insomnia and I have never really had a decent night's sleep in all that time.

I had made similar mistakes with Mt Kilimanjaro, Tanzania, and Matupit volcano on Bougainville Island, politically part of Papua, New Guinea but geographically part of The Solomon Islands. Again, I was too immature to be sensitive enough to the volcano spirits and tribal ancestors of place. Before I attempted to climb Cotopaxi volcano in the High Andes, Ecuador, I contacted the guardian spirits first.

Some years later after these experiences, the Guardian of the Element of Sulphur suddenly came to me in the middle of the night. He was so clear, as though there was somebody physical actually standing in the room with me. I sat bolt upright in my bed seeing this face peering into mine. He had long, sulphurous yellow hair and beard and he spoke these words to me, which I shall never forget, 'You have violated sacred space; now you pay the price!'

He was very angry. I asked for forgiveness; I asked for mercy and grace.

I realised from this experience that powerful spirits are part of stone and crystal, and you abuse them at your peril. After many months of meditation, we made our peace together and he is now one of my Spirit Allies. So-called mistakes are often great teaching opportunities to help us grow into wisdom.

———————————

When we returned to Loanengo village Chief Kahi was waiting for us. The Chief and I sat upon the earth and spoke at length about the ceremony and his culture. Kahi explained that he was the High Chief and that Chief Wai Wai was his younger brother who was the Kastom Chief. He continued that, when he first saw me, raising his finger to his third eye, he said he could see that I was a special man so he took me for a walk through the rain forest to the waterfall to enable him to ask me many questions and find out why I was at his village. He explained that, after the questions had been asked, he listened to my words and realised that I was a "king amongst men". He then realised that I was here in his village at this time for a special reason and that I fulfilled all the necessary requirements to be a chief. His words washed over me. My ego thought I was "special", my heart knew the truth. I was remembering who I used to be in a past life!

High Chief Kahi went on to explain that he had spoken at length to Chief Wai Wai and had personally authorised the ceremony of my initiation as a chief. Kahi explained in more detail the complexities of the tribal ranking system and that the rank of chief given to me was that of kastom chief, shared with Chief Wai Wai. This was to enable me to reconnect with their ancestors and also to my own Celtic ancestors. Shared guardianship and responsibilities would be passed over to me also. The armbands I wore during the ceremony contained the aromatic leaves which would have shown my rank. These leaves symbolise peace which is represented by the God of all plants, Majikjiki. This plant is known locally as mynesi.

High Chief Kahi then explained about the name given to me, opening his hands wide and gesticulating to the earth, but he had some difficulty with the exact translation and said that the name Iarueri was his grandfather's name, as both he and Chief Wai Wai are brothers but are chiefs of different tribes. Note: the name grandfather often means first ancestor in tribal lore.

He then continued, 'The first ancestor of our family had four sons. One died so each of the others became the chiefs and founders of three main tribes. When the men died in tribal conflict, the bloodline was lost to the sons so was carried by the women of the ancestral line from which I come.'

Chief Kahi now has three sons and, on his death, each son will become a high chief of the three tribes to fulfil the ancestral blood lineage. He also believes that their ancestors had white skins and indicated that I may fulfil the role of restoring the ancestral lineage of the fourth son.

Chief Kahi went on to say that the rank and position given to me was a great privilege and holds much responsibility and authority so that I can represent his people overseas, as well as locally.

'The ceremony to confer this position upon you was done in our holy temple, the nakamal. You must remember that always. All the other Westerners and tourists that come to our land and our village are not interested in our culture. I could see in your spirit (touching his third eye with his finger again) that you are different so I asked you many things to listen to your words. The ceremony was very important and you are the only white man to have this rank given to you. We trust, honour and respect you. The ceremony is only the beginning. It is your new foundation. To fully complete the bond with our culture, you must marry one of my daughters for I now call you my son. Do not marry a European woman. They are usually only interested in money and will give you nothing but trouble. We do not need money for everything we need is around us. In our culture, you will have no trouble with our women for the man is the head of the household and the woman does all he asks of her. She will never question you or quarrel with you. This is our way. When Christianity came to our land most of us accepted it as the bible taught us that man is superior over women. You may choose which daughter you want and I will personally perform the wedding ceremony. If you ever reach a higher rank of chief I will have to be present for that ceremony.

'You ask about the name Iarueri. This means "First One" – the first one to have his feet deep into the earth; the first one of our ancestors that nothing can move, even if it is a cyclone, war or politics. The First One stands firm to follow his spiritual destiny and to teach others. You are that person and will represent us overseas. On the night of your ceremony I gathered my family together and told them about you. See the white man staying with us, he is a special man. My children said, "why is this?" I replied that he is a chief of our people so must be given the respect and honour he deserves.'

High Chief Kahi then wrote the name Iarueri in the earth between our feet with a finger. He stood and we shook hands and embraced. He returned to tend his garden.

In the late afternoon Jerry, his two sons and I set off to climb to Yasur volcano. I knew that tourists from other areas of the island came every night to be driven to the crater rim then depart to their Western-style bungalows after a few photos. We decided to go at a time before the expected tourists arrived to enable me to pray to Yasur and to be alone with my thoughts. When we reached the crater rim it was almost dark, very cold and windy; the two boys were not used to the cold wind so Jerry took them down to the edge of the forest to the boulder plain to wait, reminding me to watch out for flying lava bombs.

I offered my thanks to Yasur, to the Guardians of place, to the Guardian of the Element of Sulphur and the Guardian of the Element of Fire. The exploding lava in the pits in the crater below me were awesome, some lava bombs landing a few hundred feet from where I stood, one actually breaching the crater rim, landing near the footpath. The sound waves and the air compression made my ears hurt and my whole body vibrated with the sheer force from the ground when it shook with the explosions. My heart felt as if it had been touched by some mystical force.

I knew at this point that the second phase of my ceremony had been completed. I felt deeply at peace, like nothing I had ever felt before. My spiritual lifelong search for my truth was over. I felt complete, knowing now that my own spiritual path was confirmed as a solitary practitioner guided by Spirit, by the Goddess. I knew I could no longer conform to manmade rules, control, regulations, dogma and creeds, as I am an individual. So my path is simply that – my path; the path I alone will seek and follow in all its mysterious ways. Nobody can correct my ritual, ceremony, techniques or prayers for they are directed by divinity from within. This sets me free. This returns my self-esteem, my self-confidence and my own personal worth as an individual human being.

I returned down the path to Jerry and the boys. We walked in silence in the darkness without using my torch until we came to dangerous gullies in the dirt road. Along the way Jerry pointed out in the rain forest the luminescent fungi which glowed like low watt, pale blue bulbs in the undergrowth, giving the forest a surreal appearance of fairy land. Jerry explained that the boys often collected these luminescent fungi to light the houses for the night; they gave off sufficient light to allow people to complete basic tasks.

On the main road we met a few people walking. All carried smouldering fire sticks so that we could identify walkers in the blackness of the night by seeing bobbing red glows here and there, like fireflies. When we met anyone nobody spoke. All shook hands very gently, almost a touch of fingers, and everybody whispered. I was told that it was disrespectful to Spirit to talk at night.

After my evening meal I retired to write my notes and to recall my experiences at the rim of the volcano. During this meditative silence I became aware of myself standing at the crater rim very clearly and a robed being approaching me from the left. He was wearing a golden robe with an emerald green tabard. He bore the symbol of the Dragon Sword upon his chest. This being then spoke to me, 'I am the Grand Marshal of the Golden Order of the Dragon Sword. You have been duly initiated into the Order as priest and knight. Remember this Order is open to all who follow a spiritual path. You have been initiated through the ancient traditions of the tribes of this land.'

Then from the centre of Yasur volcano rose a huge, magnificent, golden sword – the Dragon Sword. Then I heard the words, 'Forged through fire! You are now known amongst us and you will take your place.'

Interestingly, Jerry told me later that no tourists came to Yasur that night which surprised all the villagers.

8th May 2003
Golden Order of the Dragon Sword

Early in the morning, before dawn, I reconnected to Spirit and I journeyed in dreamtime being aware of the environment around me at the rim of the volcano. Looking within the crater I saw that it was now filled with clear water with white mist swirling upon its surface. I then saw an empty canoe coming out of the mists towards me. I sat in the canoe which took me to the centre of the lake where, through the swirling white mist, I could see a golden glow. I looked beneath the canoe into the depths of the lake. I could see the pulsating red lava of the volcano moving below and I saw the form of the Dragon of Fire. For a second I felt vulnerable and concerned for my safety. As the canoe moved nearer to the golden glow, the mist became thicker, more dense and more active in its manifestation. Here I seemed to stop before an energetic barrier or veil of some sort. I decided to speak and ask permission to continue, 'I seek permission to pass to the realms beyond.'

I waited for a reply or response for a moment. Then I heard a voice which said, 'Who seeks passage beyond this veil?'

I replied, 'I am a bearer of the Dragon Sword and, duly initiated, I seek access to the mysteries beyond.'

The veil parted and before me was an emerald green dragon or serpent (I could not define the difference) and within its coils the Dragon Sword pointing downwards. The creature faced me with its mouth open and fangs bared. I spoke to it, 'Guardian of the Magical Sword, I come not to steal or dishonour the weapon you guard for within its blade is your sacred power – your spirit which I honour and respect. This sword has been forged by fire from the centre of the earth and born through water. Your consciousness is that primal energy within the sword, for you are of the earth – her mountains, her valleys, her secret places and sacred shores. As I am a bearer of this sword, I pledge to uphold its sacred power, magic and light for I have met with you before at other holy sites and temples around the world and called upon your sacred name to pay homage to you, as the Rainbow Serpent at Uluru, the Golden Dragon in Prague and the White Dragon in Budapest. I have been initiated to the position of chief, priest in an age-old tradition that began before time and that has now remained upon the earth to this very day. I seek now your guardianship and protection, your knowledge and your wisdom, and your sacred skills of the ancient ways of my ancestors and the truth of my descendants that I may reconnect with them through the collective cellular consciousness which is deep within me. Help me to reactivate the God and Goddess realisation within through the sacred power of the Golden Dragon Sword.'

At this point the dragon serpent withdrew itself into the Golden Sword activating it with its consciousness so that the sword became alive. Now the sword could be named. The sword stood before me, its golden light pulsating like a lighthouse through the mists of time touching those who have been called to serve humanity and all life to the best of their ability. I placed my hands upon its hilt and we became as one body. I raised the sword high above my head, its blade glowing and growing magically to about twelve feet in length; yet it was light, swift and free. Within my hands I held the condensed light of the universe and I heard the words, 'It is good!'

I physically wept, realising that my Celtic ancestors of Water had merged with the Melanesian ancestors of Fire. As I raised my tearstained face, beside me stood the Grand Marshal, his gold and green robes swirling around him from the power of released light. I then realised that he was an aspect or manifestation of Chief Wai Wai.

He spoke, 'The path you have chosen at this time is a solitary path – a path of loneliness at times; a path of pain. This is still your lower self manifesting and these things will pass as you absorb more light. You must realise that the Dragon and the Serpent are one and the same and are the ancient symbols of your planet's wisdom and priesthood. As you have already been told, the Golden Order of the Dragon Sword is open to all who aspire to a spiritual path from all cultures and traditions. Most people are not consciously aware that they are members of this Order as they operate on different levels of awareness not known to them in an ordinary earthly environment. Yet their higher conscious state is fully aware of this role. All are connected to a core consciousness of truth and it is that core that the sword symbolises as well as other mysteries not yet revealed to you.

'Spiritual progress must be slow to enable your electrical circuits, shall I say, to readjust to the increase of voltage; otherwise fuses will be blown, as you have already experienced at the volcano in Africa. Slow initial progress is faster in the long term as it enables the individual to adjust, including the group and collective consciousness. This is only the beginning of this new stage of your spiritual journey with the Order. Much needs to be done, most of which you will not be aware of. Perform mundane tasks well and with a glad heart. This will help to make good spiritual progress, for the secret is your state of mind. The task you perform is secondary to the state of mind applied to it. For example: a high ranking priest ceremonially robed and surrounded by temple regalia may be thinking of something else whilst performing a rite; whereas an elderly poor man may be tending his garden praying and feeling the Divine within. Who has the right frame of mind? Who is the ordained priest? Some are ordained by man, others are ordained by Spirit.

'The ancient tribal culture in which you have participated and witnessed was no coincidence. You were brought to this ancient land at this time for this reason: that the initiation took place at the foot of an active volcano in a rain forest with your bare feet on the dark soil of the Earth Mother, connecting your ancestors with the Chief's through the energy of fire. A similar ceremony or rite could have been undertaken in your native Celtic land but the truth has been lost through the orthodox leaders not being fully aware of the holistic balance of all life. No truth, of course, can ever be lost totally as all there has ever been will always remain. One by one many individuals like yourself are now emerging and will stand to offer their lives in service to humanity, as the multitude is now leaderless because of the soul suppression by the teachers of most religions. Many like you from varied cultures, traditions and faiths are being called to serve together around the world at this time. It is your destiny; it is your time; it is the divine blueprint of you all upon your individual paths.'

The sword was returned and the canoe took me back across the lake to the rim of the volcano. I watched as the lake and mist dissolved and Yasur roared his mighty words of power once again.

I came out of meditation as I heard Jerry calling softly to me. Chief Wai Wai had instructed Jerry to take me through the rain forest today to show me the roosts of the flying fox high in the canopy of the huge banyan trees. This was important, he explained. We followed several jungle paths throughout the day and I asked Jerry more questions about his culture. When we needed something to eat or drink Jerry simply took his bush knife and opened a fallen coconut for us to eat its flesh and drink its milk. I didn't really care for the flesh; to me it tasted like soap. The reason for this was because Jerry preferred eating germinating coconuts which obviously had a different chemical composition.

We came to a group of people working in the forest and amongst them was Chief Wai Wai. When he saw me he left the men and came over to me, shaking my hand gently. But the most amazing thing was the look of pure love towards me as his brother, as his equal, as another human being. We had opened and connected our hearts together.

I received further Spirit communications about the ceremony and Order during the night.

9ᵗʰ May 2003

Ipeukel Village   John Frum Cargo Cult

After breakfast, I spoke again to High Chief Kahi about the ceremony and tribal traditions and culture. He explained more to me. I asked about the importance of the rite of circumcision.

'The boys are kept apart from the community in a hut where the women are not allowed access to them or even to see them. They remain isolated but cared for by an appointed boy or man. They are not allowed out of the hut except to use the toilet which is dug nearby specifically for their use only.'

On the morning of my arrival three boys had been circumcised with a bamboo knife so I was able to visit them when I went to the local nakamal. They remained in their bark hut for my entire visit and would only emerge when their wounds were healed. Then a major feast would take place. A man changed the dressings on their wounds as I spoke to them. The rite of circumcision is the rite of passage from boy to man. It is believed that it also makes the man stronger, healthier and less prone to disease so he will live longer. Once the "man" returns to the house he then has a higher status than his mother.

Kahi then spoke again about marriage. He said that, if I were to marry a local woman (one of his daughters), he would have the authority to confer upon me a higher grade of chief. When I return to Vanuatu in the future he would arrange the marriage and a big feast where everybody from the village and surrounding area would attend to bear witness to the ceremony. A piece of his land would be put aside for our use as members of his family and our own leaf house constructed (the land would remain the property of the tribe). In tribal tradition a high ranking chief has to marry into a family of equal grade. The High Chief has to know each individual person and their family history and ancestry in his area so that he can arrange marriages correctly and also decide on the correct punishment for offenders.

Chief Kahi left me and I sat alone in front of my leaf hut listening to the sound of the rain forest which enveloped me, enabling me to slip easily into a meditative state. I suddenly found myself standing at the edge of the nakamal before the banyan tree where my ceremony took place. In the dappled light of the rain forest I saw clearly the Golden Dragon Sword set point downwards into the dark earth at the centre of their holy temple. Surrounding this ceremonial area was a white mist or veil, almost curtain-like. I passed through it to the glowing sword, momentarily touching it, yet dazzled by its brilliance. I then had to withdraw to the outer fringes of the nakamal. As I watched and waited, the veil seemed impenetrable. I kept reconnecting through the day and it became much stronger and I could see through the opaque form, what appeared to be many people, knights and warriors together, carrying lights, filing in procession from inside the sacred banyan tree and all moving clockwise around the pulsating Dragon Sword. It appeared as though the Dragon Serpent consciousness was being directed from the magical sword deep into the earth to the volcano itself. I tried several methods to gain permission to pass through the veil to join the throng or bear witness to the ceremony taking place, but permission was withheld for some reason. I felt that a special ceremony had been undertaken at a higher level of consciousness or possibly in one of my own parallel incarnations. I felt puzzled; none of it made any sense to me.

At 2.30 pm Jerry and I left Loanengo to walk to the village of Ipeukel which is a tribal kastom village at Sulphur Bay run by the John Frum Cargo Cultists (see Glossary). We passed across the black ash plain from Yasur, the fresh ash straight from the volcano stinging my eyes and the sulphur fumes pungent to the back of my throat. The village was truly amazing – a large village traditionally built in every way. It was like going back to Neolithic times where time had actually stood still, the only exception being the Western clothing that the villagers used for their everyday routine. Among the leaf houses ran pigs, dogs, cats and naked children.

We found the village chief to be absent on our arrival but we gathered in the village square and spoke to the medicine man and the elders, one of whom spoke good English so he could interpret. We spoke of many things for some time – God, ancestors, tribal customs, including the beliefs of the John Frum Cargo Cult. The medicine man, or Yeramanu, asked why I had come to their village. So I replied, 'I am not a tourist. I am a traveller seeking my spiritual path and have come to learn about your ancient tribal customs and traditions that I may be helped to reconnect to my own spiritual truth and ancestors.'

The Yeramanu asked, 'What do you understand the volcano to be?'

I thought for a moment and replied, 'Through my understanding I believe the earth upon which we sit is our mother from whom we were all born. The volcano is God's symbol or representative of the male energy of creation as the earth is a symbol and representative of female energy. Therefore, the volcano is God manifest in physical form amongst us.'

The Yeramanu and elders spoke amongst themselves in their own language for what seemed a long time. Then they all turned to face me and smiled.

'You know the truth! Why do you ask these questions when you already know the answers?'

'I seek confirmation and self-confidence of my inner spiritual awareness from those who know the truth. Thank you.'

'Do you speak to God?'

'Yes. I speak to God.'

'Does he talk to you?'

'Yes, he talks to me.'

'We know that for we see it. You must come with us to our nakamal.'

Jerry looked at me and raised his eyes and smiled, confirming that I was being honoured. I followed the elders to their sacred temple through the village where, during the preparation of the kava, we spoke again. Elder John then asked me what I knew about the John Frum religion. I had to be honest and replied that I knew nothing about it. He seemed disappointed with my answer. He frowned and turned away. Elder John then spoke at length to me explaining that God is manifest in all of nature – the trees, the stones and their medicine.

'We take kava to keep the body light. You cannot become fat if you drink kava regularly. Kava helps us to become still within to allow God to speak to us and to help us with our problems, such as healing. God will speak to you after taking kava to help you find your ancestors.'

As the boys and men prepared the kava, Elder John continued to explain more of their ways to me, 'We refuse to send our children to school to learn the Western way, to be part of the Western culture. We do not use the government hospital but rely totally on our Yeramanu who talks to the spirits after taking kava to be instructed on which plants are to be used for medicine.'

The Yeramanu, a dark, thick-set man with a large black beard, then asked me about my beard, 'How long have you had the beard?'

'I have had it about twenty years now.'

'Why did you grow it?'

'I grew it because I felt within myself that this was the right thing to do, even though I did not know why at the time. I now realise that the beard, along with long hair, holds extra energy around the head to enable you to speak to Spirit, to God.'

The medicine man, the elders and more men, who had now gathered, spoke amongst themselves, obviously going over what I had just said.

The Yeramanu then looked at me and said, 'You speak the truth. The beard is your sign of power. It must never be removed. Today we drink kava together, you and I, we have different skins but we are as one in our hearts. One day we will walk together.'

The kava taking ritual in this village was more ceremonial than at Loanengo. The Yeramanu was the first to take the kava, followed by Elder John and I together. We stood in silence to pray, followed by the other chiefs from visiting villages, some who had travelled from other islands to receive his help and healing. Apart from the sounds of the sea crashing upon the coral reef nearby and the volcano with the occasional canine ambush on a pig, all was silent. We then all had something to eat from a communal bowl. I felt dizzy and nauseous after the kava. The food was full of ants, which we all ate. I have always been fascinated by ants, spending hours as a boy watching them at work. I considered them as intelligent and industrious. I never expected to have to eat them!

Elder John spoke quietly to me before we left, 'Nobody in Vanuatu is poor. We have no need for money as everything we need is provided for by God.' He pointed into the rain forest. 'You come from a different culture to ours. That is the path God has chosen for you but we are all one in spirit. If you need food, we give it freely. We offer you a place to sleep free. We do not ask for payment as they do in the West. What we have we share.'

A man then came forward and presented to me a woven bag and a hat as gifts.

'Much of our tribal custom has been destroyed by the church and Western education. Of what importance is it to us that we are taught at school that Captain Cook discovered our islands when our islands have always been here? Our own education of our spiritual beliefs and medicine is taught to our children in this kastom village, not Western beliefs. You are different from the rest who visit us. You sit with us to talk and learn of our ways. The others who come are not interested. They take photos then go.'

I was then led to a leaf house to rest and pray by the light of an oil lamp, as darkness had fallen, where a woven pandanus mat was unrolled for me to sit upon. Some villagers then began to sing and dance in the open square beneath the light of the moon which is their regular Friday worship period for the John Frum Cargo Cult.

As I watched in silence, I was transported back in time again to the magic of the South Sea Islands. At about 9.00 pm the music started and all gathered around the leaf thatched shelter in the village square to sing what I can only describe as a Melanesian form of hymn. As the night progressed, dancing began – the women in one area and the men in another. The dancing was more of a military march to and fro by some cult members where others swayed and moved on the spot. The women wore traditional grass skirts.

Jerry came for me later on and, after saying goodbye to the medicine man, we set off in the dark for Loanengo village. We had met as strangers but departed as brothers. It was wonderful to walk past the base of Yasur volcano at night to see the red glow in the sky and to smell the sulphur again. The most amazing thing was to see the molten red lava bombs explode high into the sky and fall back inside the crater and the flying foxes silhouetted against the moon – how magical.

10ᵗʰ May 2003
Manx flag   God Yasur

Jerry, his young son and I went up to Yasur volcano again. Jerry and the boy stayed on the boulder plain whilst I climbed to the crater rim. The volcano was awesome. Its physical force took my breath away and made me feel so frail and insignificant in comparison. Occasionally several large explosions occurred, always making me jump, and I had to strain my eyes against the bright sun to see where the lava bombs would fall. Some of these bombs were the size of a dustbin or a fridge. One explosion in particular shook the earth and caused compression waves through the air which really hurt my ears. You treat Yasur with the greatest respect. For some reason Yasur was more active today than in the past few days.

We returned to the village and I relaxed for a couple of hours to write up notes in my journal and to pray and give thanks for the wonderful experiences I had.

After lunch, Jerry, his sons and I walked several miles to the coast to Port Resolution where he lived. Port Resolution was in reality a large village, so named after Commander Cook's ship when he first landed on Tanna Island, drawn to her shores by the glow of Yasur volcano in the night sky. The deep, shark infested inlets and bays were stunningly beautiful and offered sheltered anchorage with fresh water and local food.

Jerry introduced me to his wife, a shy, slim woman and his crippled daughter, Ealise. His eldest son, also called David, was at school.

Jerry then took me to meet Chief Ronnie (Chief Noar), a small man with a smiling face and a mop of grey hair. He spoke good English and was interpreter for visiting sailors who anchored in the bay for fresh supplies. On our return, we stopped off to meet the Head Teacher of the local school, much to the amusement of the children. I spoke briefly to a class about the Isle of Man.

At about 4.30 pm Jerry, his two sons and I left his village to walk home. We had arranged to go to Chief Wai Wai's nakamal used solely for those who follow the old kastom ways of the ancestors. As I saw Jerry approaching my hut, I stuffed my Manx flag into my shirt; I always carry one with me when I travel. I wanted to show the flag to the chief and the Triskele upon it (Three Legs of Man).

By the time we arrived, the light was fading and it would soon be time for the preparation and drinking of kava. A bearded man arrived about the same time as ourselves, who I recognised as one of the dancers. He tended the wood fire inside the leaf shelter where we sat. Jerry introduced me to him. He was known as Robert but he was always called Nikwei in his own native tongue. He was a medicine man or Yeramanu, the next senior rank to the chief. He wore nambas only.

Chief Wai Wai arrived shortly afterwards and he also wore nambas only. I stood to greet Wai Wai and he invited me to sit next to him at the fire, placing upon the logs a leg of wild pig and holding a huge cream fat maggot, rather like an Australian witchety grub. This he had tied to a string and roasted it carefully in the embers, turning it every few minutes as we spoke. Chief Wai Wai presented me with two newly made pandanus palm armbands to confirm my rank of chief and a rolled up item of hibiscus bark fibre which was my nambas. I remembered the Manx flag inside my shirt pulling it out and explaining it to be the flag of my nation. The Chief and Nikwei looked at each other in a peculiar way; then they examined the flag carefully, talking in their own dialect. For some reason it appeared important to them so I gave it to the Chief.

The Chief, Nikwei and I talked for a couple of hours, Jerry interpreting as required. The smoke from the fire stung our eyes, being our only source of light in the darkness. Chief Wai Wai offered his pipe to me to share with him, the home grown black tobacco pungent and very strong – another symbolic gesture of a shared respect of a man of similar rank. When the kava was ready, I drank a little with Wai Wai. He cut a slice of meat from the leg of the wild pig for me to eat. Wai Wai went on to explain that, by placing his hand upon my head during the ceremony, he also confirmed not only the position and rank of chief but the shared guardianship of the flying fox, banana plant and banyan. Now I understood why Jerry had to take me to visit the roost of the flying fox in the banyan trees. I had to make that connection.

Chief Wai Wai took me to a place at the edge of the nakamal to show me a sacred place where the flying fox spirit stone was situated, along with the spirit stones of other creatures/plants. When he needed to communicate with the spirits of the flying fox, he would go into a trance dance and perform a sacred ceremony. Wai Wai spoke in Bislama (pidgin English) so I could understand most of his words.

After further explanation of tribal tradition, the Chief then handed me two feather sticks, the headdress of my rank. He explained that these sticks, which had different coloured feathers tied to them, were stuck in the hair just behind the ears, rather like a couple of antennae. They were about two feet long and the feathers were dyed in the natural colours of red, blue and green. Wai Wai said that, because my hair was too fine and straight, unlike their own which is thick black and curly, I would have to use a headband of some sort to tie them in position.

After Chief Wai Wai had finished speaking to me, Nikwei went off and soon returned with a carving which he was working on of a man in native dress, finishing it at the fire. This he offered to me as a brother. I was told that these items were not the usual tourist trinkets but the authentic tribal attire and totem carving made especially for me. Jerry interpreted the words of Nikwei and said that this carving was of great tribal significance and importance for me and it would always link me to his people. The carving had the arms of the man held at the waist instead of hanging by the side. This is a significant difference and means something, but I forgot to find out what.

Wai Wai asked me to learn Bislama and to return to the tribe so he could teach me the kastom way and to take my position of chief. The Chief went on to tell the story that when The Queen and Prince Philip visited Vanuatu at the time of independence he was chosen to act the part of a warrior threatening Prince Philip with a spear. I related to him my story of when I was in Vice Regal service and had served The Queen and Prince Philip as a footman. We both laughed together at the coincidence we both shared.

Chief Wai Wai then explained that Nikwei was one of the guardians of Yasur volcano so he asked Nikwei to speak to the God Yasur on my behalf. Nikwei stood and went into a trance dance falling over onto the earth several times in the darkness. It was erratic and I had difficulty in seeing him at times. After falling over several more times, Nikwei stood, obviously in a trance-like state, facing Yasur and raising both hands to his God speaking in his native tongue. Then he stood in silence for a few minutes. Jerry's young sons giggled. The Chief looked at them in such a way that they became silent immediately casting their eyes to the ground. Wai Wai explained to me that Yasur was now speaking to Nikwei on my behalf.

Nikwei gave thanks to Yasur and sat with us by the fire. He spoke to Wai Wai and the Chief said that the message for me from their God was – "thank you for coming". Nikwei had a large weeping ulcer on his thigh that was torn open after his fall talking to Yasur. Blood and pus dribbled down his leg. He disappeared into the forest, returning with kastom medicine leaves which he rubbed between his hands, applying them to the wound. Wai Wai said again that we could see that I was no ordinary person unlike the disinterested tourists. I spoke, with Jerry interpreting, that I had found these days amongst his people one of the most important times of my life and that my heart had now filled with peace. Wai Wai and Nikwei smiled broadly and looked directly into my eyes, seemingly into my very soul. My heart recognised these men as part of my Soul Group.

Both men went over my past history carefully, as Kahi had done, wanting me to explain to them that my father was dead and I was the firstborn twin and why I had had a beard for many years. All important signs apparently, including circumcision, that I was indeed a chief. Chief Wai Wai continued saying that it was very important that I was to return to "my" tribe. He went on to explain that the spirits of his people go to the God Yasur at death, back to the creative force. Yasur seemed to acknowledge this statement with an impressive explosion, causing the trees in the nakamal to sway.

As we stood to say our goodbyes, I felt sad. I had been a part of this culture for only a few days yet it felt so familiar as though I had come home in some way. I have always believed that my first incarnation upon earth was as an Australian Aborigine. Maybe I was wrong and it was as a native of this land, after all, it is the same root race.

Wai Wai again repeated to me, 'You must understand that the ceremony you have gone through has never been done to an outsider before. This is the first and only time and you will never fully realise the importance and honour given to you. Likewise these gifts that we now present to you are made especially for you as you are now our brother. You must return next year for sacred ceremony and also the following year. This is necessary for you to fulfil your role as a chief. It is for your safety also.'

I agreed, not knowing how I could afford such journeys or if I could get time off work. I trusted that Spirit would provide. We embraced each other and looked silently and deeply into each other's eyes. I felt love move between us, a bonding of human beings from different cultures coming together as one. We stood upon the bare earth beneath the moonlight in an opening in the rain forest canopy. In the near distance the volcano spoke. The flying foxes flew overhead and the cicada called from their leafy abodes under the stars of the Southern Cross. The smoke from the fire filled my nostrils and here I stood with fellow human beings in a land far from my Celtic island home. My heart was sad yet I felt at peace – a peace I had not experienced since the Goddess touched my heart and mind and sent me into a state of spiritual bliss many years ago.

The Chief spoke, 'You will know when to return, for the ancestors will tell you. They will come to you in your dreams. It is important to write down what they tell you.'

Jerry picked up a glowing fire stick and we walked back to my hut along the dark, damp jungle paths and road, my senses alert and sensitive to every familiar smell and sound around me. Tomorrow was the day I had to leave so I wanted to savour every last experience. As we got nearer to my leaf hut, I asked Jerry about his family. Jerry went on to explain that Ealise had fallen over at the age of one and had been unable to walk ever since. He spent many months in Port Vila with the toddler as she underwent surgery by an Australian lady doctor. Kastom medicine didn't help. Jerry's own words were, 'The doctor cut too many strings so my little girl can never walk again and nobody can help us.' She is now eleven years old.

In their tradition and culture a crippled girl will never get a husband. She is going to have great difficulties later in life and will have to be kept by her relatives.

11th May 2003
Departure

Today was my last day at Loanengo village. I felt very sad. Somehow I had been reconnected to divinity within and found it so easy to slip in and out of prayerful meditative states. They were such simple spiritual people. They asked for nothing, they demanded nothing. Everything was given freely and with love and respect with a gentleness that is rare in the West. I had been asked initially to return and live with them for two years to learn the ways of the Yeramanu as part of their family in their homes, primitive to Western standards perhaps but totally in balance as one with the Earth Mother. As this was impractical, I had agreed to return separately for the next two years.

My heart was full of gladness for the opportunity. My mind was full of irrational fears, doubts and conflict – fear of the unknown, fear of failure. Through my confused thoughts, my sad state, I ate my breakfast of fruit and tea. I was suddenly interrupted by the truck arriving at 8.30 am. I had no further time to ponder my dilemma so I put my bags in the truck after embracing Jerry and saying goodbye to his boys, who stood in silence nearly. One had large tears in his eyes. We looked silently into each other's eyes. There was no need to speak.

We drove across the ash plain of Yasur volcano and I offered my silent prayers of thanks to Him. We returned to the airport, passing over the mountains, which enabled me to see more of the island. Just past the airport was a lodge where I had arranged to stay the night ready for an early departure to Port Vila the following morning. As it turned out it was Mother's Day in Vanuatu. The owners of the lodge invited me to their feast. They were very gentle, hospitable people. That night several tourists stayed at the lodge. I had great difficulty in interacting with them so I went for a walk by myself along the coral reefs on the shore watching the local people who were fishing and swimming. I sat alone and I wept. I felt emotional and mixed up in so many ways. I knew that I was going through a spiritual transformation of some sort. Part of my soul was still at the Chief's fire.

12th May 2003
Lucid dream

I left Tanna on the morning flight arriving in Port Vila at lunchtime. My flight back to Brisbane was late in the afternoon so I made enquiries as to where to get my tribal artefacts fumigated as there was a strong possibility that the Australian authorities would confiscate these items because of the likelihood of harbouring pests or disease. I was directed to the Ministry of Agriculture, Quarantine, Forestry and Fisheries where I had my artefacts fumigated for three hours with formaldehyde. The official said that they needed fumigated for longer but I explained that I had a plane to catch so I asked for the Quarantine Certificate in any case.

After going through Vanuatu Immigration I sat next to a female tourist on the aircraft who wore the most nauseating perfume and who talked incessantly about trivia. I realised that probably her perfume was an average brand that most Western women would wear and, because of my sojourn in the rain forest,

I was accustomed to the natural delicate scents of nature. In effect, I had been on an intensive retreat which had heightened my perception and senses.

After arriving in Australia at 6.30 pm, the Quarantine Inspector looked at my artefacts, scraping and thumping them, looking for creepy things. He said they did not recognise the Vanuatu Government's Quarantine procedure, but thankfully I was able to keep everything.

I arrived at the hotel and rang May to let her know I was back. She was really excited. I put my tribal artifacts in the sun on my balcony to disperse the toxic fumigation. I had a meal in the hotel restaurant and went to bed early. I felt emotional, confused and disorientated. I felt really sad as my heart was still at Chief Wai Wai's fire under the open sky. That night I had a lucid dream or vision of Chief Wai Wai walking up to my bed and speaking to me. It was as if he was physically in the room with me. He spoke clearly and in a way I could easily understand, his face serious yet his eyes sparkling.

'Iarueri, it is now time for you to face your first death. Be strong. I am with you as your brother. The ancestors will call you to return after this test is completed.'

The Chief turned and disappeared through the portal into the rain forest. I sat bolt upright in bed, perspiring, wondering if this death was just symbolic or actual in some way. I felt wretched and close to tears.

The following day I went into the city to buy a travel guide of Vanuatu and clothes for Chief Wai Wai, a pair of boots for Jerry and a dress for Ealise, posting them care of High Chief Kahi. Studying the literature of Vanuatu helped me understand my experience better.

I found the people in the city aggressive, yet I didn't before. The litter, pollution and noise made me feel ill. Yet in reality Brisbane is a very clean and beautiful city compared to others. I felt spiritually polluted and realised that I was still probably energetically open to these harsh energies so I spent the rest of the day in the Botanic Gardens in a contemplative mood, calling my power and soul parts back, until nightfall. When I saw the foraging flying foxes silhouetted against the moon, I wept, falling to my knees beneath a banyan tree, crying out to the ancestors to help me to adjust to the Western life style again. I called out to the spirit of the flying fox to take a message from my heart to Chief Wai Wai. I would prefer the challenges of the jungle to the sterile lifestyle of the West any time.

13th May 2003
Embarrassment   First death

I met May at the airport at a pre-arranged time. We hugged each other and she cried. She looked frail, tired and anxious. She said her goodbyes to her family and we went through Immigration.

Once I got May settled into the business class lounge with a snifter, she soon relaxed and became chirpy and bright. She kept repeating to herself that she was going home. May was very deaf so I had to shout and she shouted louder back in turn. She wondered if she could have a cat in her new flat in the sheltered accommodation that was being prepared for her as she missed her old cats which she had to give away when she left the island. Then all of my nightmares manifested in compressed form.

'I used to have such a beautiful soft black pussy!' she shouted.

An elegant woman nearby choked on her gin and tonic. I sensed that trouble was brewing like a cyclone and tried to change the subject. May was now on a roll, extolling loudly how she often enjoyed stroking her black sleek pussy. A man opposite coughed and buried his head in a newspaper. Somebody else giggled. I prayed the floor would open up and swallow me. Hundreds of eyes looked in our direction – at least that's how it felt.

Our flight was then called. We got settled into our business class seats on the aircraft. May almost disappeared into the depths of her reclining bucket seat. We took off – heading for home! May was like a little girl, giggling. I don't know what she had had to drink but I wished that I had been given a bucket full. Then the nightmare replay began when the stewardess came round with drinks. May told the stewardess loudly all about her pussy in full gory technicolour. The stewardess smiled sweetly in her well-practised way, describing her own amazing cat in detail. I wanted to get off and walk!

May turned to me and shouted, 'David. This nice lady has a pussy with long black hair!' Everybody nearby stared. The man in the next seat choked.

I crossed my legs, making sure I made no eye contact with the young woman and looked out of the window at the cumulus clouds billowing in thunderheads over the South Pacific Ocean. My thoughts returned to the tribe. Tears welled up in my eyes and I was angry with myself for being so emotional. My heart actually ached. All this wealth and luxury around me felt so cold, dead and empty. I wished I was sitting with Nikwei at the Chief's fire, in the nakamal beneath the volcano.

When we arrived at London Heathrow, May's ankles were swollen and she was very stiff. Fortunately the travel agent had arranged for a wheelchair to be available so we were escorted through the priority channel to a waiting pre-booked taxi which took us to Gatwick Airport for our flight back to the Isle of Man. We almost missed our flight but eventually arrived back on the Island, its sweet, clean, sharp air filling my nostrils. May was welcomed by our family and her friends were there on hand to take her to her new home in Castletown which they had redecorated for her. May hugged and kissed me and, weeping, said that I had saved her life. (May passed to the realms of the ancestors in September 2006.)

On my return home I couldn't wait to tell my family and friends about my experiences. Most were not interested and changed the subject. I felt that they were simply jealous. However, the reaction of my family shocked me, especially when I said I was returning for two more visits over the next two years. I was expecting deep interest and support when all I was told was "Can't you see they are using you to get money and clothes" or statements like "they saw you coming; they are ripping you off!"

I felt deep pain at these comments. This initiation was so profoundly important for me. I had no family support. I could sense in my twin brother a fear that I was being manipulated and used because of my open, trusting nature and that he was trying to protect and warn me to be more careful in his own way. I loved him for that. Yet he had not seen or felt what I had experienced. He had not been with the tribe and had his heart opened as I had.

I felt alone again. I had no one who I could confide in. I became more withdrawn and couldn't stop crying. My body ached; I felt miserable, crying out constantly to the ancestors for help, which came in a variety of forms. I functioned in life because I simply had to but I had no interest in interaction with other people; in fact I would avidly avoid them. I wanted so badly to retreat from the world and curl up alone in an isolated cave. After several months, thoughts of suicide came into my mind. I eventually overcame these feelings, realising I had experienced my first death.

I felt so ill. I was exhausted with lots of aches and pains, especially my teeth. Energetic adjustments had obviously been taking place and I was able to get clearer sharper visions and dreams than I had ever experienced before. I felt as though I had been turned inside out.

Over the following months I experienced many visions of the Golden Order of the Dragon Sword. The other Orders I also encountered were the Green Order of the Dragon Sword and the Black Order of the Dragon Sword. All have different roles to play.

Further connections were made with the Guardians of the flying fox, banana and banyan. Interestingly, my connection to our Sea God, Manannan Mac Llyr (from whom the Isle of Man received its name) became stronger and more profound. It is said in legend that he was also known as the God of Atlantis. I felt the presence of Manannan clearly in Vanuatu and I began to wonder if Manannan and Majikjiki are one and the same deity, known by different names?

13th July 2003
Quartz stones

Several weeks previously I had received a strong impression that I had to collect two tumbled quartz stones at the shore from the Isle of Man – one for High Chief Kahi and the other for Chief Wai Wai. The significance of the stones to an outsider may not be apparent but in the tribal beliefs of Vanuatu the stones, especially small egg-shaped stones, are considered powerful magical items used for spiritual ceremonies and rites, as they hold within them the condensed power of the earth. The national currency of Vanuatu is called the Vatu which also means stone. These sacred stones are no longer allowed out of the country, as they also contain within them the ancestral memory of the tribes. To receive two tumbled, smooth, white quartz stones from the Isle of Man would be recognized as a spiritual gift, as they will hold sacred magic within them of my ancient land and culture. After a ceremony, I collected the stones from the sea at an isolated beach and posted them to the tribe.

31st August 2003
Council of Elders

Over a period of seven years, I had been a tenant in a semi-derilect old Manx farmhouse, which I had renovated, taking it back as far as I could to its original timber and rough lime stone walls, discovering in the process a large hidden inglenook fireplace. This was the perfect altar and portal for my spiritual work. When the fire was lit, this room became my temple space. Over the weeks and years that followed I passed through the portal to sit in council with the Chiefs and Elders in their different nakamals to receive their teaching. They tested my ethics and morals for the reasons I wanted to return and to continue learning their cultural lineage. Great insights were learnt.

24th September 2003
Spiritual ignorance

This evening the Council of Elders had called me to open the portal. I went into a meditative process and became aware of Spirit communication moving through me. I took up my pen.

'Iarueri, you still await a deeper call to return to the tribal lands in Vanuatu to fulfil the raising of the inner consciousness. Patience. You have had this call; it is just a question of receiving the appropriate physical response. To return to undergo tests and trials for the sake of being able to say that you have done this is of no value whatsoever unless it is based on spiritual concepts. Some cultures and belief systems subscribe to violence and suffering for initiations without any or little spiritual basis. This is cruelty which initiates the neophyte into fear only. Rather counterproductive! To undergo tests and trials that involve pain or discomfort, they have to be based on spiritual awareness so that the initiate is protected, supported and monitored throughout the process. The pain has the effect of opening psychic centres with the release of certain chemicals and trapped toxic energies from this life, past, parallel or future lives, so skilled priests or chiefs must officiate and adjust the proceedings for the individual's needs. "Blanket" initiations, rituals and ceremonies are fine as a foundation but we are all different and are all progressing at different levels of awareness. So to build upon a basic foundation is acceptable providing adjustments are made on different levels.

'When you were initiated as a chief, psychic centres were duly opened to enable you to contact the ancestors more clearly; this created intense emotional releases. You were ready at that time so the situation was prepared for you by the guardians and ancestors. Some have said, "How can this be? You were only initiated as a chief within 48 hours of your arrival. It is a fake!" This, Iarueri, is a statement of spiritual ignorance as you had been preparing and training for that moment over many incarnations. When the pupil is ready, the master will come – a common saying, repeated but very true. As you were ready at that time, there was no need for you to live within the tribe for many months or years, as had been suggested, since you had already achieved the right level of awareness. All it needed was the correct circumstances and preparation to pass you through the veil. You were expected by the Chief. Remember what he told you. This was no accidental happening.'

1st October 2003
Marriage invitation

A letter arrived today from High Chief Kahi calling me back to marry his granddaughter in a ceremony, which I am unable to do. Personal details were given about his granddaughter, which I cannot reveal, and details about his family. He had asked me to arrive with my family for a wedding ceremony at which he would officiate. I wrote diplomatically back to Chief Kahi explaining that I could not marry his granddaughter but I still wished to return for other ceremonies, if he agreed.

Interestingly, I was told by the ancestors that, before I could return to the tribal lands, I would need to have communications from Spirit and also a physical invitation from the Chief. I now had both.

25th January 2004
The Black Arts   Missionary killed

Since I wrote to Chief Kahi declining to marry his granddaughter I hadn't had a letter in return. What was interesting is that, from that point on, I developed a very painful right shoulder which manifested for no apparent reason. I used all the metaphysical skills and knowledge that I had and I still could not resolve this issue; I began to wonder if by chance the black arts of Vanuatu had been projected to me in some way as, when I was in Tanna before, I went with Jerry to Port Resolution to meet his family and Jerry showed me a series of missionaries' graves. There was one inscribed grave in particular of a female missionary from Scotland and Jerry explained to me the story behind this. This missionary defied the local Yeramanu in front of his men ridiculing their tribal customs and beliefs and she challenged him to see if he could kill her by his magic. She was eating a banana at the time and claimed that her God was more powerful than his. As she turned away, she threw the banana skin to the ground at his feet, so the Yeramanu picked it up (which obviously contained her energy), returning to his nakamal. The following morning she was found dead in her bed. The year was 1894. I will not reveal her identity. I know that this magic is still used and probably just as effective because certain secrets have been revealed to me and certain techniques have been explained and shown to me of what can be done to harm or kill another man.

I wondered whether I had caused loss of face to Chief Kahi by explaining to him that I could not marry his granddaughter and that, in some way, a psychic attack had been imposed upon me. This may very well not be the case but it is a possibility, so I wrote back to him explaining the situation to see what his response would be.

28th January 2004

I received a letter from High Chief Kahi asking if I would return at the end of February or early March. Now I have a suitable time I can plan the next stage of my journey. Nothing was mentioned about my shoulder.

12th February 2004
Humiliation

Last night I made the clear decision to return to Vanuatu within the next few weeks. There were many reasons I could find why I should not go. I needed to motivate myself. It was now time. I began to mention my decision, not taken lightly, to friends and family, looking for moral support and understanding; yet, to date, I had only received vitriolic attacks from my friends on why I should not waste my money at playing the big chief. I was being accused of egotism and naivety to think that I should be made a chief of a small tribe on a small island in the middle of nowhere, although my brother now defended me. I opened my heart to Barry and explained how I felt. He encouraged and supported me from that day on. I needed his love.

My confidence and hopes duly shattered, I began to wonder if my friends were right. I came to the decision; this was a chance I must take. I would never get another opportunity and, if my so-called friends did not, or would not, understand the importance of this opportunity that was their problem. I prayed to the Goddess and the ancestors to give me the strength and courage to continue and to bring understanding to those who were doing their best to prevent me from going to suit their own agendas and fears. Hopefully, through these experiences I would grow spiritually stronger and more aware, so that I may be able to help others be strong; to pass their own tests and trials as I have done. This was my greatest test to date.

6th March 2004

A mother's tears

This was my last day at home before departure tomorrow for the other side of the earth. A part of me was afraid; another part of me was exhilarated. My mother, Margery White, gave me the costs of the return air fares to Australia and Vanuatu. With tears in her eyes she said that she did not understand why I wanted to go to that place again but now knew it was important to me. This has taken a huge financial burden from me, so I thank her and bless her for that. If we walk the path of courage and truth, Spirit will provide.

Tonight, with the light of the full moon reflecting on the snow outside, I lit candles, leaving them burning safely all night to honour the deities of my lands and the deities of the tribal lands of Vanuatu.

PART 2

RETURN OF THE WHITE SERPENT

9th March 2004

I eventually arrived in Brisbane, Australia. I felt exhausted. I didn't go to bed but went straight away to get supplies, school stationery, and to change traveller's cheques. I brought with me from the Isle of Man various items of clothing for the tribe including shoes for Jerry and dresses for Ealise.

11th March 2004

On my arrival at the Air Vanuatu office in Brisbane, I was informed that all lines of communication were down on Tanna Island due to Cyclone Ivy causing devastating damage. What was known, however, was that most of the roads were blocked by fallen trees and landslides.

VANUATU

14th March 2004

I arrived in Port Vila and managed to get through on the telephone to Challen at Jungle Oasis Lodge. He would arrange a truck to collect me tomorrow from the airport. The hotel I stayed at was considerably damaged by the cyclone.

15th March 2004

On my arrival at the Lodge, I found that the place I had stayed at before had been totally destroyed by an earlier cyclone setting the wooden buildings on fire. Chief Kahi was in Vila with his wife, who was in hospital having an operation. He would not be back before my departure. Jungle Oasis Lodge was run by the Chief's second son, Kelson.

I had to share the facilities with a couple of tourists for a while, which I didn't like. They were very demanding and had no respect for the kastom culture or people. I made it clear to Kelson that I needed to speak to Chief Wai Wai urgently as I wanted to stay in his village to continue with my studies of tribal culture. Kelson assured me that he would speak to the Chief tomorrow. I was woken during the night by being severely bitten by unidentified insects; their squashed and bloody remains stained the sheets and my body. Traditionally, the kastom people slept between two large banana leaves on a pandanus mat.

16th March 2004

Tattoo protocol

Kelson told me he had spoken to the Chief and between them they had agreed it was best for me to stay with him at the Lodge as the Chief's village was severely damaged by the cyclone. I felt bitterly disappointed. Kelson said that I was to pay him for my keep and guides. Kelson asked for 30,000 Vatu (the equivalent of £260) for a month's stay. I had lived rough before with tribes so I was puzzled by the Chief's decision. I gave Kelson Jerry's shoes and asked him to give them to his brother.

I could hear the smug laughter and taunts of those back home and the "I told you sos". I felt crestfallen and so very sad that I had spent so much money, time and effort to be stuck in a tourist lodge.

Later that morning, Challen, a female tourist and I walked to the Chief's village. As we entered the village, the children ran ahead shouting 'Iarueri;

larueri comes,' to the beat of the tam tam drum calling the men to dance. The children cried and laughed, pulling at my clothes and holding my hands. They were genuinely pleased to see me and I them. The Chief and I grabbed each other as brothers and the others were pleased to welcome me back home. It felt so right being here.

Part way through the dancing, Nikwei appeared suddenly, looking at me and smiling, then joined the group of dancers. After the dancing, Challen and the tourist left and the Chief, Nikwei and I walked together back to Kelson's Lodge where we sat for a meeting. Kelson was our interpreter. We discussed a rough programme for the month ahead. I knew enough Bislama to realise that, during our conversation, Kelson was not telling the Chief what I was saying and not telling me exactly what the Chief was saying. Nikwei said that when he heard that I was at Itabu, he stopped his work and smeared himself with charcoal as a sign of respect to honour my return. The ulcer on his leg had healed, leaving a scar.

Chief Wai Wai said that the first ceremony would be to officially make me a chief of the tribe before a council of chiefs from around the island as witnesses, where I would have to kill a pig during the ceremony. This ceremony would take place on 21st March – the Spring Equinox!

We talked for some time and Chief Wai Wai spoke about tribal tattoos, saying that a tattoo, ear or nose piercings are marks of status or grade of that person and had to be earned. After this ceremony I would become the same grade as him and, in the future, both of us would receive the tribal mark together, which would be the next year, as the Chief could not receive his mark until his deceased father, the former High Chief, had withdrawn from him spiritually and joined the ancestors. To receive this mark whilst his father was still walking and talking with him would be disrespectful, he explained.

Nose piercings are reserved for the highest grade of chiefs in the northern islands. All tattoos mean certain things and are sacred spiritual marks. Last year, the ceremony was secret where the Chief had aligned me to the spirit of the tribe and the ancestors. This explained why I felt as I did, the emotional turmoil, the feelings of being turned inside out, the despair and difficulty of being with people. Chief Wai Wai said that he would contact and speak with the ancestors that night at the nakamal to begin the ceremony now and that I could expect to feel tired, emotional and have further spiritual or energetic adjustments taking place.

The Chief said he would like me to stay with him for a few nights to drink kava and to prepare me for the process.

I gave Wai Wai and Nikwei some gifts I had brought with me – two lightweight body warmers (as it gets very cold at night), some tobacco and pen knives. The Chief reminded me that my name, larueri goes back to the first ancestors and was his grandfather's name – he was a Yeramanu and Holy Man. It was a name reserved for a High Chief only, which was a really great honour for me.

The Chief and Nikwei left and, around 4 o'clock, Challen and I went up to Yasur volcano to watch the night sky fill with red lava bombs. Yasur was at level one activity (as gauged by vulcanologists) which is at its lowest at that time of the year. Even so, the explosions and fireworks were very impressive.

During the night, as I lay in bed, I thought about what the Chief had said in relation to staying with him, so I wondered why he wanted me to stay with Kelson. I was confused and I just couldn't understand what this was all about.

Then, in the night, I was awakened from sleep. Someone was calling me, 'Iarueri. Iarueri.' I couldn't see anybody; I was in a state between sleep and waking. I realised that it was a spirit voice and then suddenly this being began to speak, 'Tattoos are marks of privilege. These sacred symbols link the energy body to the physical through their magical and mystical application which, when created in the tattooist's mind, imprints the sacred geometry of the tribal mark. Tattoos must never be used as vulgar body ornamentation because the energetic forces or consciousness which are attached or associated with the sigil or mark may do irreparable psychological harm to the uninitiated. Never ever have a tattoo using a sacred symbol unless you have the permission and the authority to use and understand what it is. This is now expected from you, for the mark has to be earned. Once you are marked thus, the energy body is impregnated with the consciousness of all the energy linked with the sacred sigil. The outer pigmentation design is only secondary, as the true tattoo is energetic and many are marked this way, which can only be witnessed through the inner sight or vision.

'You will shortly earn the privilege of such a mark, should you choose to do so. All human life comes from an ancient tribal origin which used the tattoo mark as a warning or indication to others of the status in the community of its bearer. This mark of a cultural, tribal origin calls to it the powers of that ancient tradition, good and bad, depending upon the choices you make and the strength of your personality. These marks upon or within the energetic counterpart of your physical body will mark you for many incarnations so that you are forever linked with your ancestors, building up, if you will, a pattern of your spiritual progress which the Higher Beings can read at an instant. To mark yourself with a sacred symbol without it being earned or authorised is sacrilege and consequently, a person not strong enough psychologically, who has not been prepared through ceremony to display this mark, will suffer illness of one sort or another and what would be termed "bad luck".

'You will know from within what mark you are to access irrespective of its cultural origins, for you may have only earned its acceptance of recognition long after you have reincarnated, several times possibly, but where deep within you you recognise the spiritual calling of such a mark. Each one of you is different so a standard design, say of the Celtic knotwork for example, may need to be adjusted or changed slightly to recognise another aspect of your spiritual quest and status. Marks of this nature are often given by Spirit to the recipient through the medium of vision or dreams. Ask a person who bears a tribal mark what he or she has done to earn it and by whose authority it is given? If the bearer mocks or ridicules your questions, then they bear false witness and the consequences shall follow. Some, however, will give answers to these questions and others will not know except by a deep inner knowing that the mark is right for them and it makes them feel more complete. This is very valid, for God's consciousness comes from within. Scarification is a cruder form of this practice but nonetheless holds the same inner knowing of validity and personal progress and status. A tattoo is, therefore, an earned initiation mark.'

17ᵗʰ March 2004

Cyclone Ivy

I went to see the destruction of the lodge I stayed at last year which was only half a mile away. It was incredible to think that these leaf huts and gardens were immaculate before the cyclones struck but were now totally abandoned and overgrown to nature. The solar-powered telephone system installed by the Vanuatu government to all large villages was also destroyed, including the hut the telephone man lived in. The phone is now relocated to Jungle Oasis Lodge. Chief Kahi's home was also destroyed. The wind apparently blew in the walls causing the fire from the hearth to burn the house down. Chief Kahi lost his home, business and now his wife is seriously ill in hospital in Vila. Jerry lost his job as a guide to the Western tourists who stayed at that place, so he was in financial difficulties, especially now, as I hear he had another child.

I wanted to walk to Port Resolution school a few miles away to meet the Head Teacher in person, as previously I had had several meetings back home with my MHK (Member of the House of Keys, or member of parliament) Andrew Douglas to see if the Manx Government would give aid of some sort to the local people. Andrew wanted me to take photographs of the two local schools and get some supporting letters from the teachers and pupils. When he had the necessary information he would then approach the Minister for Overseas Aid to present our request. Duly armed with an official government letter of introduction, several small Manx flags that Andrew had given for the children, stationery that was obtained in Brisbane from a personal donation from Andrew and a charitable collection of £80 from a local church he was involved with, I wanted to make sure that I handed these items personally to the Head Teacher. Kelson insisted I took his truck and I had to pay for the privilege. I did not like this man. There was something about him which I did not trust.

The Head Teacher and school committee of teachers, parents and children were amazed and delighted with the gifts and the official letter. Cyclone Ivy had severely damaged the school, demolishing one classroom totally. The school used to be a Seventh Day Adventist property but now belonged to the TAFEA provincial government, but is not maintained in any way except by the children's parents.

I met Jerry, his wife and disabled Ealise, who was delighted to see me. She came scuttling along on her hands and knees through the cyclone debris to meet me. I met Chief Noar again, whose house was completely demolished by a huge banyan tree which was uprooted and blown over by the cyclone. He was very lucky to have escaped with his life.

Jerry and I walked to the beach and we spoke of various kastom traditions and I told him of my disappointment of being with Kelson. Jerry said mockingly, 'You won't learn anything from him, as he is a Seventh Day Adventist and is totally against the kastom tradition. Don't trust him.'

Jerry explained that, after the cyclone, the beach was silver with fish washed up on the sand. People were collecting them by the basket full. Jerry said that his wife had had another baby at the height of the cyclone so the doctors at the hospital had called the little girl "Ivy". Jerry further explained that, in their kastom tradition, his wife was not allowed to cook or prepare food or do any other job except her own laundry and the laundry of the baby. After a few weeks, Jerry would then take the baby outside to introduce her to the villagers and only at that point could the other women look after Jerry's wife. Jerry said he was not allowed to sleep with his wife until after that time.

Jerry had invited me to stay with him for the yam festival on 1st April and he would also help to collect letters of reply from the Head Teacher and the committee of the Port Resolution Primary School.

I asked him if there were any deaths from the cyclone and he said that there were a few deaths and they were all buried. He said that no-one gets cremated in his culture.

I returned to Jungle Oasis Lodge and Kelson had arranged for a local Seventh Day Adventist Children's Choir to give us a concert.

18th March 2004

Sunburn

After breakfast I sat on my little balcony watching the driving, cold cyclonic rain bounce from the dirt track. Two young white men walked around the corner, both wearing white shirts and black trousers and both soaked to the skin. They held their bibles out in front of them. I felt angry at more religious indoctrination being forced upon the simple kastom folk. Maybe they believed getting pneumonia would be good for their souls?

So who or what is God? What makes people of one cult want to force their beliefs on to others? I contemplated this issue for many days. Deity is neither male nor female, yet we have to personify the Supreme Consciousness into a finite, human form to enable us to have a level of understanding. If we are all part of the Creator, then I suppose the nearest I can get to understanding this is by realising that we are a part of the Holographic Principal. We are therefore co-creators and co-destroyers.

After meeting and talking with local people, I soon learnt that the cyclone damage to the crops had been devastating. They explained that Tanna Island had experienced drought conditions for a couple of years so the fruit and vegetable crops, including paw paw, avocado, banana and coconut, were destroyed or severely damaged. The people were suffering and also the fruit bats, since there was no fruit left on the trees for them. The local people were having to buy in rice, which was imported from China as it is not grown in the country. Because of the lack of cash, many are still in severe hardship so tourist money is essential. It is interesting that the traditional native leaf houses were less damaged than the modern concrete block buildings which they are now building as schools. These buildings have been totally destroyed, whereas relatively few of the native leaf huts have been destroyed because the wind can simply filter through them.

In the morning I walked to Ipeukel Village at Sulphur Bay to meet Chief

Isaac, the Yeramanu and other elders of the village. It was a long walk through the jungle and across the ash plain and I took the wrong turning in the rain forest ending up in the wrong village but was soon redirected to the correct village by the local people.

When I entered Ipeukel village the dogs were barking and the pigs were squealing, children were running around naked and shouted that Iarueri was coming. Even at this other village they remembered my name. The elders came out to greet me and invited me to sit with them under the shade of the communal shelter in the centre of the village. They offered me a plate of tuna, chicken and a root vegetable of some sort. The meat was covered in crawling flies. I offered them some tobacco which I had brought for them.

There was no interpreter, as such, but we could understand each other by body language, hand signs, lots of smiles and lots of laughter – the universal language. The men were very keen to know if Bin Laden was still at large or had been captured by the Americans. I said he hadn't been caught yet, so they all agreed that he was protected by Spirit to stop the American Imperialism!

I explained to the Yeramanu that I had a sore shoulder and I asked him if he could provide some tribal medicine for me so that I could experience some typical kastom healing. He fully agreed to do this and said that he was honoured that a white man should ask for the native kastom medicine and he thanked me for doing this. I agreed to return.

I left the village about midday. I had worn my shorts for the first time and, crossing the long desert-like ash plain around the base of the volcano, I felt that my legs were starting to burn. I felt dehydrated and as though I was getting heat exhaustion. To keep me going, I licked the mineral salts from the sweat on my arms and sought out the shade of a tree as soon as possible. I was angry with myself for being so stupid.

Later that evening, I realised how badly I had been burned. My legs, arms and face were red and the pain was indescribable. I had also been bitten in the corner of my eye by a mosquito, so my eye was painful and swollen as well. As I tried to lie in bed, I couldn't stand the weight of a single sheet. The sound of the volcano became very loud and intermittently there were sounds of distant thunder and lightning until eventually the storm was directly overhead. It was cyclonic; the wind, the rain, the electrical storm, the sound of the volcano. It was very primeval and it was such an amazing experience to be surrounded by it. Unfortunately, the fruit bats were very weak, so it meant that lots of local people were out that night with sticks, bows and arrows and spears hunting them since they were unable to fly away. I wondered if the Chief knew about this?

21st March 2004 - Spring Equinox
Thieves and liars   Trance dancing   Soul retrieval

Chief Wai Wai collected me from Jungle Oasis at 8:30 in the morning and we went to Itabu Village. The idea that had been arranged was for Kelson and myself to stay overnight for the ceremony. When Wai Wai came to collect me, Kelson asked him why he was coming, as there was no need for the ceremony that was planned after all. I was angry and suddenly realised that Kelson did not want me to get involved with the kastom people. I was shocked at his attitude and his blatant lies; I no longer trusted him.

When I reached Itabu Village, I explained to the chief that Kelson had said that he had spoken to him and the agreement was for me to remain at Jungle Oasis. The chief said to me that Kelson never spoke to him. Through the interpreter, I explained that Kelson had charged me 30,000 Vatu at a supposed reduced rate. They were absolutely horrified. I said that I was angry since I had now lost a whole week being stuck at Jungle Oasis with Kelson when I could have been at Itabu Village with the chief and the men, which I had wanted to do right from the very start.

I said to Chief Wai Wai that I wished to stay with him, which he readily agreed to. He had been unable to understand why I wanted to stay with Kelson. Kelson apparently had told him that Iarueri had insisted that he wanted to stay with him. So we now had to get the money back from Kelson to give to the chief and I knew that this would not be easy, so the Chief said that he would speak to Kelson and arrange this.

All of the kastom men gathered and said to me that Kelson and David Hosea were both Seventh Day Adventist Christians and that they were thieves and liars and were known so in the community. All they thought of was making money, whereas the true kastom people did not need Western money. I now found out that Chief Wai Wai is in fact the High Chief and Kahi is not even a chief at all! The only position of authority that he claims is being the pastor of a small Seventh Day Adventist Church. I felt hurt and upset, as I trusted the Hoseas and looked to them as my adopted family, as father and brother.

Nikwei is one of the Guardians of Yasur. He invited us to his village, which is part of Itabu but a separate nucleus of the John Frum Sect, different from the main group near Sulphur Bay. As High Chief Wai Wai, myself and others from Itabu approached the village, we had to stand at the boundary until directed forward to receive a garland of flowers each. We had to shake the hands of all formally, including the children, as all villagers stood in a line to greet us. They all began their ceremony by singing South Pacific hymn-like songs which were very haunting, the boys and men playing worn out guitars and drums. The spirits were then summoned while some of the men and women went into a trance dance state, spinning and falling about through the village like whirling Dervishes. It was fascinating to watch them.

Nikwei had lots of small coloured flags on sticks all around the village, all displaying either Latin crosses or equal-sided crosses within their centres. For example, there was a black flag with a white cross, a green flag with a gold cross, a yellow flag with a green cross, a white flag with a red cross, plus others, all meaning different things. It was explained to me that the cross aligns with the Guardian of the Sun, Newqusekar. His power was drawn to the cross on the flag and then directed to the person needing healing. Nikwei wore around his neck a turquoise flag with a golden cross with which he touched a sick person. Other flags were used to sweep around the person, rather in a manner to clear their auric field.

Nikwei took the white flag with the red cross and walked around in a state of trance touching others who came to him, who then whirled off in a state of trance themselves. The women, not trance dancing, performed their usual John Frum marching dance and singing. When the Yeramanu or the chief needed to speak, he then took the white flag with the red cross and planted it firmly in the earth and all remained silent until he had finished his speech. Those receiving healing were swept either energetically or physically with different flags, including receiving massage and energy projections. The healer took the "bad energy" to the flag to be dispersed or cleansed in some way. The trance dancers then spoke to their patients, telling them the cause of their conditions via the spirit ancestors and that they then had to ask for forgiveness three times to Majikjiki. Some of the healers flailed their arms around wildly, others whistled in a peculiar way.

I asked Nikwei for healing for my injured right shoulder, so I removed my shirt and sat on one of the logs used for healing to the surprise and the wonder (fascination, I suppose) of the villagers. I was told that they had never had a white man in their village ever before and they were honoured that I had asked them for their medicine. The energy from Newqusekar via the flag was focused and directed towards me, whereupon an old lady healer went into a trance dance. Through Moses, my newly appointed interpreter, a tall, athletic young man in his late twenties, she asked me if I had been inside a volcano? I assumed she meant Yasur so I said I hadn't but had been to the crater rim several times. Then I suddenly remembered about Nyiragongo volcano in Zaire in 1976, so I shouted out, 'Yes, yes, I have been inside a volcano,' and briefly explained what had happened. I was absolutely astounded! She said my spirit was still held there and she wanted to know if I wanted it back? I said yes. She then went into a long trance dance and Moses explained that the longer the dance the harder it was for her to bring back the trapped spirit. The old lady then fell all over me, sweeping my body, especially my head, with her hands. I felt heat rising up my spine and in my belly, then felt a little nauseous and weak as if I could easily faint. In fact, had I not been sitting, I suspect I would have done so. As this was taking place, other villagers were working on my bad shoulder. I felt much better afterwards, "cleaner" somehow and more at peace with a sensation of clearer eyes, a sensation of being more centred and grounded (all sensations of a successful shamanic soul retrieval).

After the healing, High Chief Wai Wai and I were encouraged to dance with the villagers so we were attired in the traditional female grass skirts, much to the amusement and delight of the villagers. Another shamanic tradition – after healing, you dance your spirit back or dance to honour spirit. It was absolutely fascinating that, irrespective of the individual culture, there is a core essence of shamanism throughout the globe. I felt near to collapsing and really wanted to rest and lie down, but stayed on my feet to dance with the High Chief.

A local meal was provided of unidentified root vegetables and chicken. The plate was filthy and eventually somebody found a dirty spoon. After our shared meal, several speeches were given by Chief Wai Wai who explained why I was here and what would take place for my ceremony. I had to give speeches in response to others, explaining the story from my viewpoint and thanking the villagers for their hospitality towards me. Nikwei and the other villagers spoke also. They are great orators and storytellers.

Nikwei then officially presented to me a carving he had made especially for me of a man in a nambas. I had to give another speech of thanks before the village in response. All clapped. I continued to explain how important it was for them to maintain and keep their traditional kastom way. I said that Spirit had brought me to their home to learn about their culture so I could teach my people again how to walk the true path of Spirit. All clapped.

When we left, all the villagers lined up as before to shake our hands. We returned to the chief's house and kitchen to be given another large meal of rice and vegetables.

Kelson arrived late to stay overnight for the ceremony because he had to see to the arrival of different tourists, no doubt to make sure he got his money. Chief Wai Wai and his son Donald, whose tribal name is Natonga Kwat Rawi, took Kelson into the hut to speak to him regarding my stay at Itabu Village and for him to pay back what I had given him. Kelson emerged some time later and made an inspection of the toilet and washing facilities at Itabu, which I thought was the height of cheekiness.

After more discussions, he said that he had now arranged that I would stay with High Chief Wai Wai to enable me to focus upon my kastom studies. I felt disgusted with his blatant lies and he knew that I was aware of what he was up to, but he didn't want to lose face. Kelson said that he would check my situation on a daily basis and had instructed the Chief how to look after me. What an absolute cheek! Kelson then left. I apologised to Chief Wai Wai for his behaviour and attitude, as I sensed Kelson was trying to use me as a means of upsetting the Chief.

By the time the family politics had been sorted out, along with the bad weather, it was decided to postpone the ceremony until the next day when, I was reminded, I had to ritually kill a pig. I was secretly dreading this. We all went to the nakamal to drink kava.   A message was then sent round the island by different runners to inform all the chiefs and their representatives of my grading ceremony the following day, inviting them all to attend as witnesses for the official ceremony of making me a chief of the tribe publicly.

The Chief's family were very nervous of my being in the village, as no white man had stayed with them ever before. They tried so very hard to do the right thing for me and were very kind and courteous but had no idea what an average Westerner needed. I felt so happy and thankful to be with them, to be living in a simple leaf hut with my friends, the ants, amongst the local kastom people. This is what I had dreamt of all along. I was ecstatically pleased.

22nd March 2004
Initiation as Chief   Binding rite

It rained very heavily all night with extremely strong winds. I wondered if another cyclone was approaching as it sounded like Concorde was about to land on the roof of my hut. The noise of the wind was indescribable. The hut began to sway and move and I could hear flooding water outside as the torrential rain beat down upon the earth. Coconuts fell all night because of the high winds and occasionally I heard a tree crashing and breaking in half. Should a coconut have hit a child, it would have been fatal. In fact several deaths each year are caused by falling coconuts.

I felt tired after a sleepless night because of the weather and also because of the effects of the kava. I spoke with Moses and asked him several questions and he explained different aspects of his culture to me. He explained that, during the ceremony, High Chief Wai Wai would also perform a binding rite where a handmade coconut fibre rope would bind me to the kava, pig and nakamal and one part of the rope would remain bound around a branch of the banyan tree as a reminder to all taking part in the ceremony. I was to take the rest of the rope back home to bind it to a tree so that I too would remember the ceremony and the tribal connections to it and this is where it would have to remain until eventually it rotted and fell away of its own accord.

I felt a little nauseous this morning, but thankfully I wasn't sick. At about 8 o'clock Donald and his brother Jack collected me. Jack is the second born son of Chief Wai Wai and his tribal name is Namas. Together we went to Jungle Oasis Lodge to collect my bags. I asked Kelson to give me back Jerry's shoes but he refused, saying, 'What use does a kastom man need of shoes? I will use them for church.' He walked away. He stole his brother's shoes! It poured down the whole time we were walking so we got thoroughly wet. My bags were soaked and the clothing inside wet, which remained so for days, very quickly going mouldy. Interestingly last night as I lay in bed listening to the cyclone approaching, the rain fell on my face from the open windows and from the gaps in the thatch. It was a weird feeling lying in bed getting wet indoors.

When Moses spoke with me again, I asked him different things and he confirmed that Iarueri was originally a High Chief and Yeramanu. He was a Holy Man and he was the son of High Chief Maruki from whom the tribe takes its name. Maruki's father was High Chief Rawi and this is as far back as memory recalls. Moses explained to me that when the missionaries came they destroyed as much culture and lineage as they possibly could, so nobody can remember back from their great great grandfathers.

It was stressed to me again that Iarueri is a holy name and reserved only for a High Chief. I therefore will be the same rank as Chief Wai Wai, as the binding rite will unite us both as brothers. This I felt was so incredible and beyond my comprehension!

I was told that the first ceremony would be held at about 3:00 pm and go on until midnight, when the High Chief and I would sit alone in the nakamal in a vigil to the ancestors. I asked if Jerry could attend and was told that a few days before he had damaged his leg in an accident, falling on to a split branch which tore the flesh on his leg. The men brought him in a truck, which I paid for. When the truck arrived just before 3:00 pm, the men had to help Jerry out of the back and carry him. Interestingly, the truck driver also was on crutches. The wound on Jerry's leg was ulcerated, swollen and looked really horrible. Kelson was also expected to attend to represent so-called High Chief Kahi, but I secretly hoped he wouldn't show up.

As we waited for the ceremony to begin, Moses explained to me about different aspects of his culture. He said that marriages are arranged through the chiefs at the nakamals, where pigs, kava, mats and food are the bridal price agreed to, in accordance with the rank, or grades of the individuals. The most valuable pigs are the ones with the biggest tusks (these are the oldest), especially if the tusk is circular and grows back in on itself in a perfect ring. Seventh Day Adventists, he told me, refused to eat pigs, something to do with the Bible, so they only eat goats.

Moses said that everybody has a particular job to do which is traditional in their lineage in the tribe, such as the tattooist or story teller.

The Chief then explained that only a High Chief could be ritually marked on the ear lobe, cheeks and shoulders. No other person was permitted to receive such marks. The Chief said to me that I was not yet strong enough to receive these marks. I understood exactly what he meant. He meant that spiritually I was not ready yet to receive the energetic forces and guardians which the mark draws to it. I marvelled that both of us were not yet ready to receive these marks until next year for different reasons. It was amazing how it was fitting together for me like a giant jigsaw puzzle!

I was told to go and have a body wash. A bucket of water would be left for me in the bamboo wash house and I was to pray and prepare myself for the ceremony which lay ahead. Tribal time, or Vanuatu time, was not the same as Western time! I had realised that, if somebody says 3:00 pm, it could be anytime between 1:00 pm and 5:00 pm! I loved how the kastom people lived in cyclical time, not linear, as we do.

Men from all over the island were gathering now, the chiefs were already sitting in a hut keeping warm by a fire, trying to keep out the rain which poured in through the roof. The weather was getting worse; rivers actually flowed down the main thoroughfare and trees were going down, the wind was increasing and mudslides were sweeping down the hillside. The cyclonic rain and wind were now getting stronger. Rivulets flowed down every path, making it dangerous to walk. I was told that some of the 4 x 4 vehicles couldn't even cross the river, as it was in spate, so some chiefs couldn't come to the ceremony from that side of the island. Runners brought news that different rivers were flooding, preventing other chiefs from attending the ceremony, including those in the mountains as the tracks were too dangerous and erosion was sweeping away pathways all the time. However, about 15 chiefs or their representatives managed to get through, some staying overnight, so we couldn't postpone the ceremony a further day to enable them all to get back to their villages.

Not only was it very wet and windy after several days of cyclonic rain and overcast skies, no sun had got through so it was also very cold. I felt really cold, so the locals must have found it very difficult.

The ceremony commenced at about 3 o'clock with all visitors huddled in the nakamal hut, except for a few brave souls and myself who did the ceremony outside. I stripped to my waist and the men placed around me a sarong of the recent native Vanuatu culture, called a lava-lava, and somebody attempted very kindly to hold an umbrella above my head to keep off most of the rain. The umbrella instantly blew inside out.

High Chief Wai Wai put on nambas and the men sang and danced two songs. There would have been more but, because of the terrible weather, the coldness and the floods, the planned ceremony had to be shortened. The Chief made a formal speech to welcome me to the nakamal and officially conferring upon me the position and title of Chief Iarueri, Guardian of the sacred stones of the flying fox, banana and nabanga tree, before the assembled chiefs. A bundle of kava roots were bound with the coconut fibre rope which lay alongside a little black sow, bound by its feet.

After the rank or grade of Chief was given to me, my name Iarueri was called out before all present and I was given the ritual club to kill the pig, held by the hind legs by Nikwei. The pig escaped just before the ceremony began, but was soon recaptured by the dogs and the boys. I was instructed to hit the pig sharply upon its forehead, which I did as best I could under the circumstances, as I could hardly see with the rain in my eyes. We had to shout above the sound of the wind. Nikwei turned it from side to side whilst I hit it twice more. I felt really upset for two reasons: firstly, that I was taking a life for a ceremony specifically for my benefit, and secondly, one strike should have been sufficient, so the pig suffered at my clumsy and inept hands. I was told it was vital that the blood of the pig soaked into the dark earth of the land.

As the weather became even worse, the High Chief apologised to all for such a short ceremony, as he had planned to have lots of singing, dancing and feasting before and afterwards. Everybody was wet and cold, even those huddled around the fire in the nakamal hut. The High Chief went on to explain that the principal criteria had been accomplished and completed and that the ceremony had been officially witnessed by the visiting chiefs, and that I had killed the pig. I was then told to untie the bundle of kava roots and to hold the rope with the Chief as he bound our joined hands together as brothers of equal rank and grade of the same tribe.

The pig was butchered by the hut and hacked in two halves with a machete. A hind leg was given to Jerry with some kava root to take home with him. The fire in the hut was made larger, so bits of pig flesh and organs were stuck on sticks to cook over the open fire by all. These sticks were stuck into the ground with sharpened points at a 45 degree angle so that the meat cooked, each person slicing off a bit at a time.

The boys prepared the kava in the usual ritualistic manner. To show and to confirm my equal rank and status, High Chief Wai Wai and I held the first coconut shell of kava together, drinking alternately. Only two people of the same rank are permitted to do this and this tribal etiquette is followed strictly at all times. It was a great honour and privilege for me and I remembered doing the same thing after the first ceremony last year. This was official confirmation of my grade before the council of chiefs.

We all spoke around the smoking fire, two bits of flesh were cut and given to me to eat after the High Chief had the first piece. They were black on the outside and raw on the inside. The problem was that I kept seeing the face of the little black sow looking up at me! As a strict vegetarian I really struggled having to eat meat on my first visit, but knew this sojourn would be difficult, as the kastom people have no understanding of this concept. They only eat vegetables if they fail to hunt. To refuse their food would also be an insult. I reasoned that all the meat I would have to eat would be organic so free from growth hormones, antibiotics, adrenalin and fear which saturates abattoir slaughtered creatures in the West. The spirit of every creature killed is honoured at the nakamal.

After more talking amongst ourselves, the Chief told me to leave at 6 o'clock and to return to the village to have my meal. I was originally to remain with him alone until midnight to communicate with the ancestors through a vigil but, because of the atrocious weather, this had now been scrapped. I hoped that we could do it for the second part of the ceremony later during my stay.

Jerry left after the ceremony had finished, carried back to the four wheel drive vehicle. It was hilarious watching the truck driver hobbling behind on his crutches. Donald and Moses went back with Jerry to Port Resolution, where he lived; then they had to return on foot, walking through the night in the pouring rain. Before he left, Jerry said to me that he didn't feel well enough to travel but, because I was his friend, he made the effort to be at my ceremony for my sake. I knew he was in great pain so I gave him some healing. He told me he was standing in the sea to clean the festering wound.

Before I left the nakamal, half of the coconut fibre rope was presented to me to take home in remembrance of this ceremony. I felt disappointed with the weather, for I was looking forward to a full ceremony and singing and dancing, plus the midnight vigil, but I dare say all who had to be there were there and all that which was necessary took place. This is all to do with trusting Spirit. It was ironic that there was less rain and wind last night than tonight. The rain was incredible, so heavy you could hardly see a few yards at a time. It seemed as though I had passed an initiation of water!

At the edge of the nakamal and at the base of the great banyan tree are the sacred stones of the flying fox. This is an area which is taboo for other people. Those who ignore this custom rule become sick. Only the High Chief and I are allowed in this area. All native life forms, insects, plants, animals, weather, etc have their totem guardian stones holding their power and spiritual presence. The chiefs of the area are responsible for certain sacred stones. Everything in the tribe has its season to be hunted, sown or harvested in accordance with kastom and tribal law.

23rd March 2004

Kastom medicine   Bleeding wounds   Eating bird guts and guano

The rain continued to be very heavy in the night with very strong winds but by 7 o'clock in the morning the wind had stopped and the rain had eased. Most people are up by 5:00 to 5:30 am. Sometimes I could hear other tam tam drums beating in different villages, awakening the people to work. The volcano seemed very noisy and active this morning. There is a very large hole not far from my leaf hut in the centre of the village, rather like a quarry excavation which emits sulphur smoke at times. I have been told that this hole is the "Ear of Yasur". The hole is about 50 feet deep by 80 feet across, full now of tropical plants in a garden setting, but apparently when you make a sound it echoes back and this is why it is called the Ear of Yasur.

At 8:30 am, I set off for Ipeukel Village at Sulphur Bay, escorted as usual, but this time by Moses, Donald and Tom, all in their best clothes to impress the other villagers, who belong to a different tribe. The arrangement made last week was that I was to return to get some kastom medicine for my bad shoulder. Chief Wai Wai was not pleased with me for going, for he said that I should stay within the spirit of Itabu, as energetic changes were taking place within and around me and that, by going to another village which has a different spirit, it would not be good for my development at this stage. I apologised, understanding exactly what he meant, but I explained that I had made an agreement and I couldn't go back on my word. He honoured me for that.

We arrived in the village an hour earlier than planned and met the Yeramanu, the firstborn son of Chief Isaac, along with other elders. After questioning me thoroughly and through the interpretation of Moses, the Yeramanu sent off two small boys into the rain forest to collect the necessary herbal supplies. He left shortly afterwards. We waited in the meeting lodge and a huge plate of sweet potato, taro and a whole chicken was given to me to eat. I ate a small portion to be polite, the rest eaten thankfully by the others.

I looked around me watching the villagers repairing the cyclone damage to their houses and, after about two and a half hours of waiting, with many questions and answers in between, I saw the Yeramanu approaching carrying a bottle of water which he shook vigorously, which I thought very interesting. It was rather like he was making a homoeopathic remedy and succussing the contents. I was called to one side by him between two huts, where I was given the bottle of green liquid, obviously a blend of herbs which had been added to the water. I made a bad mistake while I was receiving the medicine. When the Yeramanu gave me the bottle of green liquid, he instructed me to remove my shirt so I attempted to place the bottle of medicine on the ground to enable me to do this. He stopped me very abruptly and was clearly very upset, snatching the bottle from me. Then I understood that, for some reason, the medicine must not touch the ground, possibly because of an energetic transfer to ruin the medicine's energy, again probably on a homoeopathic principle.

The Yeramanu rubbed and massaged my shoulder, arm and right torso front and back with the green leafy concoction and I was told to drink half of the medicine now, which tasted quite pleasant, just like cabbage water. The other half of the medicine I was to drink that night. Kava root was given to me to take that night also in our nakamal. They wanted us to stay to have kava with them but we said that we had to return. They told me to return on Friday for kava and more stories.

On the journey back to our village, I was told the history of so-called High Chief Kahi. Moses spoke fluently and he explained that he is not a native man but his father was from Tonga who worked for the British Colonial Government when Vanuatu was known as the New Hebrides. Kastom law states that the blood line passes through the male side not the female side, so David Hosea is in fact not recognised as anything, let alone a chief. As he is very strong and big in comparison to the smaller, more refined stature of the Ni-Vans, people are afraid of him. But I am told that he has never been through the kastom ceremonies I have been through, so I am in fact of a far higher grade than him. Nobody knows the grade of his father when he was in Tonga but, if he were a chief, this has no influence in Vanuatu. He would lie about it anyway! He never goes to the nakamal near his home or wears nambas. In that particular nakamal, there is disunity, as there are four chiefs vying for supremacy, all of equal grade, but no High Chief. In our nakamal at Itabu, there is no discord or trouble, as everybody knows that High Chief Wai Wai is the senior chief over many villages. David Hosea is, therefore, an imposter, liar, cheat and thief, like his son Kelson. These were the words of Moses. Donald and Tom nodded vigorously and smiled.

Chief Kahi wrote to me twice inviting me to marry his grand-daughter, who he said in the first letter was 18 years old and in the second letter 20 years old. In fact, she is a child of 13! When I told the men that Kahi wanted me to marry this girl, they were amazed and said that he had no authority to do this in kastom law; therefore, it would have had to have been a Seventh Day Adventist marriage service, of which of course he is a pastor. Moses said that Kahi remained in Port Vila because he knew I would find out about all of his lies, so was avoiding me.

As we walked back, a local person told Moses that Kahi would be phoning from Port Vila to speak with me at Jungle Oasis Lodge and that they wanted me to be there. Moses asked me what I wanted to do, so at first I said that I refused to speak with him after all the lies and deceit. Then I changed my mind and I said that I would ask the advice of High Chief Wai Wai and whatever he suggested I would do. The Chief said not to speak to him as he would tell me more lies and would try to influence me against the kastom people. I did not go for the telephone conversation.

After a brief rest, Moses, Donald and I went to visit some sacred caves formed by the activity of Yasur volcano. These were long, narrow and deep, but most were open to the sky, rather like deep walled pathways, now full of debris from the cyclone; some had bottomless shafts. These caves were where those who were being persecuted by tribal warfare in the past would run through to avoid detection and capture. Once they reached the Itabu nakamal, they received sanctuary and safety from the high chiefs and their warriors. This is where the name Itabu comes from: it was taboo, or forbidden, to hurt, take or kill any man who asked for sanctuary, which the enemy had to obey, for the Itabu tribesmen would bear arms to protect the High Chief and those seeking refuge. This was quite revolutionary in those days of cannibalism and head-hunting. In the far off days, all chiefs had armed bodyguards with them at all times. Itabu, therefore, translates as Forbidden Village, which everyone knew was a holy, sacred place and the place of a powerful Yeramanu, High Chief, High Priest.

We descended into the caves down a very old wooden ladder. All the rungs had rotted except for one about four feet from the bottom, the poles were still in position, leaning against the wet mossy rock face including all the pairs of rusty nails sticking out either side where rungs were originally fixed. Donald went down first, followed by me. I caught my trousers on a nail near the top, which tore them; so, as the poles were green and slippery, we had to use the edges of our feet to get a foothold on the remaining nails sticking out all the way down, which was a depth of about 15 feet. About three-quarters of the way down, I lost my footing and fell on to the bottom rung which gave way instantly, causing me to fall heavily on to a set of protruding rusty nails. I fell to the ground amongst the cyclone debris, holding my chest, trying not to wince or cry out in pain, but Moses and Donald realised I had been hurt; not only that, I was covered in slimy mud which stung what I presumed were bleeding wounds under my torn shirt. Donald and Moses asked me to open my shirt so that they could see my chest. They were horrified at what they saw and visibly upset because there were deep scarifications across my chest, which were like tramlines. They were bleeding and I felt that I had cracked a rib under my right nipple. As I had been in their care, they said that Chief Wai Wai would be very angry with them and I could see clearly that they were afraid. I laughed it off and said that I was OK, but never mentioned the pain I was in. It appeared that I had offered my blood to the guardians of this land!

I insisted on continuing our exploration of the cave system before the climb back, which was equally dangerous, but with firm hands from Donald and Moses, top and bottom, and a hoist under my backside at the top from Moses' shoulder, I got out of the cave structure safely. When we got back into the bush, Donald picked some herbs and squeezed the juice on the wounds. He said that this was to stop infection.

We went to a few places near the edge of the nakamal about 100 yards away where several very deep, uncovered holes were hidden in the undergrowth with sulphurous deposits around their rims. These could not be seen unless you knew where to look for them. Donald went to the nakamal and got a stick from the fire, banging it over the holes, causing a shower of red sparks to fall into the cavities. Within seconds copious quantities of hot, sulphur smoke and flames poured out of the holes. It was truly amazing, especially when you considered that the village was built upon volcanic vents and a very thin crust, beneath which was obviously a sea of molten magma. All these holes were extremely hot when your hand was held over the opening. It would be a horrible place for a child or pig to fall into. Moses said that these were the breathing holes for Yasur.

We then went to the nakamal for the usual evening prayers to the ancestors where Chief Wai Wai assisted me on putting on my nambas. I was no longer embarrassed about this. The Chief was horrified and angry when he saw my wounds but I said it was my fault and I was fine. He glared at Donald and Moses who clearly winced. I participated in two dances and singing as best as I could, but my chest was too painful. These dances and songs were meant to have been performed yesterday at the official ceremony, which was postponed because of the cyclonic weather. Some of the visiting chiefs were still present, who witnessed the dances. I managed to drink two shells of kava. A small bird had been shot with an arrow, which was cooking over the open fire on a stick, like a kebab. I was given the back half to eat; it hadn't been gutted or cleaned! I struggled with the raw guts and the guano still inside, feeling and tasting the bitter dung and the crunchy grains of seeds. I managed not to vomit, but purposefully kept letting bits of the bird fall to the ground, which the dogs took. With the nakamal being a holy and sacred place, I didn't know if I could throw the remains on the ground or not, so I asked Nikwei. He said, 'We are brothers,' and he scoffed the lot, including the feet.

During the kava ritual, I was offered the first cup, or shell, by High Chief Wai Wai. After facing towards Mt Mareun in the west, you then spray the last mouthful of the kava on the ground, shouting 'Tamaffa'. This is a greeting to the spirit of the nakamal, known by that name and to initially call in the ancestors, praying aloud for what help or thanks were necessary. This ritual took place every night. All the other chiefs and men then followed in the same manner, according to grade. After the kava, a small portion of food is eaten, but never immediately before.

As usual, I felt my head spinning and became dizzy. After years of taking kava, the locals don't seem to feel any effects except that of becoming quiet and still to speak to their ancestors, helping them to go within, as opposed to alcohol which has the opposite effect. Alcohol is not permitted in Itabu village.

The banyan tree in the south of the nakamal represents the stability and strength of the Chief, so this is where the Chief and his guest of honour, or myself, sits or stands to speak. It was wonderful to sit naked, except of course for the nambas, beneath a tropical sky and the rain forest canopy, listening to the volcano and the screaming fruit bats and the silent whispers of the praying men as they communicated with Spirit. Again it transported me back to the Stone Age where, except for those wearing T-shirts and shorts, there would have been little change. I cannot express in words how I felt being amongst these devout men, the only white man privileged with this honour of being accepted as one of their own. I felt deeply at peace with all life.

The Chief was also horrified to see the red weals all over my body due to the incessant mosquito bites – or was it the bed bugs? He apologised but could do little about it. Some of the men wondered if I had a horrible disease and, when I explained it was mosquitoes, they laughed and clapped me on the back with their hands.

I took the rest of the herbal medicine from the Yeramanu at Ipeukel Village in the evening before I went to bed.

A snippet of ancient tribal protocol given to me was that of a punishment. In the past if a Chief said that a boy and girl must marry and one of them refused, a piece of black palm rather like a long skewer (the same wood that is used to make arrows to kill a man) was used to pierce the ankle at the Achilles tendon. This spike would eventually cause septicaemia or ulceration and would be very difficult to remove, causing excruciating pain, possibly causing lameness for life. There were occasions when people had endured this torture for two weeks or more until their foot would have to be amputated or until they died.

24ᵗʰ March 2004

Creation myth   Black and White Serpents

The Chief insisted that it was very important for me to visit the sacred site of the tribal creation myth. This site is taboo for Tannese people not from the Maruki tribe and no white person has ever been permitted to visit this site before.

The guardian spirit of this sacred site was contacted by the Chief at the nakamal prayers to the ancestors last night for my permission to enter and for my safety. I was told that my safety was now guaranteed. The Chief said that I must see this sacred site with my own eyes and walk upon the land in person.

The full journey from Itabu village to the sacred site and back, plus visiting other important sites en route, took six hours of hiking through the rain forest and hills. I was thankful for any rest I could get; I was dehydrated because of the strenuous walking and sweating, plus the high humidity and the heat.

On the way to the site of the tribal creation myth, we stopped off to visit a small spring in the rock some distance from the village, where I was told my drinking water was collected from daily in a gourd. This was another sacred site and the legend attached to the site is that the Chief's father, the former High Chief Wai Wai, heard water running whilst walking through the forest with his wife. On investigation he found a small spring, so he quickly returned to the nakamal and called the tribe together via the tam tam drum and, when the men had assembled, they killed a pig and prepared kava. He told the men of his new discovery and called upon the spirit of the nakamal to inform him who was the rightful owner of this new spring? The spirit of the nakamal told him that he was the rightful owner, and his tribe. Since that new discovery, more spring water has emerged, which appears to be volcanic in origin, and oozes out from the rocks.

After a further two and a half hours of hiking up vertical slopes, we came to the sacred site of the Maruki creation myth. This site again is very volcanic, high on the slopes of Yasur, being stained with sulphur deposits with hot and venting gas. This place is known as Mt Horredy.

As the future High Chief, Donald is being trained for this role, which includes memorising tribal myth, legend and history, in a similar way, I suppose, as my Druidic ancestors did. Nobody below a certain grade is permitted to know this story. As the Chief needed me to know our ancestral lineage, he authorised Donald to reveal the hidden wisdom to Moses, as my interpreter, to enlighten me.

Donald spoke slowly and deliberately, in great detail; his facial expression was that of a wise elder imparting a great secret. I have permission to reveal it in condensed form.
The Myth

In the beginning of time, a God Man and God Woman came from the stars and made their home in this land. The God Man was the first great High Chief, called Tangarua. He was the black and white serpent of the sea (interestingly, the God of the Isle of Man, Manannan, is also God of the Sea). The God Woman was called Pieria. Tangarua and Pieria had two sons, who were twins, the firstborn called Majikjiki who was white. The second born son, who was black, was called Kumesen. (This myth is similar to the Biblical myth of Adam and Eve, in that a tribe developed, but without saying how.)

When Tangarua realised that he was now mortal, he instructed Pieria that, when he died, he was to be buried with his head above ground, face up and his skull covered in volcanic clay. Tangarua favoured Majikjiki, the firstborn, sending Kumesen away into the jungle. When Tangarua died, Pieria buried him as instructed, covering the skull in clay. From his right eye sprang the waters of a sacred pool. From the dead Chief's left eye sprang the first coconut tree and all of creation. His wife kept this sacred source of water dammed with wild canes and told her white son that it was the High Chief's wish that he would be guardian of this holy pool, which was to be kept secret from his black brother and all the other boys. Now that the God man was dead, Majikjiki became the white serpent, Kumesen the black serpent. (These twins are the first ancestors.)

One day, whilst Pieria was working in the garden, the white twin allowed his black brother and the other boys to see the sacred pool and then to swim in it, against the Chief's wishes, thus breaking kastom law. Pieria heard the noise of the boys and came to investigate. The black twin and the other boys saw her coming so ran away and hid themselves in the mountains. When Pieria saw that the sacred pool was dirty, she knew that Kumesen and the other boys had been swimming in it and when she asked Majikjiki if this was so, he lied to his mother saying that he alone had swum in the pool. Pieria was angry that he had broken spiritual and kastom law and that he had blatantly lied to her. She took up her axe and broke down the pool's barriers, causing the sacred waters to flood out. The white twin tried to stop the flood waters by pushing over two trees across the entrance, one on either side, creating a large X. (These two trees still in this form were shown to me.) This did not stop the flood and where the holy waters soaked into the earth, arose the origins of the oceans, sweeping the white twin away on a tidal wave to the far side of the earth, to the west. As the surging sea rose up from the earth, flooding the land, two more tidal waves broke free, causing in total three tidal waves which swept across the face of the earth in three different directions.

As the black twin had remained in his tribal lands, he survived. He and his descendants are buried in Tanna Island, the first island in the world to be formed after the Great Flood. The myth speaks of the black twin waiting for the return of his white brother, the white serpent, to come home and this myth has been passed down for many generations. The white son's name is Majikjiki, as previously explained, and he is considered a national holy man, the God of Nature, his black aspect being Kassosu, and it is this image that is shown on the national currency of Vanuatu.

Moses took me around the mountain to a place where hot sulphurous white deposits were coming out of the earth, so he collected some, moulding the substance into his hands, and he said that this was what they traditionally used for soap. When it had dried it was hard and a little bit like a lump of chalk.

Donald and Moses, in their telling of this part of the creation myth, said that High Chief Wai Wai believed that he is the incarnation of the black serpent, Kumesen, and I am the incarnation of the white serpent, Majikjiki. Both are one, hence the ceremonies to initiate me as equal rank and grade to himself. I now understood why I had been singled out. It is also interesting that, just days prior to my second arrival, Cyclone Ivy swept clean the energies of the island, creating a flood of water. A new change of energy perhaps, preparing the way energetically somehow for the myth to become fulfilled in a way which was beyond my comprehension. Maybe, somehow we are all being used as little pawns in the cosmic game of chess? I remembered the Chief saying quite clearly and specifically last year after the first ceremony that I had "returned home". Kahi also said to me that a white man was expected to return to the tribal lands.

The local people are adamant that Noah built his ark on Tanna Island, on a rise overlooking this sacred site and the coast below. Donald and Moses took me to this very place where a banyan tree stood, where its aerial roots contained many stones placed there by the villagers. This place didn't seem to be taboo. The Maruki tribe believe that Tanna Island was the first island to be created, not only in Vanuatu, but the whole world. All other islands in Vanuatu, 80 plus, are formed from corals, sand and shells, proving that these islands were formed from the sea, therefore, developed after the three tidal waves. However, Tanna is formed from volcanic stone, so Tanna was created before the sea formed and before the flood.

After we returned to the village I was glad of the rest, as my chest hurt, then went to the nakamal with the Chief and put on my nambas. It is usually only the High Chief, Nikwei and myself who wear nambas, all the others seem to prefer T-shirts and shorts.

As usual, all the men either called me Chief or Iarueri and I received the shell of kava either before or the same time as the High Chief to mark my status. Those who have grey hairs, such as myself, are not expected to prepare the kava, which is left to the younger men and the initiated (the circumcised boys).

The Chief explained that his father, the former Chief Wai Wai, was imprisoned for refusing to give up the kastom path because of pressure from the Establishment, that is the colonial government of the day, and the interfering church. Many other kastom men were imprisoned also for their spiritual beliefs in the old ways. During the Second World War he, along with a thousand men from Tanna Island, was taken to fight or support the war effort by working for the Americans based in the New Hebrides, fighting the Japanese. After the war he and the others were released and he continued to carry on the kastom path, teaching the current High Chief, his son, the sacred way of Spirit.

Sadly, as each generation passes, a little more ancient wisdom and knowledge is lost. Was this natural human evolution I wondered or just simply human stupidity?

The High Chief said that the missionaries gave a gun to his father and he killed a man with it. He was unclear about why this occurred and what the circumstances were or consequences, if any, except to infer that the missionaries were responsible. The Chief was very interested to hear the story about my own father being called up by the state to fight in the Eighth Army at El Alamein and Tobruk as a tank driver and the injuries he received after his tank was bombed by a German Stuka. We have so many interesting stories that are similar in each of our lives; it is really quite remarkable.

I helped the men collect wood to make the fire for the nakamal. The men continued to wonder about my mosquito bites and were very sympathetic when they knew what the weals were. I looked like I was covered in measles. The men were very kind and thoughtful; one put a filthy rag over my log for me to sit on to protect my delicate white ass. Maybe nobody wanted the task of pulling out the splinters!

After the two kava shells were drunk and the evening prayers to the ancestors said, I returned to the village to have my meal of rice and chicken. It was a new moon that night. My legs were still painful from the sunburn and now peeling. I must have looked a pretty awful sight – peeling legs and red weals everywhere on my body. I was told that the Chief was very angry when I fell down the ladder into the caves, cutting my chest. Before our day's outing today, I remembered him telling Donald and Moses to bring me back in one piece!

The Chief explained that when they wanted to kill a flying fox, he would put a certain type of leaf upon the flying fox's sacred stone in the nakamal and that night a flying fox would remain in a vulnerable position to give its life for the benefit of the tribe. When the flying fox was shot with an arrow, it would be carried over the shoulder to the sacred stone and laid upon the earth, the men chanting to honour the spirit of the bat. After the first kill of the season, the men could hunt at any time, providing that the spirit of the bat was honoured. Anyone found hunting out of season would be severely punished. It was not permitted to photograph the sacred stones which looked like small, smooth tombstones.

25th March 2004

Eating bat   Manannan

The High Chief and I spoke together with Moses regarding the kastom legends and he explained many more things to me. When I asked about the specific spelling of particular names, Moses simply said, "It's something like this."

In effect all the words and names are spelled phonetically and I have tried on several occasions to cross-reference these spellings with other people. We also went through the family tree of High Chief Wai Wai and I asked the Chief what his name actually meant. Moses explained that the name Wai Wai means "He who walks swiftly with Spirit".

'The translation,' Moses said, 'is a bit difficult but that is the nearest that I can get to it.' (See Appendix B for Family Tree)

Contemporary tribal law also states that you can only go back four generations because of the dark days of colonial, trader and missionary persecution, murder and tribal slaughter, either through armed conflict or the systematic spread of Western disease on contaminated blankets and clothing. The past generations of the tribal lands which, through legend storytelling, went back to the dawn of humanity were systematically destroyed by the church and state to the effect that nobody can claim a true tribal heritage or lineage to the ancient ancestors now. Mistakes would be made as the kastom people have no writing skills; all is oral and is passed down from generation to generation. If the legend-keepers or wisdom-keepers were killed, then tribal history and ancestral lineage were destroyed. The church knew this; this is why they tried to target the storytellers.

When High Chief Wai Wai dies, Donald, his firstborn son, will become the new High Chief Wai Wai. The Chief said that he would traditionally have been called or given the name Iarueri but Donald was not mature enough; the person who bears this name has to be a holy man! After the Chief's death, 15 days must pass and then all the chiefs will gather to lay their hands upon the kava and pigs and then to the High Chief elect, who will   be Donald. After a big ceremony Donald will formally be initiated as the new High Chief before the council of chiefs.

The Chief repeated that he believed that Majikjiki had returned through me, he being the black brother. This is why he instructed that I visit the site of the creation legend so that I would return back to the source of my ancestors. The Chief said that he could see my spirit and it is very powerful and that God and the ancestors walk with me. 'We are two brothers now again, reunited, of the same rank,' he said.

Whilst his father, the former High Chief Wai Wai, still walks with him in spirit, he has to keep his beard cut close and is not permitted to bear the tribal mark of the High Chief until his father fully withdraws to the spirit realms of the ancestors. Then he can let his beard grow bushy, the outward mark of a chief in this part of Tanna Island. And next year, he told me, his father will have fully withdrawn, to enable us both to receive the tribal marks of the High Chief together.

The Chief said I needed a rest day today as the spiritual alignments to Majikjiki would make me feel tired. Donald and Moses were required elsewhere rebuilding houses damaged by the cyclone. All circumcision rites have been postponed due to the problems of cyclone damage.

The High Chief said that he had flying fox on the menu for me that night. We went to the nakamal as usual and put on nambas. It was showery and very cold; so only a few men meeting. Luckily, I only had one shell of kava, so I didn't feel too sick. The mosquitoes were exceptionally bad that night. Even the men were complaining about them. I was in great distress; I think this was why the Chief let me leave the nakamal earlier than normal to change and then to have my meal of bat. The meal looked very presentable in the dim light of the oil lamp but, because of the hot sauce, onions, beans and rice, I wouldn't have known the difference between bat flesh and say beef.

At the nakamal another man who I had not met before, called Absalom or Nakuhu, explained that the fire at the base of the banyan tree was the most sacred place in the nakamal. If the ashes had to be removed for any reason, kava had to be drunk and a pig killed. This is because the fire represents God in physical form at the base of the tree, which represents the High Chief. He also said that they would only meet in the wooden meeting house in the nakamal if the weather was exceptionally wet.

During the rest, I received a vision of Manannan, which surprised me. I was taken back to the place of the tribal creation myth and saw Manannan clearly on his white horse, Enbarr. At first, I watched the earth in the clearing start to crack and split open from the centre. Then I saw the point of a golden sword thrusting up from the ground, followed by Manannan upon Enbarr, the soil and rock cascading from them as they emerged from deep within the earth. Manannan held up the sword high and, from above, I clearly saw a shaft of white light strike the sword like a lightning bolt, causing the sword to pulsate with intense light and energy.

Then I heard the words, 'Iarueri. It is done. The myth is complete. God has brought you back to the land of your birth that, through you, he may fulfil the prophecy of this ancient land. The past is swept clean. A new beginning now dawns where black and white will walk together in peace and respect as sons of Spirit. God or Spirit uses each one of you in different ways which are beyond your comprehension, for the human mind is weak but the mind of God is great, which knows and sees all things. You have been training and preparing for this moment for many lifetimes and at times the burden has been heavy for you, for you have not fully understood what the ancestors were doing with you. You had agreed many incarnations ago to bear this responsibility at this time, to fulfil the myth. For, until a chosen white man had walked upon the earth at this sacred place and had honoured and respected the spirits of the land and its guardians in their kastom way, nothing could have occurred.'

As I watched, the ancestors of this ancient land emerged from the sides of the volcano and stood about us in a circle. It was very powerful and moving.

Manannan continued, 'See about you now that all the ancestors are gathering to witness the return of power upon their kastom tradition. This is the path chosen by you to fulfil. Last year, you made your mark energetically and spiritually through the sacred ceremony with Chief Wai Wai, reuniting you to the ancestors of this land. You suffered emotionally after the process of realignment, not fully understanding what was happening to you but realising that it was God's will. You trusted Spirit. Iarueri, you have earned your name. Soon you will earn your tribal mark. It is not a mark of adornment but an ancient symbol linking you to the ancestors energetically. When spirits see this mark (or its energetic counterpart imprinted within your collective consciousness) they will recognise your link to the tribe of Wai Wai and the guardians of this sacred land.'

Manannan then thrust the golden sword deep into the earth and the sea returned to fill the sacred pool. Manannan and Enbarr then disappeared beneath the waves.

I was glad to get to bed early that night. I didn't do much today, as it was a rest day for me and I was glad of that to be honest. The cuts on my chest were turning septic, so I had to use some antiseptic ointment from my first aid kit for the first time, as I had been receiving herbal concoctions from the kastom men up until now. It was a good job I had a tetanus injection. There were very large spiders in my hut which ran across the mosquito net and my face during the night. I found them fascinating.

26th March 2004

Women's kastom dancing

Moses, Jack and I went to the Ipeukel Village again to get more kastom medicine and treatment for my shoulder. Another bottle of green liquid, which tasted like spinach water, was provided. They wanted us to hear their legend stories and to drink kava together, but Chief Wai Wai wanted me back at Itabu by lunchtime and really didn't want me to go there in the first place because of their different energy. The Yeramanu and the others in the village wanted to know why I wasn't allowed to stay and why Chief Wai Wai didn't want me to go to their village and drink kava with them. This situation became very tense and awkward for all of us, especially for Moses and Jack.

I received more herbal remedies rubbed into my shoulder by the Yeramanu and he wanted to know what the cuts were on my chest, which I explained to him. He was impressed! Wounds give warrior status in most tribal cultures.

As we left the village, Moses explained the following snippets of information to me: pigs are more expensive than cattle or goats because of their ancestral, tribal tradition. Cattle, goats and horses are recent introductions, along with the Indian minah bird, so none of these animals have tribal spirit stones, as the native mineral, plant, animal or elemental ones do. Things like volcanoes, rivers, the sea, reefs, mountains, pools, etc also have their spirit stones and some are taboo to all people. Some sacred sites are guarded by spirit guardians that have been communicated to and worked with for countless generations, so are very powerful entities and beings. Some people will become sick or have soul parts removed, or even be killed if they are found in these sacred areas since they haven't gone through the required rituals. This is all very real and is still applicable today.

In the first days when cattle were introduced, the only way the owner could catch the beasts was to chase them through the jungle with dogs and then slash a leg with a machete; then, when the beast fell down, the opposite leg was slashed, cutting the tendons, preventing it from getting up and running away. Then its head was cut off with a machete or an axe.

If a kastom man killed another man, the chiefs would meet at the nakamal to discuss the murderer's fate, which could also be death. Often, and usually what would happen, is that a young woman from the murderer's family or village was exchanged for the lost man, so that eventually when she became pregnant, usually against her will, and produced a child, especially a male child, that child would replace the man who had been murdered. The girl would virtually be working as a slave for the rest of her life.

As we walked, a government UNICEF truck stopped and gave us a lift back to Itabu village. Lunch was prepared and after eating the Chief took me on a tour of his garden to explain all of the plants to me, what they were used for, either now or in the past. There were certain plants that you could put in food to kill somebody and others where the sap was placed on to an arrow point to kill a man. All of the arrows I have seen are flat-pointed ones that knock the bird or bat out of the tree. He explained that, if you had a pointed arrow and shot it into a tree, if it missed the bat or the bird, it would stick into the branch and would remain there until it rotted; whereas, a flat-pointed one would simply fall out of the tree and could be used again. Nowadays, they use arrows which are metal. Long wooden spears have three-prong barbed wire points. These are also used in tribal warfare.

Some plants, when used with spirit stones, can induce rain, causing the volcano to form clouds, whereas others can induce sun. Only certain people or Yeramanus, in particular, can use rain plants and only certain others can use sun plants. One plant in particular can activate or quieten the volcano. Plants can be used for any sickness, that is traditional sickness not necessarily a foreign-induced sickness, or medical condition from constipation to contraception and infertility.

Because of the amount of starchy food I was eating at the time, such as rice, taro, manioc and sweet potato, I was constipated. This was not helped by the fact that I was constantly dehydrated even though I drank as much water as I could. I felt I was also low on salts, especially mineral salts due to excessive sweating in the hot, humid conditions, so I constantly licked my arms to get some salts back into my system. No salt is used in local cooking which makes the food taste very bland. In the past, when local people wanted salt in their food, a boy would be sent a long way to walk to the sea to collect some sea water and this water was then used for cooking. I presumed the coastal people had no such problems.

Sugar is a recent introduction, with sugar cane growing in gardens now. I am told that this would not have been used in olden times but I expect that the ancient Melanesian and Polynesian ocean going canoes would have brought such things with them in search of new lands to settle in.

Later in the day, I watched dancing by the women of Itabu led by Mitac, who is High Chief Wai Wai's wife, normally known as Martha. Her official title is High Woman, or known locally as Big Woman. Mitac is a very beautiful woman. I am not quite sure how old she is because nobody really knows what their age is officially, but I would say that she would probably be in her early 50s. She has a beautiful facial bone structure; her eyes are like pools of liquid light and, when she looks at you, your heart melts, but deep within her she has formidable strength, bearing and courage. She is a true leader, a true matriarch, very wise, very knowing and full of the Goddess energy.

Mitac organised the women's kastom dancing. The tam tam drum was played but at a different beat and note to the men's call, and all the women gathered and took much time and effort to paint their faces and to adorn themselves with sacred leaves, ferns and their colourful grass skirts. They looked absolutely beautiful. They have their own sacred area, or nakamal, which is usually taboo to all men, but now they allow the male tourists or visitors to see these dances. Only if a white man is present can local males watch the dancing. Whilst I sat at the edge of the nakamal with Moses and Donald, watching them dance, two young men arrived and very nervously sat next to me. They whispered to me, 'We have never seen this ever before,' and they looked frightened, looking around themselves expecting there to be trouble.

Several dances were performed but one in particular was important to watch, I was told, for this particular dance re-enacted the creation myth of the white and the black twins being joined together – the return of the black and the white serpents.

After the dancing, Moses, Donald and I went to see the flying fox roosts, a large banyan tree from which the spirit of the guardian of the flying fox comes to enter Wai Wai's nakamal. Because of cyclone debris we couldn't get up the valley to the tree. On the way the boys found a weak flying fox so knocked it out of the tree with stones and pointed sticks thrown like boomerangs. The poor bat was badly injured and crying like a baby. I felt so sick and sorrowful. This is their kastom way of hunting; it is not for me to judge or to become involved. The guardian of the flying fox had now told the Chief that hunting can resume, so one bat is always given in sacrifice, in other words places itself in a position so it is easily caught, as normally they are at the high tree canopy level, out of the way of harm from the men on the ground. The bat was left hanging on a low branch for collection on our return, its wings pierced so that it couldn't fly away.

Because of cyclone damage, there was very little fruit available for the fruit bats now so they were hungry and venturing lower and lower and nearer to human habitation. Many are weak and seem unconcerned about human activity, whereas before they would have kept very well clear. They are now sitting targets for the catapults, sticks, stones and arrows.

Now that the bat guardian spirit has permitted the flying foxes to be hunted and eaten, the hunters must gather at the banyan tree where the bats are roosting before the cockerels crow first thing in the morning. When the hunters have killed many, the bats are tied to a pole and the pole is hung between two special trees, where the bats are dressed with vines, sacred leaves and flowers to honour their spirit. The pole of bats is then ceremonially carried over the shoulders of two chosen men into Wai Wai's nakamal, where they approach the bats' spirit stone chanting and singing and performing a dance, rather like a unified shuffle to honour the guardians.

A chief from an area where fruit bats are scarce, who has been given permission to hunt, receives the first fruit bat and in return he has to exchange this sacred gift by offering to Wai Wai a pig and kava. Anyone who hunts the bats out of season or without permission from the High Chief will be severely punished or fined, as he is breaking kastom law. For some reason flying foxes are very important in their culture.

After our hike, Moses and Donald collected the flying fox from the branch and returned to the nakamal. I put on my nambas. A fire was started and kava was prepared by the boys. The flying fox was brought to the fire in the nakamal. The wings were cut from the body and a stick pushed into the bat's mouth until it came out of the anus. The hair was then singed off the body in the flames and the wings used to beat away the singed hair. When ready, the stick was stuck into the ground at a 45 degree angle over the fire for the bat to be roasted. The wings were put in the same pot as the manioc and the pig meat. Nothing is wasted. The pig's organs were also cooked in the same way over the open fire.

The Chief speaks to the men at the nakamal, instructing them in the kastom way and the kastom laws, sorting out disputes, marriages, deaths and funerals, circumcisions and other rites and important issues while the kava is being prepared for drinking. At this time tobacco is smoked, either in a pipe or loosely in any paper they can find, including my letters. Once the kava has been drunk by all, everyone falls silent to pray to the ancestors. After kava a small amount of food is eaten, which may have been prepared beforehand and brought to the nakamal by one of the men. Kastom law states that no man can touch the food with his fingers, in case the hands are dirty through having been to the toilet or touching his woman intimately. All use small sticks, like oversized toothpicks, or larger sticks to take food from the pot. This practice prevents or reduces the spread of bacteria and disease.

At the base of the banyan tree is a log, or in our nakamal two logs, where only the High Chief or High Chiefs may sit for official business. Both High Chief Wai Wai and myself have our logs. I sit at the right of him and he sits directly between the fire and banyan tree.

About 5:00 pm, or round about early dusk, no woman or girls are permitted near the nakamal and any female who meets a man on his way to the nakamal must leave the path and direct her gaze away, out of respect, to acknowledge that the man goes to speak to the ancestors for the benefit of them all.

When kava has been taken at dusk at the nakamal, one of the elders stands on the perimeter of the sacred site and yodels or calls loudly in a particular, peculiar way, until he hears a man across the valley at another nakamal responding. I have often wondered if this was a chain reaction across the island. Men and boys call to each other from dawn to dusk through the rain forest by this yodelling sound.

The Chief sent me back to the village, escorted by Moses. I went to the toilet in the middle of the night, which was simply a hole in the ground surrounded by a few bamboo poles, and walked into the corner of a thatched hut as I went. I felt something cold and clammy land on my head. I knocked it off quickly, causing it to land on my shoulder, from where I saw it was a gecko lizard. I held it in my hands, its eyes sparkling in the moonlight. This is what I loved; our "houses" are alive with life.

27th March 2004
Dream dance   Chief Kabari

The rules of the village are strictly adhered to by all according to what the Chief tells them to do. If Moses and Donald have to work, I am told I have a rest day, as I am not permitted out and about by myself. If the Chief says I need to have a rest day, then I have realised by now that there is a good reason for it, as he himself is instructed by the ancestors regarding my needs and adjustment energetically. I have clarified the point regarding the status between the High Chief and the Chief. A High Chief is a chief over many nakamals and chiefs; whereas a chief is simply a chief of a village and one nakamal.

During my morning's rest period, I went into prayer and meditation and received a clear vision of a particular dance I saw the villagers perform involving clubs or sticks and the presence of Majikjiki. I made a careful note then enacted the dance I had seen to High Chief Wai Wai, Donald and Moses. As I was performing this dance, I was aware of a large bird's shadow gliding over the open area of the village. Chief Wai Wai seemed excited about what I had described and the dance I had performed and said to me that this particular dance I had seen in my dream is only performed by the villagers of Itabu and is called the tokka. He said that before his father died he revealed to him a similar dream and the dance which is peculiar to this village. Other villages have different tokka dances.

He went on, 'Iarueri, you have passed the tests. You are truly my brother.'

Moses said that the bird which had flown over us whilst I was performing the dance is the Maruki tribe's sacred spirit bird to prove what I was saying was true. Interestingly, the bird that flew overhead was a harrier of some sort, which is only seen over the plains and volcano, not over the rain forest canopy! It is known as the "eagle from the volcano" by the tribe.

The Chief said that, as I had been given the same dream as his father, then the ancestral guardians had given me this secret, which was a great honour and privilege. The dance is strictly secret and I have been instructed that it must not be revealed to anyone. The Chief said that only he, his father, Donald and I were aware of this dream and now, obviously, Moses who he made promise not to reveal to anybody else.

The Chief said that he has given me the spirit of Majikjiki, which is like a small baby at this stage. He said that care is needed for it to grow and develop. When the time comes for me to compose a song, the spirit baby will have grown into a spirit child until it has fully grown into a spirit adult. I understood what he meant in that the energy adjustments are small at the moment and, as I become more attuned and stronger, the energies would grow and expand significantly. I would become more enlightened until I could bear the full potential of the power of Majikjiki in relation to what my life's role is to become. Further attunement will not take place until the next full moon on 5th April, when another ceremony will take place and where I have to perform a ceremony for the High Chief. As a full chief I am expected to behave with dignity, honour and bearing. I am not allowed to swear, steal or take another man's woman; I am not allowed to drink alcohol; I have to agree to a strict code of ethics and morals, which I have done.

After lunch, a party of us from Itabu, plus a son of the chief from a neighbouring village we were going to visit, set off to visit Chief Kabari at Ianakun village in the hills above the valley. The path was very steep and very narrow and, when we eventually got to the village, I was introduced to a village elder before meeting the chief. This is their protocol. The village elder then went to the chief, explaining why I had come and who I was.

The village had received considerable cyclone damage; its guest bungalow, which overlooked the valley to the volcano opposite, had been flattened. A truly magnificent view, especially I am told at night time when the sky lights up with glowing redness. The bungalow, or leaf hut, would be repaired by the end of April.

I was told that Chief Kabari has six sons and one daughter. Chief Wai Wai showed me the sacred stones for the element of fire and taro at the base of the banyan tree in the village nakamal, of which Chief Kabari is guardian. If a fire is lit in the Ianakun nakamal, it is taboo for me to touch a stick, otherwise I will get burned. Each nakamal is the holy place to hold the sacred stones of the creatures of this land and each chief is guardian of these stones and responsible for the welfare of these creatures or plants in the traditional kastom way. Other chiefs need to get permission to interact with these stones and their guardians. Part of the role of the chief is to advise and talk about spiritual matters so, as the kava was being prepared, I was asked to talk about many things through the interpretation of Moses. I explained the importance of not losing their tribal kastom to the pressures of Western civilisation. I spoke about the four elements and gave Chief Kabari some healing and some chakra balancing.

The kava was strong and I felt rather ill, thinking of the trek back down the mountainside on the slippery trails. During the kava ceremony, in the silence, I saw a vision of a black boar with three curls to its tusks emerge from the centre of the nakamal from a pool of rainbow light. The boar went up to Chief Kabari and knelt on both front legs before him, placing a white, lily-like flower at the chief's feet before returning into the rainbow pool and disappearing back into the spirit world. I then saw three ancestral warriors emerge from the centre of the banyan tree, who stood before the chief to honour him before disappearing from whence they came. I told the chief what I had seen and Moses interpreted it to him. This seemed to be a good omen.

These villagers, I was told, were trying to get help from the TAFEA provincial government to get a road built to their village, but they will not do it as it is too expensive. Because the track to the village is up a very steep mountainside, it practically cannot really be done, so everything has to be carried up to their village on their backs, including the corpse of a villager who had died in Port Vila a few days ago.

Mosquitoes were especially bad at this time due to lots of standing water after cyclonic rains for them to breed in. Chief Wai Wai's wife, Martha, came from Chief Kabari's village so this is why they are related by marriage and have such a close connection.

A great honour was given to me at Ianakun village, which was related to me when I arrived back home at Itabu. Moses explained that, when our little party arrived at Ianakun village and we were speaking with the village elder, Chief Kabari asked his ancestors about me, saying, 'Who is this man that comes to my village?'

The chief said that he received the reply clearly, 'This man walks with God.'

Also, when it came time to drink kava, I drank the same time as Chief Kabari, even before High Chief Wai Wai, a mark of great respect and honour. The chief was especially impressed with me when I spat out the last of the kava dregs from the shell, shouting, 'Tamaffa.'

28ᵗʰ March 2004

Tests and trials   Sick baby

I was kept awake again by a rat chewing constantly between the gaps in the double-skinned bamboo walls of my leaf hut. I kept shining my torch in its face during the night but it stared back at me. We were now on first name speaking terms! Rat droppings were everywhere, over my clothes and my bed, each night.

This reminded me of a time I lived in a remote stone cottage for seven years on the Isle of Man. I had no electricity or telephone and, if the water pipes froze in winter, I got my water from a stream in a bucket. My lighting was by oil lamps and candles and I often cooked basic food on the open fire. When it rained heavily, the cottage flooded, especially the kitchen, so I had to wear rubber boots. This meant the field mice would come in out of the cold and wet for some warmth and food which I left out for them on a saucer. I used to sit by the fire with a wild mouse sitting on my shoulder or head as I read or meditated. When I went to bed, it or another one, for I couldn't tell, climbed on to the bed and, making a nest in my beard, slept with me for a few nights.

After breakfast, the Chief asked me if I would do some healing on a small boy, so I agreed and said that I would do my best. I waited until someone went to fetch him. I thought that he must have lived some distance away as I had to wait a long time.

I now realise about the tests and trials I am expected to overcome. I assumed that they would be physical things, for example, throw the white man into a pit with a pig and see who climbs out first, but nothing of the sort. It was all very subtle and, interestingly, I never found out until later that everywhere I went and everything I said or did was reported back to the High Chief, so I was actually being tested and not knowing I was being so. The way I was tested was through things like healing, counselling, teaching, public speaking, acceptance of their customs without question, for I know my safety is paramount in the Chief's mind. Also the courage to face strangers and say what I believe and standing up to the likes of Kelson on behalf of the Chief and the other uneducated kastom men – this is far more difficult than facing physical danger.

Two hours later, Donald's wife, Namu, came with a babe in arms, who only lived as it turned out two minutes walk away, and who is the High Chief's youngest grandson. The child, also called Wai Wai, was in obvious distress, crying, screaming – the same scream I had heard every night I had been in Itabu village and wondered where it came from. The Chief told me that Wai Wai's older sister, who was also an infant, dropped him on his head whilst carrying him. Looking at the baby, he had a swollen neck, which was so inflamed it was the colour of a beetroot. His head was swollen and he was very agitated and obviously in great pain. I felt his neck and it was burning hot. I felt concerned because it appeared the child had either broken his neck or fractured his skull and I was afraid not only for his welfare but for the seemingly impossible task which I now faced. The Chief said to me, 'Heal him!' It was more of a command than a request.

Men gathered around us, holding bows and arrows, machetes and spears. I felt very vulnerable and I asked for help from Spirit. His mother tried to hold the child still but the baby struggled and screamed even more and was unable to turn his head, which needed support all the time. He had also never seen a white person before so I expect that he was freaked out and afraid of me. I prayed constantly to the ancestors and to God and did some spiritual healing as best I could, working with the child's aura for he didn't feel comfortable with me touching him. My fingers became very hot, which had never happened to me before.

The mother and babe then left, but a queue had formed wanting healing from me, so I then had to perform on the High Chief, then Martha, Rachael, who was the woman who was cooking for me, Donald and Enoch, who is the youngest son of the Chief who appeared to be 12 or 14 years old. Both his legs were so badly ulcerated that not one fraction of healthy skin showed. The ulcers were leaking, constantly oozing pus and fluid and the flies swarmed about him all the time. I felt so sorry for the boy, as he was very pleasant with large brown eyes that melted your heart with compassion and love.

I fetched my dowsing rod and dowsed each person's aura before and after the healing session so that they could see that something had actually taken place, to kick in their belief system to allow them to know that they can heal themselves. No-one can heal anyone else. I can be a facilitator but inevitably that person has to heal from within.

Afterwards, the Chief, Moses and I sat around the table and the Chief asked me for some simple advice on setting up a small business, as he hoped to attract a few tourists, especially eco-tourists to stay at Itabu village to get some cash for things like tools, machetes, Western clothes, pots and pans. I did my best although I'm not skilled in such matters really. By the time we had finished, it was after 4:00 pm and more people had come from far and wide asking for healing from me.

That night there were different men at the nakamal, so I was asked again to explain the difference between the church and the kastom way, as some villagers said they were getting very confused. I could only tell them how I personally experienced the church and the kastom path and explained that it was their choice and that it was quite possible and permissible to combine the two. I explained that whatever was right was for them to find in their own hearts. I urged them each time I was asked to speak to teach their children and their children's children the way of the kastom tradition. If they wanted to go over to the church, that was their choice, but I asked the men to teach their children about the kastom path, so that they could make their own choice.

They seemed pleased that I stood up for their tribal beliefs and appeared to understand what I was saying. I found out that, in basic primary school, most people were taught English and so they understood the principal things that I was saying, provided that I used simple words and spoke slowly.

29th March 2004
Cyclone damage at school

The High Chief reminded me again not to wander off into the bush by myself, as some men did not agree with or approve of my being made a chief and he said that they may try to approach me and harm me. It rained most of the day.

When Moses, Donald and I went for a walk into the bush, we went to the local area where a couple of years before Cyclone Una destroyed the local lake at Isiwi and its hot springs, filling the area with silt and debris. In the past, the locals had swum and fished in this particular lake which was very near Itabu village. Everything now was choked up and it just looked as though it was a piece of ordinary ground. It was quite remarkable.

The boys told me the story of the John Frum Cult and how it was now split into three different splinter groups, all wanting power and control. One of the present leaders, a man called Fred, had travelled the world on a Taiwanese fishing boat and then a larger cargo boat to West Africa and brought back African magic, rather like voodoo, which was powerful and confusing to the local people. He must have appeared like a magician to them. Tribal warfare had broken out in the past because of Fred's teachings.

We went to visit the local primary school called Iaqurimano. The Head Teacher was called Willie. (I tried to create a link with the Port Resolution and Iaqurimano schools with the Manx schools and the help of the Manx Government through Andrew Douglas, MHK.) I presented the official government letter to Willie from Andrew Douglas. Willie said that the aid they needed was not stationery but that they were desperate for desks and a new classroom. The school had received damage from Cyclone Ivy which the local community was trying to repair. The current main building was built of concrete blocks and was the third school to be built on Tanna Island in 1967 by the British Government. It is in need of urgent repair. The school has no water tank for drinking water, so the Japanese Government is going to fund a water tank and supply for them. When it rains the school has to close because of severe leaking from the roof.

Each child takes to school a roasted sweet potato, or similar, wrapped in leaves in a string bag for their lunch. Iaqurimano school has 140 children at present and it is expecting 150 next year. The International Red Cross has given the school a blue plastic tarpaulin to cover the roof of one of the most severely damaged classrooms. The children have to sit on the ground in some classrooms or squash up at any available desks or chairs.

We met a woman on the road wearing a huge dead green stick insect on her head like a hat, which she would have been taking back home to cook. These are wrapped in leaves and bark and baked in the ashes of the fire. The women and boys collect several at a time and set off to search for them by singing a particular chant to the spirit of the stick insect. My clothes were wet through, even with the use of an umbrella, the only way to dry them was simply by wearing them.

Donald's baby was brought to me again for more healing. He seemed to have had a better night. There was less screaming certainly and I was told that he could now turn his head a little. I did some more work with him and I found that he was not quite so afraid of me. I was able to do reflexology to the head and neck reflex points on his feet.

Moses told me more about the tokka dance and the bird I saw flying over my demonstration of the dance that I had seen in my dream. The eagle's feather can only be used for the tokka dance which is held every four years. They use special sticks for this and the sticks that he described were the same that I had seen in my dream.

Because of the terrible rain, I stayed in my hut until 4:00 pm when Moses, Donald and the others took me to a certain place in the rain forest. They showed me the area where scientists had been drilling for something. All the local men knew that the scientists had discovered valuable finds and collected some

73

stones to take home for fossil identification. (I found out later that they were probably ferro-magnesium deposits, but the local men said that the scientists wouldn't tell them what they actually found.) In the area we found a hornet's nest nearby and Moses, very unwisely in my opinion, started to lob stones at it. I was surprised at him doing this on two counts: firstly, all life is sacred and secondly, they could have killed someone with a mass attack. The hornets were huge and a bright yellow colour. It later transpired he had done this because he was afraid.

On the way back to Itabu, we passed through Nikwei's village. We saw the remains of his original house, which was washed away by torrential flooding. Chief Wai Wai's father's house near where Donald lived was flattened and then burnt down at the same time.

I went to the nakamal as usual. A chicken was decapitated and gutted and then thrown into the fire's embers. It was raw inside and black burnt on the outside, as usual.

30th March 2004
Majikjiki's spear   Cloak of black and scarlet feathers

It rained heavily all night with strong winds. I felt cold and miserable. The rat had eaten my bar of soap in the wash hut and I couldn't retrieve the bits that had fallen between the bamboo floor.

The Chief told me to stay in my hut until lunchtime and he would collect some herbs to massage my bad shoulder. I heard no screaming from baby Wai Wai last night or this morning. During my stay in my hut, I took the opportunity to connect with Spirit and the ancestors and I found that I moved quickly and easily through the veil into the energetic counterpart of the nakamal, or parallel universe, where it was night time. There was a full moon and the red glow from the volcano was very bright in the sky. A group of native men danced in a circle, then they parted to reveal Majikjiki and the council of elders. Majikjiki threw his spear at me, where it landed between my feet. He wore the most amazing cloak of scarlet and black feathers of a bird I recognised seeing locally but did not know its name.

He spoke to me, 'Iarueri, you are known to me and the council of elders already. We have walked together as brothers in this sacred land before at the dawn of humanity. Take this spear and throw it into the banyan tree and tell me what you see.'

I threw the spear high into the tree and from where it struck I saw a ring of white light move outwards and from within this circle of light flew countless scarlet and black birds, like honeyeaters, which covered me all over. The birds settled and became still, transforming themselves into a cloak similar to the one Majikjiki wore, but this time it was living. I told Majikjiki what I had experienced.

He replied, 'What does this tell you, Iarueri?'

'I don't understand what you mean, Majikjiki,' I answered.

'Iarueri, this shows you that you are of the same grade or rank as myself so you have no need to ask for my blessing, for you already walk with Spirit in the highest way. You simply do not fully understand this yet. You will be marked according to your grade in due course, but you still have to learn how to align yourself to Spirit correctly, for you are not doing this yet. Chief Wai Wai will assist you in this process, but it must be done slowly, otherwise you may become sick by the extra power of Spirit.

'A seed takes time to develop and grow and it must be carefully nurtured. From this small seed a giant tree can grow and flourish. The tree needs to develop initially strong roots to anchor it to the earth before the branches form, otherwise the cyclones of life may rip you from the ground. When you are truly anchored in Spirit, then there is no stopping you from manifesting divinity in your life. The cloak of scarlet and black represents the blood and the people of this land. You are part of this place now in Spirit. The blood of this land flows in your veins so this cloak will protect you and nurture the seed developing within you. You have the ancestral right to wear the cloak of the black and scarlet feathers. Be patient.'

Majikjiki then clapped his hands and all vanished. Further visions and teachings followed over the coming days.

I did some more healing after lunch, including little Wai Wai, trying some craniosacral work and chakra balancing. Chief Wai Wai did some kastom medicine on my bad shoulder by squeezing fresh herbs on to my skin and massaging in the juice. The leaves and plant were a beetroot colour and this was to cleanse the blood he said.

It rained all day so I went to the nakamal at about 5 o'clock with Moses, who spoke of more spiritual stories while the kava was being prepared. Donald had shot a bird. He had spent the whole day hunting because, in their culture, if somebody does something to help a man, they are obligated to repay that person. So, because I had been doing some work in healing his son, he'd spent the entire day hunting for something to give to me, because he cannot pay me any other way. Donald turned up at the nakamal with his bow and arrow and a very small bird and this was for me to eat. It was a small green bird called a silver eye, the size of a sparrow. Donald offered this bird to me as a gift for helping his son. He held the dead bird out to me in both of his hands and he bowed before me. I felt emotional at the gentleness of this man. His eyes looked up into mine and they were full of tears. I held him close.

The bird was prepared and, as before, it was cut in half; he had the front half and I had the bottom half and, as before, I got the dung bit – the raw entrails, the guano, the legs and all those things which are unmentionable. Donald got the head, the juicy brain, the eyes and the beak. I gave the wings and the feet to Nikwei; he was quite happy with those. This is the second time I have had to eat raw bird shit. I can assure the discerning reader that it is an acquired taste!

1st April 2004

Saving life of baby   Boar hunting

It rained heavily again with strong winds, lots of thunder and lightning. Donald's baby was brought to me again today. When Wai Wai was brought in his mother's arms, he looked at me and could turn his head fully around and no longer cried. The temperature and inflammation had reduced considerably. Three large ulcers, or large boils, had appeared on Wai Wai's head, one at the neck, one at the base of the skull and one on the other side of the head, more or less in a line all on the right side. Much pus was drawn out by the mother last night. Chief Wai Wai said to his grandson, 'You are a very lucky boy. Iarueri has saved your life!' It seemed I had passed another test!

Everyone was very pleased and I was totally amazed! The High Chief held me tightly in his arms and Wai Wai's mother cried, touching me gently on my hand. The baby looked at me with eyes full of light. I could see the universe within them. I felt very emotional and I gave thanks to Spirit for this truly amazing miracle.

Again it was another rest day because of the bad weather, so I went into a meditative state and I found that these times were very valuable to me. I connected immediately with Majikjiki in his cloak of scarlet and black feathers, but this time he wore boar's tusks at his chest.

He spoke to me, 'Iarueri, I am known by many names. The name is unimportant, for what is necessary is for you to link to God. Beings such as myself serve humanity in this way to help those who are responsible and dedicated upon the path of Spirit. You wonder why the boar is so important to our culture? The reasons are because in ancient times, it was the only available food source in the animal world which took great courage and skill to capture or kill. The boars with the largest tusks were very dangerous and could kill a man. Some would take small infants from families, so it was a creature both feared and revered. When tropical storms devastated natural food sources, such as birds, fruits or root crops, the wild pig was known to be a resilient, strong survivor – the qualities required by the tribal peoples. Often an initiate, a young boy moving into manhood, would have to prove himself as a warrior to hunt and to kill a boar with his skills of bow and arrow, spear and stone. The boy was often killed or severely injured in this process. It was an initiation of courage to overcome fear. The boy who returned to the settlement with the boar was hailed as a man and honoured as such, especially if he displayed hunting wounds. He then took his place in the war canoes.

'I am not suggesting that all of what occurred in the past was right. It was the tribal way just as in your ancient culture you too had brutal initiations and ways, which today would be unacceptable. All of us have come from a tribal culture. When the boy warrior returned with his first kill, if the boar had large tusks it was seen as a greater prize, for greater skill, daring and risk were involved. He would be elevated in tribal society accordingly and the story of the hunt and the kill would be told for many years, sometimes moving into tribal legend.

'If the pig was too large to carry or drag back to the settlement, then the boy would return with the head. The boy knew that he would be hailed as a great warrior if he were to return with such a prize so smaller pigs would be left alone until a larger one was found. Sometimes, if the boy was away from the settlement for several days and nights, he would be weak, wet, cold and frightened. Occasionally the boar would find the boy first and he would never be seen again. Make no mistake; this was a very dangerous task.

'After the feast and celebration, the chief would present the tusks to the new warrior to be worn as an indication to others of his status and courage. To wear the boar's tusks calls to you the spirit of the pig and the spirit of the hunt, that is the spirit of the warrior. To wear the tusks without earning the right could make you ill, for you are not strong enough in spirit. Care must be taken when wearing tribal artifacts. The tusks are not worn as decoration, remember that. The man who wears them is seen to walk with Spirit and is to be respected, for the spirit of the ancestors walk with him.'

I told High Chief Wai Wai what Majikjiki had said in this meditation and he agreed wholeheartedly and said that this was their way. Then I told him of a story about when I faced a wild boar as a jackaroo on a sheep station in Queensland, Australia. One day my boss asked me to do some boundary riding to check the fences and billabongs of the property. I worked on a small property of only 28,000 acres and we had 9,000 head of sheep, so most mornings I would get on the motorbike and my dog, called Buster, would sit on the petrol tank between my arms. Across my back was a .303 rifle, which I was told I had to carry everywhere I went to protect myself against boar attacks.

On this particular occasion, as I was checking fencing, Buster happened to see a very large wild black boar in a billabong. He jumped from the motorbike and started to harry the boar, biting at its back legs. The boar turned round and charged Buster and I saw with horror that it was the biggest boar I'd ever seen. Buster yelped and ran back to the motorbike, jumping on to the tank hoping for a quick getaway. What of course happened was that he hit the bike so hard that he knocked me off it and the bike careered down the track for a few yards, crashing in the bush with its back wheel spinning.

By this time the boar was heading towards us in charge mode – it was intent on attacking us. I scrambled on my hands and knees to the bike, pulling my rifle from my back and laid it against the motorbike, the rear wheel still spinning. Buster had gone to hassle the pig again and prevented me from getting a clear shot. Then the pig attacked Buster and hurt him in the shoulder. The dog yelped and moved away, limping. The pig then looked at me and the intention, I could tell, was that he was going to kill me. I steadied the rifle against the bike and I took careful aim and shot the boar straight in the forehead, but I was shocked to see and hear a whistling sound as the bullet hit the boar's skull and ricocheted up into the sunlight. The boar shook its head and issued a deep, guttural grunt at me, pawed the ground and charged again. I put a second bullet into its head, which equally ricocheted off. This made the boar extremely angry and he just kept charging at me each time. I aimed another couple of bullets at his skull, which made no difference whatsoever and then I knew that I must not panic or be afraid because, if I did, I would be dead. So I took careful aim and put a bullet into his shoulder, which made him drop to the ground. To my horror and dismay, the boar stood up and on three legs charged again. I put another bullet into his head, which made no difference, and then with my last round I stopped him with a bullet to the chest. The boar landed on the motorbike in a cloud of dust, its face in my face. I was absolutely frozen to the spot, the rear wheel of the motorbike still driving, still on its side, the sound of the barking dog in my ears, and the guttural last cries of the pig. I felt extreme fear, yet admiration for this beautiful creature which I had killed. I honoured it in the only way I could by placing my hands upon its head. I didn't know what else to do. I wanted to vomit. I cried. The acrid smell of cordite hung in the air. My hands were covered in blood.

As I relayed this story to the High Chief, he said, 'Iarueri, you too have won the right of the warrior to wear the tusks of the wild boar,' and he placed his hand on my shoulder and smiled. 'Did you take the boar's tusks?' he asked. No, I didn't.

The Chief massaged my shoulder with more of the kastom herbs. They were a very deep beetroot colour with an unpleasant odour and he reminded me that this was to strengthen my blood and to link me to Majikjiki. It seemed ironic that my shoulder injury (I never really knew what had caused it) was facilitating a closer link between me and Majikjiki by using these sacred herbs on my body.

Namu brought little Wai Wai to see me. He reached out both of his hands and held my beard tightly, giving me a look, eye to eye, the look of an advanced soul, trapped in a frail physical body.

After lunch, the rain eased and we all went to a different village to meet another chief. Again, we had to reach this village by climbing a steep slippery mountain track. The nakamal and village were at the top of a mountain range and were very exposed to the wind, rain and cold. The chief was called Chief Tukuriary and the village Nakauren. We carried with us lots of pots and pans hung on poles over our shoulders and these were filled with different types of food, for we were going to this particular chief's village to honour the yam festival. The track was dangerous and vertical. Two of us fell.

When we arrived at the village, I was asked again to speak at length to the villagers, including the women who were preparing the first yams of the season, regarding who I was, why I was at Itabu and the difference between paganism of my culture and theirs and the way of the church. I did a traditional dance with the other men in a circle, moving anti-clockwise. Long speeches were given by the chief to welcome High Chief Wai Wai and myself, and as today is the first day of the yam harvest, the High Chief must have the first one. This year the harvest was poor because of the cyclone damage. The chief's speeches were then responded to by High Chief Wai Wai who gave thanks for the first crop and gave a blessing to the yam spirit. This chief and nakamal are guardians of the sacred stones of kava, pig and yam. (Apparently, there are different grades of pig stones.)

Moses pointed out to me a strange looking stone situated at the base of the banyan tree in this village's nakamal and he explained that this was the Yeramanu stone and only the Yeramanu was permitted to sit on it. The position or rank of Yeramanu is equal to, but very different to, the chief, in that the Yeramanu is the holy man or medicine man, witch doctor, who could do good or bad magic, almost by the sound of it like a magician. Secrets were told to me regarding techniques used by the Yeramanu of this village to kill a man or make him sick. They could also make a person well.

I was given kava as an honoured guest, which was exceptionally strong, plus prawns that had been obtained from the market, which were added to the yam and root dish. I was meant to go to Jerry's for the day to celebrate the yam festival at Port Resolution but Jerry still had a bad leg and I really felt that I didn't want to go there, as the spirit was not right for me there now. I knew that Chief Wai Wai would not have approved anyway.

We had a long slippery climb back down the mountain at dusk. I felt very ill. When I got to Itabu, I vomited in a flower bed. The Chief was most concerned, and was disappointed that I could not eat my meal, which was a chicken dinner especially prepared for me. I had been feeling unwell for a couple of days now, with headaches, sore throat and the runs. I had been taking my homoeopathic medication on a daily basis.

I explained to the Chief and Moses that I needed to stop taking kava for a while as it made me feel so ill. The Chief looked upset and I realised that I had made a bad mistake. Had I failed the test? This put the Chief in a very awkward position because the kava ceremony is so important to their culture. Was this now seen as a weakness of mine, or lack of respect? I had to find a way to connect with the kava spirit for help.

I explained to the Chief that, as the circumcised boys chewed and prepared the kava root nightly, then later drank it, they were brought up with this ritual over many years, whereas I was not. Kava is unobtainable in this raw form in the West, so to drink two full shells of a strong narcotic brew straight off was something I was not used to, so it made me very ill. The Chief looked woefully sad as though I had insulted his reputation so I felt bad. Because of the illness, especially dizziness and nausea, I rested for the morning and, guess what, it was dry and the sun was shining.

2nd April 2004
Chief Tukuriary   Sore titty

About 11:00 am, Chief Tukuriary arrived with a small party of villagers wanting healing from me. The two chiefs talked together, then Chief Wai Wai pushed forward from the crowd a shy woman, saying to me, 'This lady has a sore titty, heal her.' After the usual preparation, I asked her which breast was painful. She pointed to the left one. I showed her the reflex point for the breast on her left foot and did some reflexology pressure massage. She shouted in pain! Two men from Tukuriary's body guard stepped forward with machetes. I stood up and told them to move back. They were surprised, looking at Chief Tukuriary for his response. He nodded. They backed away. The woman looked frightened now. I asked if her husband was present; he stepped forward. I showed him where to massage the foot reflex point. She felt much better she said.

I did healing for a good hour and felt ill the whole time, but I did my best. I would never have done healing feeling that way under normal circumstances.

After lunch, I rested gratefully for the rest of the day. The Chief asked me to do some more healing for a man at 4:30 pm. Some people had walked for miles to come to see me. It was a great honour and thankfully I had no kava that night.

3rd April 2004
The Forbidden Pool   Nuie

Many of the places I was being taken to were taboo for everyone else, including local people, as they are sacred sites for the spirits and ancestors of a particular nakamal, village or tribe. I still had a sore throat but I felt better. My chest was painful from the nail wounds and possible cracked rib today and my shoulder was seizing up again because I was unable to exercise.

It rained all night with strong winds but it was sunny today. Chief Wai Wai said that he put a sacred leaf upon the sun stone today to bring the sun out for me especially to cheer me up. He told me that he wanted to take me to see the sacred pool of Itabu, the forbidden pool. Not even Moses, my interpreter, was allowed to accompany us, for it was a sacred spiritual place and he said to me that anybody who is found there is killed, and this still applies today. The Chief explained to me as we left the village that only three people in the world are allowed to visit this sacred pool – himself, Donald his firstborn son and myself. What an amazing honour and privilege. The spirit of the pool had guaranteed my safety when the Chief spoke with it at the nakamal last night.

We turned off the main road and followed a path which took us further and further into the mountains, into a small valley. It was lush with tropical plants and flowers and butterflies flitted around our heads as we disturbed them from feeding on the mineral salts in the mud here and there.

A woman was bathing and washing in a pool as we arrived at the end of the valley. The Chief coughed diplomatically and we stood a moment to allow her to adjust her dress.

We then moved forward, near to the pool where there was a large standing stone. This was the volcano stone and it was a peculiar colour of red and black. The Chief explained to me about the stone, yet he never spoke to the woman and I felt awkward about this as she lowered her eyes, staring at the water, which she sat in. She was ill at ease and embarrassed.

When we climbed up the bank from the volcano stone, the Chief told me that bits were taken from this stone for kastom rites. Then we passed into a very narrow, rocky gorge. It was very slippery due to cyclonic debris. There was a series of pools which cascaded from the upper level of the valley down to where the woman sat in her bathing pool at the base where the volcano stone was.

At the very top of this gorge there were clearly two entrances into this series of pools. I suddenly realised that it was a large Y shape, the very same shape as the archipelago of the islands of Vanuatu. Then the Chief showed me which of these pools was the sacred pool of Itabu and I was amazed to find that exactly where the sacred pool of Itabu was is the same positioning that would correspond with the island of Tanna on the national map.

The Chief explained to me again that if anybody came to this particular pool to drink or to wash, then they would become ill and he said that, if he found them there, then they would be killed. The Chief squatted down by the pool which was full of debris from the cyclone. I asked the Chief if I could remove some of the branches and sediment that had filled the pool and he raised his hand and said, 'No, leave it.' He said that the rains would come and wash the pool naturally. I was not permitted to move anything.

As we looked into the deep water of this pool, it was interesting to see that there were lots of gaseous bubbles rising from deep below. These were obviously gases from volcanic activity of Yasur. The pools on either side of this one did not display this particular phenomenon. High Chief Wai Wai explained to me that, if anybody from the tribe died overseas or in one of the northern islands, he would come to this pool at night and here he would do a sacred ceremony, and he showed me with his hand what that would be. He splashed the water moving the surface with the palm of his right hand, creating vortices which seemed to go down deep into the pool. He kept splashing the surface of the pool very gently. He said a stick was then broken and burnt and the person's spirit was then able to pass into the world of the ancestors via the pool into the volcano to the Well of Souls.

If rain is needed, leaves from a particular banyan tree are put into a kastom basket with a stone and then placed into the pool. Then in the evening at the nakamal, when the rite of kava has taken place and Tamaffa called, the rain would come that night.

The Chief also showed me the kava stone which was standing in the Y part of where the two rivers met and flowed into this cascading series of pools. This stone is also taboo to all others, especially when sacred leaves are placed upon it to enable the people to plant and harvest a crop. The planting of kava can only be done when it is raining, I was told.

The Chief did not permit me to take photographs of the kava stone or the sacred pool. He said he has given me the right as Chief Iarueri to visit these sacred sites; in so doing I cannot be harmed by the guardian spirits. This fulfils the legend. He said that it was important for me to visit this pool and then to see what dreams or visions I had when I slept. The Chief explained that the only pool that the villagers could use for bathing and washing was the pool that the woman still sat in at this time. She seemed afraid to move and continued to sit in the centre of this pool, waiting for the Chief and I to leave.

The Chief then frowned and looked at a rock; then he took a twig and reached into a crevice at water level and a large yellow-green spider, about three inches wide, scuttled from the rock face and ran underwater. It must have been a water spider of some species as it remained submerged in the dark depths of the pool.

I asked the Chief the name of the guardian spirit of this sacred pool and he said that the spirit was named Nuie. He also said that the guardian spirit was male.

After paying allegiance and honouring Nuie, we left the sacred pool of Itabu, passing the woman still sitting in the centre of her pool, eyes cast down, and returned to the village. Along the way I was again shown the different herbs and plants used in the kastom medicine and rites. In particular, the Chief showed me the leaf of a wild ginger plant which is rubbed and then used to aid the healing of circumcision wounds. There were lots of very black rocks on the ground that looked like lumps of coal or anthracite.

The aerial roots of the banyan trees are held or tied out in a straight line with pegs and vines so that, when they grow and develop, a perfectly straight timber pole is created for use in building houses or lodges.

We emerged from beneath the rain forest canopy to a clear, blue sky.

Something wet and hot hit the top of my skull with such force that I instinctively threw my hands up to my head, feeling a thick, mucus-like substance that hung from my fingers like snottites. The smell was dreadful and, in the heat and high humidity, I felt an oily slime run down the back of my neck and spine.

I gasped, trying to flick the putrid jelly from my fingers. The Chief was bent double in fits of laughter at my plight. No bird could have produced that amount of guano, it must have been a flying dragon! No matter how many times I washed my hair and shirt, that smell stayed with me for many days.

The Chief wanted me to rest after the visit to the sacred pool to communicate and connect with Nuie.

I went into meditative mode and connected with Nuie at the sacred pool of Itabu. I suddenly saw a large black boar with three curls to its tusks. A veil hid the pool so I asked for permission to pass through. The veil parted and it became night time where a full moon reflected onto the deep, still water. Then a small red pig emerged from the pool and stood looking at me. From the reflection of the silver moonlight on the water emerged the water spirit and guardian Nuie.

He spoke to me, 'Iarueri. I am both male and female, earth and spirit, for I am all things to all people; my place in the realms of spirit is where sacred waters lie deep and from whence I manifest. You have earned the right so that I may link with you through the sacred waters of your native land. Wherever holy waters lie, I shall be there to nurture you and care for you as you are now a guardian of this sacred place and working with the element of water, as you are working with the element of fire through your connection to Yasur.

'The spirits and the animals of the forest have every right to be here, for they have always walked this land. Man has lost this right so the privilege now has to be earned with permission given by the guardian chief. For those who desecrate or misuse holy sites such as this illness will follow. You understand this process, I know.

'Look deeply into these waters, for within the blackness of the sacred deep, your ancestors will appear to you, for water is a gateway to the spirit world – a portal. Water is sacred, along with all of the other elements – earth, air and fire. All are gateways to the spirit world when used with respect and care. This pool is deeper than your physical senses perceive, for remember that we are using the energy of spirit which has no boundaries and cannot be tamed by the weak mind of man. Where there is a natural opening into the earth, such as a cave, a hole or a pool, there is an energetic counterpart which will go much deeper into the realms below – to the realms of the ancestors. Man has the God-given right to work with us with respect and honour that we may walk the path of Spirit together in peace and harmony. But man will never conquer us as he is trying to do in the West. Disaster will occur!

'Deep within the spirit waters of this pool slumbers the consciousness of the sacred serpent of these islands, linked to all other spirit waters deep beneath and within the earth. When the time is right, the slumbering serpent shall rise to the surface and a new dawn of humanity shall commence, for when it does rise it shall bring with it a new form of energy or consciousness. Each of you has this sacred serpent deep within yourselves, sleeping at the base of your spine, waiting to rise up to enable you to become God-men and God-women. Each time you visit a sacred pool or site, you take a little of that sacred spirit with you and you leave a little of your energy behind. Make sure you leave behind the right sort of energy, otherwise you will pollute a holy place and the consequences shall follow.'

Nuie then disappeared back beneath the still waters of the pool through the reflection of the silver moon. The small red pig also disappeared beneath the surface of the water and the veil opened to allow my exit. The black boar and I then left and entered the bright sunshine.

At dusk, the Chief and Nikwei called for me at my leaf hut to go to the nakamal. Moses explained to me that kava was my greatest test because of the effect it hand upon me. I put on my nambas, along with the Chief and Nikwei, and I took two shells of kava. I did not want to put the Chief in an awkward or embarrassing position, so I made a point of drinking the kava and honouring Tamaffa in the usual manner. The Chief looked very pleased.

4th April 2004
Miscarriage Extraction medicine

At 8:00 am, Moses, Donald and I went to Shark Bay. We spoke to the kastom owner who said that the sea was too rough for the sharks to come in too close, so I could go and visit the headland without any charge. My two "guides" hadn't been here before so we got lost in the jungle several times. When we eventually reached the cliff face, a spectacular drop to the shore below revealed huge white breakers crashing on the rocks below and then foaming on to the beach of black volcanic sand. There were no sharks anywhere. The only thing that we did see was a large green turtle of some sort. It was really wonderful to get some sea air into my lungs again, for Itabu village is in the mountains next to the volcano, quite some distance from the sea. I felt a little homesick but felt much better after breathing in the salt air.

Everywhere I've been there was severe damage from the cyclone and there were lots of nets and floats on the shore down below, which Donald said were from Taiwanese fishing boats. The local people often scramble down to get these fishing floats; then they cut the top off and use them as water carriers. Sharks that had been washed up on the beach were skinned, then, once the skin was dried, used as rough "sandpaper" for their outrigger canoes.

The sea air reminded me to ask Donald if the Chief had received the quartz stones I posted to him. Donald explained to me very simply that the package of white tumbled quartz stones which I had sent to the Chief from the Isle of Man were given to Kelson by the postmaster at Lenakel. At that time, the Chief was in Vila so Donald eventually got the package from Kelson, but he said that the package was opened and he thought that some of the contents were missing. Donald said that quite often when I sent a package to the Chief it had already been opened by Kelson first and they didn't know what had been taken out. The Chief did not have his own post box, so everything went into Kelson's box. (I gave the Chief the money to open his own post box at Lenakel. Other people can also use this box now.)

On our return we went to Nikwei's little village. Even though it's a satellite village of Itabu, it still has its own name – Kapaapen.

We went again to see the John Frum Cult dancing, which is only held on certain days, also the healing through the trance dancing. The Chief, Nikwei and I donned the grass skirts again to dance and the women laughed. I did two healings. One on a woman who I was told afterwards had had a bad miscarriage and who was bleeding uncontrollably and had great abdominal pain with leg problems. She was lying on a mat in her smoke-filled hut. As I sat earlier, this particular woman came up to me in a trance dance. She was helped up by her family and began the dance with the aid of the others and, when she moved herself to where I sat, she bowed to me placing her head upon the seat next to me, which was the first indication of spirit intervention and the early stages of healing commencing. I didn't fully understand what was taking place but the older women healers nodded gravely with each other and they said to me, 'Heal, Heal.'

A mat was brought out from the hut and the woman was laid down upon it. I tried to clear her chakras but couldn't get the lower ones cleared at all, so I called for a feather, which surprised everybody, and Nikwei went and brought to me a curled tail feather of a rooster, so I explained to him that I needed a long, straight primary feather from the wing of a bird. Eventually he came back with one and I began to do some shamanic energy clearing using the feather (extraction medicine), which I ran through some smoke to cleanse initially. All the villagers were amazed to see a white man working in a tribal manner and, out of respect, all remained silent.

Soon after sweeping her auric field, she began to quiver or shake. After I had finished the four sweeps, she was assisted up and told her husband that she was burning up with the heat, so he and another woman poured water over her head to cool her down. She was then led away by two of the elder women to her hut. I was told some time afterwards that she had felt better after the treatment.

Back at Itabu, Chief Tukuriary and another group were waiting for me for some healing. They asked me to talk about spiritual matters to them and, while doing so, a boy from a different village set fire to the undergrowth beneath the large coconut trees. The fire soon spread and the flames shot up the trees, probably to a height of about 15 feet because there was a lot of dry debris around the base of the trees. The boy was chased by some of the others and the Chief and the other men beat out the flames with anything they could find at hand. This was unbelievably stupid because the fire was near the thatches of the leaf huts and the lodge. I wondered why he started the fire deliberately. Everybody questioned this. It was a bad omen.

The Chief bought a basket of locally grown kava root for tomorrow's ceremony, 1,000 Vatu worth, which was 10 bundles. The Chief's kava is said to be the strongest in the whole of Vanuatu, simply because it is grown in the deep, moist, mineral rich soil from the volcano; therefore, many people want to buy his kava. The problem, of course, is that because the Chief needs money he tends to sell his kava, which means that when he wants some for himself he then has

to buy it in.
5th April 2004

Receiving boar's tusks   Shot in throat

As a chief I had been asked to perform a ceremony from my Celtic kastom tradition and for High Chief Wai Wai and his men. This was all part of the tests, trials and training for my experience. This was to be done later in the day.

First thing in the morning, after breakfast, we had to wait for the owner of the pig to arrive which had been purchased specially for the second stage of my initiation and of my being presented with my boar's tusks – the sign of the chief. Just before 9:00 am, the man arrived with a helper with a beautiful large pig hanging from a bamboo pole, bound by its feet, squealing and wriggling in an attempt to escape. I felt sick and sad to know that I would be responsible for this beautiful and majestic creature's death so that I may go through a sacred ceremony to ironically gain my boar's tusks. It is not for me to judge their custom. It is part of their tribal ancestral culture and it is extremely important to their belief system which goes back to the ancient days. I prayed silently – rather I pleaded silently to the ancestors and to Majikjiki that I would not have to kill the pig myself.

When the High Chief, Donald and the others were ready, I had to follow the pig in a procession from the village to the nakamal, the pig screaming the entire journey. When we got to the nakamal, the pig was laid upon the ground, still bound but the pole was removed. I remember clearly thinking that it must be in great distress and discomfort because its feet were red raw from the chafing of being bound to the pole and carried probably several miles through the jungle this way.

Already a large amount of kava root had been placed in the nakamal, then the pig laid carefully next to the sacred roots. This is very powerful and symbolic to the kastom people that the kava and pig, both probably the most sacred things in their lives apart from the ancestors, are laid side by side in the centre of the nakamal to precede any important ceremony. Both the kava, with its ability to induce a state of stillness within to contact the ancestors, and the sacrifice of a sacred animal sending it to the other worlds, plus the ceremony, tribal dress, etc, is a powerful energetic phenomenon, which cannot be fully and properly described in my crude, simple words.

High Chief Wai Wai then emerged from behind the banyan tree, resplendent in full tribal attire. On his head, he wore a coronet of leaves. On his right arm, he wore a pandanus band which contained sacred aromatic leaves to Majikjiki. Around his neck hung three boar's tusk necklaces with pale blue seeds and fourth necklace of pale blue seeds with a black button at the end (I do not know the significance of this, maybe just a decoration?). He wore the nambas as usual and on his brow a black mark of charcoal running across the forehead at the third eye from temple to temple. This mark, I was told, could only be used by a chief in an important ceremony. It cannot be used by anyone else, since the tribal marks have to be authorised or earned to be displayed. Each means a different thing, like the tattoo. I was told also by the men who helped to prepare me that, should anybody copy this mark, I have to kill them!

The High Chief stood by the kava and the pig waiting for me to be fully prepared. I stripped naked and the nambas was tied on to me. Kwaramu, or Willie as he is also known, a tall thin man, mixed some charcoal and coconut juice together and I was given the same mark as the High Chief upon my brow. Herbs were massaged into my chest and back, leaving me feeling sticky, yet smelling of chlorophyll (I smelled green), obviously to be absorbed through my pores and into my bloodstream. I wondered what effect this had upon my energetic counterpart, the etheric body?

Dancing then took place with chanting and the usual rhythmical stamping of the men's feet, which had the effect of sending vibrations up and down my spine and making me feel all "goosebumpish". It was truly magical. Here I was beneath the tropical skies of the South Pacific on a remote island far away from home. I really cannot describe the feeling of inner wonder, magic and joy of this unique experience which would change my life forever.

When the dancing stopped, I was told by the High Chief to club the pig to death. He offered the ceremonial club to me and indicated that I had to give it a single hard blow to the forehead (remembering my last efforts at dispatching pigs). I looked at him and he obviously sensed my unease. Being a sensitive and wise man, he instructed me to symbolically strike the pig with the club so that I didn't actually deliver the fatal blow. The important thing was, he said, that I make contact with the club to the pig's head. He also said it would be an honour for me to pass the privilege of killing the pig to another man; that was my right as Chief and there was no disgrace in this. He then instructed me to pass the right and the privilege to Moses, who formally accepted this honour by bowing and dispatched the pig humanely and instantly with one expert blow. He gave it a second blow to make sure that the pig was killed, but it was obvious that the first had dealt the fateful blow. Blood gushed from the pig's skull and mouth, the dogs drinking the hot blood from the reservoirs of the ears as it flowed into the black earth. I felt sad for the pig but gave thanks to its spirit and for the part it had played in the ceremony.

The Chief then spoke at length to the assembled chiefs and their representatives of the surrounding villages who had gathered of how I came to Itabu and the full process of being made Chief Iarueri through the instructions of the tribal ancestors. Every so often men in the assembled crowd nodded. Formal welcome was made to me and the presentation and transference of the boar's tusks and the leaf coronet. The sacred aromatic leaves of Majikjiki were also placed around my upper arm.

I gave a speech giving thanks and tried to express my gratitude at the honour and privilege given to me. I thanked the men for accepting me and inviting me to be a part of their tribe and their culture. I know I shall never fully understand this culture, but then maybe I'm not meant to do so, since I have been used by Spirit to fulfil a legend in their eyes? Most of what will or what has occurred takes place in the realms of spirit.

More dancing, chanting and stamping took place and I was invited to participate, which I did as best I could. It was important to join the dancing to create the vortices and the sense of creating a serpent spiral on the ground. I wished my young nephew Aaron was here to experience this sacred time and ceremony so that he would understand the importance and the privilege of this hereditary position passing on to him automatically at my death.

After the final dance, we all raised our hands and cheered and laughter broke out. Ceremony was a joyful event (when it wasn't in cyclonic rain!). After changing we returned to the village for lunch. As the meal wasn't ready the Chief took me to see the women folk prepare lap lap, a glutinous, starchy traditional dish made from tubers, cooked in the stone and earth ovens, whilst the men butchered the pig ready to cook for the feast. The earth oven was quite remarkable – volcanic stones were heated in a shallow pit by burning large timbers on top of them. Whilst they were becoming very hot, the women prepared the food, wrapped up in banana leaves and then tied with vines. When the stones were hot enough, the timbers and embers were removed with sticks and this was quite incredible when you consider that all the women were barefoot. Then more banana leaves were laid on top of the hot stones. On top of these, different leafy branches were laid, then the wrapped packages of food. These were then covered by more leaves and finally soil. When the soil had been mounded up into a volcano-like cone, a kava leaf was placed in the top. When the leaf became brown, the food inside the oven was cooked and ready to be dug out and eaten – an organic oven timer!

After lunch, the High Chief and I returned to the nakamal where the men had prepared the pig, removing the lungs, heart and liver to cook over the open fire. I had to undergo another "test" of following a trail of leaves through the rain forest set by the men under the instruction of the High Chief. This was to see how perceptive I was. At the end of the trail, I was told, would be a prize. The High Chief said he would accompany me, laughing like a young boy. I had never seen him so jolly before. Bit by bit we followed a particular type of leaf that had been scattered here and there by the tribesmen whilst I was at lunch. We followed the trail to a hut and then backtracked to the back of a banyan tree where the prize was found – a shell of kava each! Also next to the shells of kava was a bunch of flowers picked by the men. I thought this was a real privilege that these warrior men had actually taken the trouble to pick a few flowers. The Chief took his shell and the shell that was left had a large spider drowned in it. I felt like giving it the last rites. We both carried our kava shells to the nakamal, where we gave our thanks to Tamaffa and drank together.

Now it was my turn to prepare and perform my sacred ceremony for the High Chief. With help from Moses, I set up my sacred circle in the nakamal, making sure beforehand I did not do anything which was against the tribal customs. I drew a large circle using two sticks and a thin vine, then had four small fires lit at each quarter manned by four volunteers to keep the flames burning. Around the circle, I spaced evenly all of the tumbled quartz white stones from the Isle of Man which I had previously sent to the Chief, including one which was kept by myself to be "offered" to the guardian of Yasur. This one was placed in the centre of the circle.

A half coconut shell containing water was placed into the ground at the west, representing the element of water. A larger fire was built at the north, representing the element of fire and a fire with green foliage upon it was built in the east to represent the element of air through the smoke. Finally a local stone was laid in the south, representing the element of earth. This was the traditional Celtic circle or medicine wheel. The elements of earth and fire were reversed since this ceremony was being performed in the southern hemisphere not in the northern hemisphere (fire is near the equator, earth is near the pole, as a guide).

By the time the circle was ready and the High Chief and guests assembled it was about 3:30 pm and, since it was getting late, the ceremony had to be brief because the men would want to take kava at the nakamal in time to precede their prayers to the ancestors.

The Chief and I went to the small wooden hut at the edge of the nakamal, undressing and putting on our nambas. Many chiefs, elders and men had gathered, sitting in circles around the perimeter. When I looked through the cracks in the hut walls I felt nervous, knowing that my performance was going to be scrutinised as a chief. High Chief Wai Wai looked at me and smiled. We walked silently through the crowd of waiting men. One man in particular was bent over laughing, slapping his hand on his thigh as my very white hairy ass passed him. I felt sick!

We entered the "arena". There was no turning back now. I prayed to the ancestors and Majikjiki for help and courage. I guided the Chief into the circle through the southeast quarter, standing in the centre of the circle. Then I called in the guardians of the four quarters and the guardians of the four elements, including the ancestors below (truth) and the masters above (wisdom), joining all at the heart. I led the Chief to each quarter as I called in the appropriate element, consecrating myself and the Chief accordingly with each.

I had placed the coconut fibre rope, which was used previously in the Chief's binding rite, in the north. The person manning the fire set it alight! I then performed a simple binding rite, binding our right forearms together to show the assembled chiefs and guests that, in my kastom also, High Chief Wai Wai and Chief Iarueri were equal as brothers, irrespective of culture and skin colour, before the ancestors and all men. I gave thanks to all guardians as we reversed the procedure and opened the circle. I thanked the men for coming long distances to witness the ceremony and asked them to enjoy the feast afterwards.

I explained briefly what I had done and why to the assembled men and received standing applause with speeches from many different guests to thank me for sharing my kastom traditions with them, something that had never ever been done before. The chief who had laughed initially spoke at length, interpreted by Moses, of his amazement and wonder at the way the ceremony was performed. He congratulated me and welcomed me into the community. I could sense that he felt embarrassed for mocking me. I smiled at him and nodded; he returned the gesture. They all seemed to be fascinated by watching a different ceremony and to see their High Chief taking part.

The fires were then put out and we did a kastom dance. I trod on a glowing ember from one of the fires and burnt my bare foot. Chief Wai Wai saw this and he picked up the ember and threw it to the edge of the nakamal. His expression was "are you OK?" I nodded and smiled.

All the white stones were gathered up and given to the High Chief to be kept for healing. I asked him to place one of the stones in the sacred banyan tree to remind him of our simple ceremony. As customary, I then presented him with some gifts I had, as he had presented to me the boar's tusks. There is always an exchange of energy of some sort, otherwise obligation causes tribesmen to lose face.

By the time 5:00 pm came, the kava was flowing freely for the feast and I would estimate about 50 or more men were present, all or most representing different nakamals and chiefs. After the pig was butchered, the offal was cooked immediately by the skewered stick method over the fire; in other words, the outside was burnt black and the inside was red raw. Large pots of cooked vegetables were also brought. I had the customary kava shell with the High Chief at the same time to show equal grade and rank; then followed by senior chiefs. I was expected to take a second in succession but had to refuse as I had already had an earlier cup and a third was beyond hope. Tonight was a full moon. She was called Owni.

The Chief asked me to do some more healing, which he had never done before whilst at the nakamal, especially before such a gathering. One old man was brought forward out of the crowd, a man who I recognised from Nikwei's village, Kapaapen. I had treated him before after the trance dancing and recognised and remembered that he had a problem with his throat. The Chief asked me if I would do another session with him.

I placed my hands on his shoulders to make the connection and looked into his energy body. I clearly saw a red barbed arrow in the man's throat in the energy counterpart. I called upon his higher self council and the ancestors for permission to remove the arrow. After some time and with several difficulties, I had to make sure that the arrow was withdrawn correctly at the same trajectory that it had entered into the energy body, so great care was taken with this. Once the arrow was removed and the energetic wound healed in the energy body, I explained to Moses what I had done and Moses translated to the old man, assembled chiefs and men.

The old man apparently had been a kastom storyteller, composer and songwriter but had gone over to the Christian church and forgotten and abandoned the tribal spiritual path. When, after several "warnings" from Spirit, he still refused to fulfil his allotted hereditary kastom role (a very important one, I may add, as the storytellers and songwriters hold the ancestral myth and legend, rather like the Druidic bards), the ancestors blocked his throat by shooting him with an arrow so he couldn't speak, sing or communicate properly. The old man said, when he realised what a major mistake he had made as a young man, he was horrified and beside himself with guilt and grief. He left the church and returned to the kastom path, hoping and praying for healing and forgiveness that his voice may be restored and the dreams and visions returned to him.

He spoke with difficulty and had problems with eating and swallowing food for many years. I asked Spirit for a blessing for him and asked the ancestors to have mercy on him and to give him their grace once again. The old man's eyes were full of tears as Moses explained to him the words I spoke.

He told Moses that he "applauded" my inner vision through the ancestors and said that I was indeed a man who walked the true path of Spirit. He thanked me many times, bowing and holding my hand. As we shook hands, tears rolled down his cheeks, his lower lip quivering, his voice a murmur full of emotion. I too began to feel emotional and said to him, 'Go forward now, my brother, and sing your songs and tell your stories that the younger generation may hear the truth of the ancestors through you.'

He wept openly. He repeated my name over and over, 'Iarueri. Iarueri. Iarueri.' Moses explained to me the importance of the role of composer and songwriter in their tradition, as they compile songs that record the history of the tribe. Moses said that he would compose a song about Iarueri now! I felt so unworthy to be among such wonderful, simple, spiritual people. Words failed me; they really did.

The women had produced a massive amount of food for the feast, which they had cooked in the earth oven. This is known as island food; in other words, native traditional food without Western influence. I took sufficient food to be polite. Even though I knew that everything was clean, organic and fresh, it still tasted dreadful.

Today had been a very memorable day. I would say one of the most significant days of my life. The energetic consequences would not only affect this life, this incarnation, but past, parallel and future lives. I wondered what my second "death" would be like afterwards and what would be the trigger.

Willie, the Head Teacher of Iaqurimano Primary School came to the feast and brought with him his official letter in response to Andrew Douglas's letter for Manx Government aid, including many letters to the Minister handwritten by the schoolchildren. This had been an exciting project for them, he explained.

I had to be up at 5 o'clock the next morning to get an early breakfast so that we could be ready to catch the first trucks of the day going to Lenakel, so I could reconfirm my flights. My throat was still painful and my burnt foot red, although not blistered.

6th April 2004
Tribal warfare begins

Up at 5:00 am and had breakfast at 6:00. The Chief, Moses, Jack and I left for Lenakel to get supplies. We had left too late to catch the first truck, so we set off walking in the hope of catching the next vehicle (which could have been many hours and many miles away, but of course much cheaper). During the walk, Moses said that the woman I had done healing on in Nikwei's village had received a vivid dream that night and saw a shining spirit. She was so frightened that she rose from her bed and ran out of the house screaming and was eventually stopped deep in the jungle by her husband who chased after her. It was from him that Moses got the story.

High Chief Wai Wai then told me of his dream which he saw that night. He said that he saw an ancestor standing next to a star. He was then drawn into a circle of light, the same circle as he had been in during my ceremony, but this was of pure spirit. He became afraid, so the circle disappeared! I felt disappointed not knowing the possible outcome that this dream could have given. He would not talk anymore about it.

We walked for two hours across the volcanic ash plain, wading across the river. I was quite happy to remove my socks and boots, but Moses insisted that I should be carried upon his back, which I was. We met Kelson's driver returning to the lodge. He said he was returning to Lenakel shortly with a tourist, so he would pick us up if we wanted to wait.

We met two local men who hailed the High Chief and came to sit with us. The Chief and two men then moved some distance away. The Chief looked grave. They talked seriously and I could tell there was a problem. Then Moses explained that the tribe at White Sands, very near to where we were at that time, had begun to capture John Frum leaders because of a breakaway voodoo sect led by the man called Fred, who had influenced Nikwei. The two men said that fighting had already broken out, which would mean that tribal warfare could escalate. As nearly as I could understand, this was mainly due to the fact that the John Frummers had begun to plant and harvest yams against kastom law, but there seemed to be some confusion and there was clearly much more involved. Chief Wai Wai looked very worried.

We got a lift to Lenakel. I sat next to the female tourist in the back of the truck. She was squeaky clean and smelled as though she had just come out of a bottle of disinfectant. I felt overwhelmed, I was so used to the women of my village smelling in a particular way – smelling of nature, smelling of natural body odours. To sit next to this young woman, smelling of a synthetic perfume, made me feel a little nauseous.

On the way to Lenakel, the truck broke a front wheel bearing so, driving slowly, we eventually arrived, where we were stuck for three hours until another vehicle could be found to take us back to Itabu. I bought two long-handled axes and some machetes as gifts for Moses, Donald, Rachael and Nahu. Nahu is High Chief Wai Wai's daughter and her job was to carry water for me daily from the spring in the mountains and to make sure that I had sufficient water to drink and to have a body wash from a bucket each day.

The Chief bought me a bottle of water and a local dough stick cooked in hot oil. When we found another truck, we stopped off at a store, meeting Kelson who also bought me another dough stick, which I thoroughly enjoyed. The truck was soon full to overflowing with other travellers and their goods; it was a very rough ride back to Itabu sitting on a hard wooden seat in the back, bouncing along on the rough roads. We were covered in red dust as other vehicles passed. I was very glad it wasn't raining.

At about 5:00 pm, Jack called me to go to the nakamal, but the Chief and I did not wear nambas. This was the first time and I was secretly glad because the mosquitoes were very bad. We performed the kava ritual and I managed not to vomit. The men spoke of fighting at White Sands and the John Frummers. Everyone was serious and worried. I couldn't identify the meat for that evening's meal.

After the pig was butchered yesterday, I wanted to ask the Chief what happened to the pig's guts after the butchering, expecting him to say something along the lines of: they go to the dogs. But he said that the guts are taken down to the river to be washed and cleaned out so that they can be cooked to eat. I wondered if they used the intestine like sausage skins.

7th April 2004

Spirit stone of the secret dance   Ambush

I had a vivid clear dream last night in which I saw a river of blood sweeping into a hole in the earth. As I followed the river of blood to its source, I found a massive boar, which had been slaughtered, lying on top of a kastom village. The village was destroyed and all the people had gone. Encroaching towards the village at a steady pace was a Western style city of skyscrapers and concrete. The message, I felt, was clear that kastom life was becoming destroyed because of the Western influence. It must be stopped or controlled in some way before everything which is tribal, traditional and spiritual is destroyed forever. The Chief instructed me to report all dreams to him. It was an important part of the kastom way to gain insights.

I could see the influence of this dream upon the likes of David and Kelson Hosea with their lies, thieving and deceit, their hunger for power, status and wealth, for the trappings of Western civilisation at all costs against their own culture. Moses told me that, when I first came to Itabu village, High Chief Wai Wai gathered the young men together at the nakamal and said, 'Which one of you will be Iarueri's guide?'

Nobody wanted the job! Moses said he wouldn't do it because he had a wife and family to look after. Nobody else wanted the miserable job because of their lack of English. Moses said that, because he could speak and understand English better than most, he was told he had to be my guide by the Chief. He said he felt devastated! I laughed with delight and punched Moses playfully on the shoulder. We both laughed at the situation but we had "grown up" together during this time and became very fond of each other's company. Moses said that he was glad that he was given the job of looking after me because now he knows more about his own culture and spirituality than ever before through the legends and myths told by Donald. (The legends and myths of the Maruki tribe have traditionally been passed from each High Chief to their firstborn son, the heir, so some of these stories or secrets about them are never revealed to the ordinary villagers. In Moses's case, the exception had been made because the High Chief needed me to fully understand the stories properly. Moses therefore knows more about his own heritage revealed to him for my benefit.)

Moses said he had been fed up with village life and had planned to go to live back in Port Vila with his family again but, since he had been to the sacred sites with me which he had never seen before and which were taboo for the ordinary man, he now realised that his culture is unique and very important. He admitted that he had learnt a lot about his own heritage. High Chief Wai Wai is in fact Moses's uncle.

Moses said that everyone liked me and the High Chief saw me as his brother. Moses said that Chief Wai Wai was already upset at the thought of my leaving and going home. He said that the Chief wept. I didn't know what to say!

When I spoke to the Chief later he told me of a dream he had had last night, seeing the two of us in the sacred circle at the nakamal. The sun shone above us and we were both lit by its light. He then saw us holding arms and being bound by a cord as spirit brothers. Confirmation again of Spirit working through ceremony, or is it the other way about in that the true ceremony has already occurred in spirit and the physical ceremony is just an enactment of memory?

The Chief said that we would go to visit some caves at 10 o'clock but that there was a large group of people waiting for me to receive healing, all women except for one man. Some of the women had been on the end of wife-beatings by their husbands and were clearly afraid. I was amazed at the apparent rise of domestic violence in Vanuatu, mainly caused through alcohol abuse – another Western influence! One old woman on a previous visit had to stand, then sit constantly because of so much pain with her knees and hips. On the last visit to see me, she could stand with the aid of a staff and on this occasion, after I had finished with her, she stood without any aid at all.

I finished my "clinic" at about 11 o'clock when I went back to my hut. Shortly after a woman knocked on my door and asked for healing for her babe in arms who had problems with both ears. I went with her to the village square opposite my hut and did what I could. It was difficult and I hoped people didn't expect too much from me.

It rained torrentially so the cave visit was cancelled. I had a rest and, during this period, I had a vision. I went to the spirit world and saw Majikjiki. We both sat down upon the grass and before him was a flat brown stone, the size of a dinner plate, and two thin fire sticks which were crossed between the stone and his feet. Upon the flat stone now appeared a round tombstone-like stone, about 18 inches high and 6 inches thick, which was formed from Majikjiki's hands, from the volcanic earth.

Majikjiki spoke, 'Iarueri. This is the spirit stone of the secret dance, which will be placed near the base of the banyan tree in Chief Wai Wai's nakamal. It is a stone created by Spirit for Spirit. It is a secret stone not known about in the physical realms. In the physical world, you place your sacred stones in important places. It is the same in the spirit world, but these spirit stones cannot be seen by the average person, only those given permission to guard and use them. This stone will connect the spirit of the dance to this nakamal where new ideas will be passed to the kastom composers to create new dances and to bring more power to the earth. To be given this privilege and right to be a guardian of a spirit stone is not given lightly, but Chief Wai Wai has earned this right and respect as he is known to us in the spirit world for walking the path of truth.

'Other nakamals may have many physical stones of power, which have their spirit or energetic counterpart, but few nakamals are considered sacred enough to be blessed with a spirit stone, not of this earth. This is in recognition of the Chief's dedication to the kastom way, even though he has been ridiculed and mocked by others less enlightened. They are secretly envious of his connection with Spirit. This stone, therefore, is a gift from Spirit to the spirit of this nakamal. All ceremonies that take place at this nakamal will draw upon this stone's consciousness and power. The more ceremonies that take place at this nakamal, the greater the spirit power that will build up. Nakamals that are used only for socialising and drinking kava have little spiritual value. It is the kastom ceremonies and those who take part within which build up and maintain this spirit energy through the collective consciousness of the focused group mind and intent. Kava used in the correct manner to enhance the divine being within is quite different from drinking it socially.

'Spirits walk with those who honour them; they do not walk at those nakamals where they are not honoured and respected, no matter how important the chief may think he is. The heart of the chief is not necessarily within the form of he who claims to be in this position.'

I went to the nakamal for the kava ritual at dusk. The Chief was sitting beneath the banyan tree. A tense discussion ensued between the Chief and the people from Nikwei's village because yesterday and today their sect, a breakaway sect from the John Frum Cult, were lucky to escape having their limbs hacked off or from being killed by an ambush party of kastom men from another tribe, using their axes, machetes, clubs and bows and arrows. Many had to drop everything and flee into the rain forest and the mountains, only emerging at dusk last night and again tonight, coming straight to this nakamal for sanctuary. Many were terrified. High Chief Wai Wai had to preside over the proceedings and, if necessary, the authority and the right to sentence a man, or men, to death or corporal punishment.

The High Chief indicated for me to sit next to him beneath the banyan tree. We heard the men's tales and stories, translated to me by Moses, who knelt behind me and whispered into my ear. I felt like a High Court Judge and realised the enormity and great responsibility that the position of High Chief held, literally the power over life and death!

The John Frummers were constantly breaking kastom laws by doing such things as planting and harvesting yams at the wrong times throughout the year, so damaging or interfering with the energy consciousness of the yam spirit in relation to their cycles of tribal life. It was too complex an issue for me to fully comprehend but, by the tones and deep concern displayed before the High Chief, it was obvious that many lives were now at risk of a brutal and bloody death if this tribal war could not be brought to an immediate stop. Apparently witnesses said that villagers, including Nikwei, were tipped off by a traveller who informed them that an ambush party was ahead waiting to kill them – this is literally. If they had not been warned and fled into the mountains, Nikwei and his party would have been butchered and hacked to bits, causing wholesale tribal warfare throughout Tanna Island. It seemed like the old feuds were resurfacing again.

I was told also that Chief Wai Wai would have been butchered along with the other chiefs before the ordinary villagers, so that they would be leaderless. This of course implied that, as an official chief of the Maruki tribe, I would have received the same fate or would have been expected to lead a party of warriors into battle in hand to hand fighting! The thought of my home and all that I loved on the Isle of Man now made me choke.

High Chief Wai Wai sent a message with a runner to the fighting men to say that he had told Nikwei and his people to stop their John Frum singing and trance dancing immediately, so as to halt the hostilities for the moment. This was to allow discussions to take place. The people were now fearful of a night attack and Moses explained that, should this take place, everyone including all animals would be butchered and Kapaapen village burned to the ground with everything destroyed. This was very worrying, as Nikwei's small village is only half a mile away, if that, from where the Chief, his family and myself slept. All I could do was to pray to Spirit and to the ancestors to protect us all and to bring peace.

8th April 2004
Bird myth   Armed gangs

We had an early start to go to the bat caves. I felt concerned, wondering if it were safe to travel with the fighting in the area. Moses, Jack and I set off, passing a huge, rusty tin building. I asked Moses what it was used for and he replied, 'It was the Apostolic Church. They were not very nice to the kastom people but not as bad as the Seventh Day Adventists.'

It was a strenuous climb up and down the slippery, wet, narrow mountain tracks. On the way we passed through the grounds of the local Roman Catholic Church and school run by the French. Moses explained that this church was built in this remote area for a reason. Even though rainfall was plentiful in the wet season, most of the year the mountain ranges were dry, so locals had to walk long distances to collect water. The church built large water tanks on their property and only those who agreed to send their children to be indoctrinated and taught lies could use the water, providing they spoke French and rejected their kastom tradition. He spat on the ground!

We eventually reached the village of the kastom owners of the cave. Moses asked me to bring my dowsing rod to do some healing on the father of the family to be visited, who was one of his relations.

On the way through the rain forest, I spotted a scarlet and black bird, the same as in a previous vision of Majikjiki and I asked Moses what it was called, but he didn't know the English name except to say that it was known as Majikjiki's bird! (I later found out that this bird's official name is a Cardinal Honey Eater.) I was amazed at this revelation as I had not discussed the previous vision with the Chief or Moses. I was excited because it was another piece of the jigsaw puzzle fitting into place for me and a wonderful synchronicity of Spirit, proof that I was on the correct path spiritually. I eagerly asked for more information and Moses said that the bird story was given by the ancestors of the tribe, connecting Majikjiki.

The Myth

A giant went around the island capturing and then eating people. One day he caught six people and put them into a pen and told them that he was going into the mountains to get some taro and other food for them to eat to save them the problem of looking for it themselves, as they were all hungry. The giant left. In reality, he was collecting the taro to eat with human flesh as the main course.

As the people waited for the giant to return, Majikjiki came along and asked the people why they were penned up? They told him that the kind giant was going to get food for them as they were hungry, but Majikjiki knew that the giant was lying. So he told the people that the giant was in fact going to eat them. Majikjiki broke down the fence and the people escaped.

When the giant returned and saw his captured people gone, he smelled the wind in each direction, north, east, south and west and followed their scent until he caught up with them. Majikjiki, being a magician and holy man, called to an oak tree to sink to the ground to enable the people to climb into its branches. Then Majikjiki told the spirit of the oak tree to grow so high that the giant couldn't reach them.

When the giant found the tree, he noticed the reflection of the people in a pool beneath, so jumped into the pool thinking that they were there. When he realised that they were not, he looked up into the tree and asked the people how they got up so high. They told him different methods, each of which he tried but failed. Then Majikjiki, who was also up the tree with the people, threw down a rope to the giant, explaining that this was how they all climbed up the tree. The giant climbed up the rope, reaching the very top of the tree. He tried to grab the people but Majikjiki cut the rope, sending the giant crashing to his death on to the rocks below. Majikjiki then called to him a small black bird and instructed the bird to fly down to the giant to see if he was dead or not. The little bird flew down and went inside the giant's large mouth, moving through the limp body until he came out of the bleeding wounds. This is how the little bird became scarlet at the front, remaining black at the back. He became known from that day forward as Majikjiki's bird.

———————————

After the healing, the man and his family thanked me as I told them of a vision I had received during the healing process, which they understood symbolically as a mistake the man had made in his life before and his illness was a result of this error. Hopefully peace and health may be brought to him now.

We travelled again with two of the man's sons as guides, as well as Jack the Chief's second born son, but he was very lazy finding the height too difficult so he left, returning to Itabu. Initially the men refused me access to go to the caves because they thought I came from Kelson's Lodge. Moses explained who I was and why I was at Itabu. Moses said later that men felt guilty and sorrowful about their misjudgement of me, so insisted that they acted as my guides for free to correct their mistake.

We travelled up and down steep and very dangerous jungle trails to visit another village high in the mountains to enable me to give healing to a very old lady. The mountain trails, which never saw sunshine because of the deep descent into the narrow valleys, were treacherous and wet and I was getting very tired and my bad knee started to ache (an injury I received in 1976 after being hit by a car).

We crossed deep crevasses and streams by slippery smooth log bridges. This I found difficult because I wore boots. For the guides who were barefoot, there was no problem, of course. Eventually we reached the village of the old lady. The old lady had only seen white people in the valley below many years ago. Due to her age she had remained in her remote village for many years, where I was the first white man to ever visit. She was nervous of me as she had never had a white man touch her before or even speak to her. Moses explained the procedure I used of shaking hands initially to make the energetic contact and to dowse the energy field of the body and do the chakra balancing. I always started by placing both hands on the person's shoulders. She said she felt much better after the process and thanked me. She looked at me and smiled in a girlish way. I winked at her; she giggled.

Eventually we reached the bat caves but the lower entrance leading into the large open hole, formed by volcanic activity millennia ago, was blocked by cyclonic debris of trees, branches and stones. It was difficult and dangerous work climbing through and over this barrier but eventually we reached the cave entrance and, on the far side of the quarry-like hole, no bats were seen! Bat droppings were in evidence and their pungent smell but unfortunately nothing was seen of them. According to local myth, this was the place where Yasur volcano originally formed and emerged into the sunlight from deep beneath the earth.

We returned to the men's village, where they had obtained some rice and killed a chicken. We had a very good meal. We were told by the High Chief to be back at Itabu for about 11:30 am because of the fighting. We returned at 3:30 pm. Moses was in trouble again!

On listening to the Chief and the other men speak, we caught up with the news on the tribal warfare situation and how the armed gangs were still very much active and hostile, waiting for the people of Nikwei's village to be attacked and killed. They were now stopping all trucks with road blocks to search each vehicle for the people known to follow the sect, to capture them and take them away. Their fate was unknown. I was told that the woman I did healing on in Nikwei's village, who ran out of the house, had haemorrhaged badly again after a fall, so they needed to get her urgently to hospital in Lenakel but could not take her because she and all who accompanied her would be killed. The Chief and Donald were trying to find a way to get around the road blocks to get her to hospital. The situation was very unstable and getting worse.

9th April 2004
Bat caves   Hanging   Myth of volcano   Refugees
I took some homoeopathic remedies against malaria. Apparently Moses saw the woman and child who had the ear problem visit my hut the other day whilst he was out hunting, so reported the incident to the High Chief. The Chief summoned the woman before him and she was told that she should not have disturbed Iarueri without first seeking permission from him. All who come for healing, I have been informed, have to get High Chief Wai Wai's permission. Consequently, the Chief had the two gates tied shut to force non-villagers to stay on the village perimeter as a reminder of kastom protocol. The gates stayed closed for several days. I wondered why they were shut.

Earlier that morning, whilst sitting in meditation, I received a communication from Spirit that I was to visit the bat caves on the inner plane. I went with the boar to the middle world where we had to wait under the natural stone archway to stand beneath the hole, which is a natural physical and energetic formation and portal. As the boar and I stood beneath the portal, we became irradiated with light and a voice asked me who I was and why I had come to the sacred cave? I said I was Chief Iarueri and that Spirit had instructed me to visit the cave. We were then permitted to enter through a veil of energy into the large, round, quarry-like gardens before and beneath the cave entrance. This formation had sheer sides which would be impossible to climb physically. A stream ran from an opening beneath the cave entrance, the whole area filled with flowers, butterflies and birds, including the Majikjiki bird.

I then heard a voice, 'If you are truly following the path of Spirit, you will be light enough to rise to the cave. If you are false in your ways, you will be too heavy.'

I was then covered in a multitude of rainbow-coloured butterflies. I cleansed my energy body to become filled with light to enable the butterflies to lift me up to the cave entrance. Then I head the words, 'Iarueri. This cave is a sacred place from where the first human emerged on this island. We speak of the spirit of man, not the physical body. From the depths of the Earth Mother came forth life, for your physical body firstly had to be formed in spirit, then created from all of the elements of the earth and cosmos. Without the spirit body, you could not have the physical body. The spirit is first, the physical body second. This is what is meant by the saying, "You are formed in the image of God." God is Spirit, the Spirit of all creation. This cave also has its spiritual form and its sacred guardians and any committing an act of sacrilege against these guardians will have to bear the responsibility and the karma of that situation. You understand this, I know.

'Deep within these dark passages, at least to your eyes, are the eyes of the sacred ones who watch and listen to what takes place. They invite those to visit, whom they permit to experience the deep solitude and holiness of being within the womb of the Earth Mother. We were aware of your mark of respect in touching your brow with the damp earth of the cave, a small gesture but one that was noticed and honoured. Thank you.'

The butterflies returned me down to the garden to where the boar waited. We both returned back through the veil of energy. I came out of meditation feeling lighter.

After breakfast, four ladies returned for more healing. All claimed that they felt better. I asked the High Chief if Kelson had paid him the money I gave him yet? The Chief said that Kelson refused to give him the money. This made me very angry. The Chief had been looking after me and paying for food, especially rice which he had to buy, so he was out of pocket. This meant that, if Kelson would not pay Chief Wai Wai the money he obtained by deceit, then I would have to pay the Chief another 30,000 Vatu. Kelson said he put the money in the bank and he couldn't get it out now. He has had a month to pay the Chief back; he obviously had no intention of doing so.

I discussed this situation with the Chief, who introduced me to a man called Kenneth. Kenneth was from the neighbouring island of Erromango; he was a warrior and, like most of the men, always carried a machete with him, so the Chief, Kenneth and I set off to Jungle Oasis to visit Kelson.

When we arrived Kelson was organising a birthday party for an Australian tourist. Kelson realised why we had come, inviting us in to join the party. Kenneth pushed his machete into a bush near the doorway so that he could get quick access to it in case a fight ensued. Kelson set three extra places at the table and told the assembled tourists that I was a big chief to try to gain control of the situation and to "preen my ego". He placed the three of us between the tourists, trying to trap us in, but, when the speeches were over and it came time to sit down to eat the meal, I stood up and I said to Kelson that we were going and not staying, as we had not been invited to a private party. I knew that this walkout would be taken as a rebuff and an insult in the kastom hospitality and was not good to do but, as Kelson was a Seventh Day Adventist and not a kastom person, I didn't really care. I knew he would use this against me later as an excuse. I told him that we would call again tomorrow for the money.

After returning to Itabu, we put on our nambas at the nakamal and had the ritual kava. I felt ill with it tonight as it was much stronger than usual. Moses and I, plus five others from the village, climbed up the volcano to see the fireworks at night. I felt ill all the way up there and back and, on my return, vomited in the flower bed next to my leaf hut. The dogs cleaned it all up! I couldn't eat dinner. The Chief was upset that I was ill again due to kava. He told me that I shouldn't exercise after kava as it was used to bring stillness to pray. Knowing that I was going up to the volcano that evening, I wondered why he allowed me to drink kava beforehand?

Moses then told me that a Presbyterian John Frum leader had been captured by the armed gangs at Sulphur Bay and was bound hand and foot and carried off into the bush, slung from a pole like a pig (this was the traditional way a man was carried to a cannibal feast). He was taken to a secret location. He then had a rope put around his neck and was pulled about and jostled. Another member of the church located him through information received and went to the warring tribe to plead for his release. Moses said mockingly that he thought he was a big warrior. This man also had a rope placed around his neck and was hung until dead from a tree. Moses said that the small contingent of police at Lenakel were doing their best to stop the problem but they were hopelessly outnumbered and had now called in the army from Port Vila to quench the tribal warfare. Moses also said that some of the John Frummers were fighting back on horseback like cavalry using their machetes like sabres. There are many wild horses on Tanna used by the local people.

After breakfast, Donald and Moses told me of the myth of Yasur volcano. I had difficulty in understanding this myth fully for some reason. Donald spoke clearly but Moses seemed unable to translate the story properly, maybe too much kava the night before! Again, Moses had never heard this story before either, since it is a secret myth of the Maruki tribe. I was not sure how secret secret meant in this case. Before with the tokka dance, I was instructed clearly by the High Chief that this story was not to be repeated to anyone else.
The myth of Yasur volcano

In the beginning, before time, Yasur began to develop underground at the place of the bat cave but it was too hot since he couldn't reach the sea with his hand to cool himself down. He then began to move about like the spirit of a pig but destroyed the island cabbage at Ianiptoka village, from where the tokka dance originated. The villagers moved Yasur on nearer the sea so he could be cooler. When Yasur moved, he made a noise like a grunting pig "so, so, so", which is the name of the God spirit now known as Kassosu, which is the black native side of Majikjiki (it is important that the reader understands that the black side of Majikjiki means the dark, Melanesian native side, not satanic in any way). Majikjiki gave the villagers spirit tools, such as the gift of composing songs and dances, such as the tokka dance.

As Yasur moved to his final place, two women called Saibai and Monga were making lap lap. The spirit of Yasur, which resembled a large pig, lay upon the top of the hot stones so the two women quickly covered the pig with soil to cook him. As they worked, they created a whirlwind which began to create a large crater around them until they were lost into its depths. This was the crater of Yasur volcano and remains to this day.

Just as I had finished listening to this myth, two men arrived in Itabu village carrying weapons from the warring tribe to take away Nikwei. Rachael, who had just finished doing my breakfast, was very frightened and she quickly ran out the back door to get Chief Wai Wai, as Nikwei and his people were still in hiding. The Chief was told by the men that, if Nikwei did not come back with them now or did not give himself up voluntarily, he would be tied and severely beaten and an armed raiding party would attack the village, killing everyone and destroying everything. Moses explained to me that similar incidents had occurred over the past couple of years; on one occasion many from the John Frum breakaway sect were held hostage and tied with ropes and chains which were put around their necks. The army came in, landing by sea, and stormed the stronghold whilst another part of the army stormed the stronghold by land simultaneously, converging on the kidnappers with a shootout. The kidnappers were all killed; the captured hostages were set free unharmed.

High Chief Wai Wai told the armed men that they couldn't have Nikwei or anyone else and that he would make Nikwei stop what he was doing, and to prove it to the warring tribe he would get Nikwei to burn his own village down to the ground along with all of the flags he used for his trance dancing. The Chief dismissed the men. They looked angry.

Interestingly, earlier on before breakfast started, Nikwei arrived in the village and asked Moses and I to walk with him back to Kapaapen. If we had done so, we would have been attacked by an ambush party lying in wait, but Moses suspected this and said, 'No. Not without the Chief's approval.'

Nikwei then ran off on his own, knowing why we had refused. Maybe he thought that, if a white man was with him, he would not be attacked. This, of course, would have made little difference.

The Chief went to the village but Nikwei was in hiding, as expected, so he gave sanctuary to Nikwei's wife and children and all of the villagers left behind. The women and children were to stay with him and his wife at Itabu. Most of the villagers had fled into the mountains, so Donald and the others from Itabu went to search for them to bring them back to the village to enable the Chief to talk and reason with them. Donald and the other men were armed to protect themselves in case of attack by the warring tribe who were also searching for Nikwei and his people in the mountains. Donald knew that, if he didn't find them first, they would all be butchered.

When the villagers saw Donald and Moses and the other armed men from Itabu searching and calling out to them, they became even more frightened because they believed that the men from Itabu were also hunting them down to kill them. The villagers all split up and fled again deeper into the mountains.

Now Nikwei couldn't be found and his life and the lives of the others were in great danger. Moses said that, if they caught him, they would hang him from a tree and hack him to bits before cutting his throat. The situation was now very dangerous and tense for everybody; everyone was nervous and on edge expecting an attack at any time of the day or night without warning. The High Chief planned to go to White Sands with Moses and Tom, all fully armed, to meet the High Chief of the warring tribe to try to negotiate a peace settlement.

'All of us could be killed,' Moses said as they left Itabu.

It was a very dangerous and courageous task they were to perform. I felt worried for my friends – no, my family. We heard that tribal fighting had now started in a full bloody battle at Lake Isiwi. The police had arrived and fired tear gas to disperse the warriors in an attempt to stop them from fighting. Unfortunately, it was too little too late.

As I stood at the edge of the nakamal, I saw a trail of bedraggled and frightened women, children and old people walking in single file through the undergrowth to Itabu village led by High Woman Martha, a very important and symbolic act. Before her was a very small child, possibly only four years old, and she carried on her head a single coconut. Martha kept pace to the progress of the small child. The child's face was stained with tears. Martha was very courageous and looked very regal; I admired her greatly. I stepped off the trail and cast down my eyes to honour the refugees. In tribal custom, this was acknowledged by Martha with a slight bow of her head.

All the refugees carried what they could. It was very moving, sad and emotional and the reality and enormity of their plight touched my heart. They were about to lose their homes, their gardens and their livestock. I offered to carry items from the village but was not permitted.

I did not demean or offend them by taking any photographs. This would have been very insensitive at such a traumatic time. The refugees made camp in and around the Chief's house and next door to my hut. The Chief and Martha moved out of their own home to a small hut, to me a very important, symbolic and supreme act of chivalry, to allow the refugees with small children to sleep inside safely. I have come to see that High Chief Wai Wai is a very exceptional person who carries out his duties and position as no other could.

I watched the High Chief leave with his two armed bodyguards, Moses and Tom, who I knew would protect him to the death. I had mixed feelings; I wanted to be a part of the tribal history and go with them and I felt devastated at the great and real risk of them all being hacked to bits and never seeing them again. I also knew that, if the High Chief was killed, then all who belonged to Itabu would be butchered, including myself. It would come down to hand to hand fighting, slashing and spearing.

I wished I were safely home on the Isle of Man now so that I could see Aaron growing up. I didn't want him wondering why his mad Uncle David had been murdered in some far off foreign land. I felt emotional but strangely I felt an inner calm and courage. I was not afraid and I didn't understand why I was not afraid. I was told that, if Nikwei did not hand himself over by tonight, we could expect a night attack by the warring tribes to occur at any time.

The Chief, Moses and Tom returned much earlier than I had expected, much to my relief. They had met and spoken with the council of warring chiefs. They had managed to calm the situation down temporarily, but only for a respite to try and get hold of Nikwei, get him to listen to the Chief and burn down his own home and village as proof of finishing this secular practice. To burn down a village seemed drastic in the extreme but better that than loss of life. The village can be rebuilt, of course. The Chief was being very smart with this. I hoped that Nikwei would see how the Chief was thinking. Police were now at Sulphur Bay permanently attempting to calm things down; senior police officials came in from Port Vila to talk to the warring chiefs.

I went, as usual, at dusk to the nakamal to witness the Chief and the elders discussing the situation. Again we wore no nambas. Suddenly, out of the gloom of the forest, a figure appeared. Nikwei slipped in from the bushes and came and sat right next to me on my log, for some support I felt. I made a point of shaking his hand and smiling at him and I put my arm around him, holding him close. The others seemed to ostracise him for the problems brought on by him to the village. Nikwei didn't speak but had arranged for someone to speak on his behalf. He was frightened and had agreed to burn his flags but not his village. The kastom men tolerated the main John Frum Cult at Sulphur Bay but they would not tolerate the other two breakaway sects, one of which Nikwei was the leader. The situation was extremely tense.

It also occurred to me that, if the warring tribes were lurking in the bushes near the outer perimeter of the nakamal, since Nikwei was sitting shoulder to shoulder with me, I could receive a spear in my back. I tried desperately to put my irrational fears to one side and to act as a chief should do, calm and centred, showing no emotion.

Word had come through by somebody from Chief Noar's nakamal at Port Resolution that he wanted to see me urgently.

11ᵗʰ April 2004 – Easter Sunday
Armed guard   Live or die!   Threatened

There was a lot of activity last night between 10:00 pm and midnight. Men were running and shouting, carrying lamps and weapons. I knew that under my bed were two axes and machetes that I had bought in Lenakel as gifts and I wondered what I should do if the worse happened and I was attacked. If

I were to use them to defend myself, I would be hacked to bits for certain. If I stood unarmed, maybe they would leave me alone. I doubted that also. I decided to get fully dressed in case I had to fight with the men, so I uncovered the axes and the machetes, hiding them under the blanket in my bed. One thing I knew instinctively was that High Chief Wai Wai would have an armed guard watching my hut all night and he would have clear instructions to protect and defend me to the death.

I did not sleep very well; I was too hot for one thing being fully clothed in the heat and humidity. During the night, I looked about my hut and worked out appropriate escape routes should a flaming arrow land on the thatch or a spear ram through the thin walls. The two best options were small windows at the back or lifting a couple of loose planks on the floor, covered by a pandanus mat. I decided to drop through the floor, since the leaf huts are built on short stilts.

Moses was waiting outside my hut when I emerged at 6:00 am. He told me that Nikwei had been found in hiding and was now being sheltered in a hut near mine. As predicted, the Chief had posted armed men around the village last night and I learnt that Jack was specifically to guard my hut and myself. He was ensconced in the lodge directly across from the village square with clear views of my hut, except for the rear, where other guards would have been watching. Donald and his men were posted in and around the nakamal where the path from Itabu to Kapaapen passed. Moses and his men were posted on the main road and surrounding paths. The Chief had the village surrounded, other armed men being hidden in different parts of the bush. Any large war party would more than likely pass by or on one of the main paths to get to within attack range.

Moses told me that early in the morning, he and his men became bored so crept up to the nakamal and made a mock attack upon Donald and his men, startling them so badly that they ran into the bush in all directions before regrouping and launching a counterattack on those who now stood in the darkness in the nakamal. Luckily, they recognised each other at the last minute and nobody was hurt. I thought this action was very immature and irresponsible by Moses and his men for, not only could men have been killed or wounded on each side but if the warring tribe had attacked the village at that time, a very serious situation would have occurred, in that the Chief, Nikwei and myself could have all been killed or captured. I knew that, if Chief Wai Wai found out about this, Moses would have been in big trouble again.

I spoke to the Chief after breakfast and he said that Nikwei had now agreed to burn his village to the ground as well as the religious flags. I thought to myself that I was the first white person, and the last, to visit Nikwei's village and to witness and photograph the trance dancing. I have this rare and unique sight never seen before in the West on film. Nobody else will witness it ever again! I prayed that the film would not be harmed in any way by the airport X-ray machines or the humidity of this climate.

The Chief said that Nikwei had agreed to abandon the John Frum Cult and to return to the kastom law. The Chief now had to ratify this agreement by sending a pig and kava to the High Chief of the warring tribe to prove it was all over. The pig's spirit would free the bad spirit of Nikwei's village, I was told, as a sacrifice. Nikwei was still being a little awkward from what I could deduce, which was surprising considering that he had a clear choice – live or die! The Chief told Nikwei, 'You have to surrender to me or I have no choice but to allow the armed men to kill you.'

It was now Nikwei's choice, bearing in mind that, should he fail to surrender to High Chief Wai Wai, not only would he be hacked to death but everyone else in his village also.

I went to Jungle Oasis to see Kelson with the Chief but he was not there and had spent the night in Lenakel for some unknown reason. The locals were presuming he was trying to avoid me.

In the afternoon I went to the nakamal to hear the Chief speak to the Kapaapen villagers. Nikwei sat isolated and alone. He looked very dejected and afraid; he remained silent. Another man spoke on his behalf. Nikwei had finally agreed to surrender to the High Chief. His flags, a pig and kava were sent to the warring High Chief that afternoon. The armed conflict had now calmed down in this immediate area but other armed gangs were still fighting the John Frum Cult members around the Sulphur Bay area and were still controlling the main road with road blocks and searching every vehicle for the breakaway sect members.

Challen, Kelson's son arrived with tourists to see some kastom dancing at Itabu and said that his father had not returned from Lenakel yet, but Martha overheard this and told us she had just seen him. More lies!

Moses and I went to Jungle Oasis immediately to confront Kelson. We spoke about how he had lied to me and stolen money from me by deception, knowing all along that I wanted to stay with High Chief Wai Wai at Itabu village and not at Jungle Oasis Lodge. Kelson said that it was a tourist law in his country that, when money had been paid, there was no refund. I reminded him that I had been invited by his father to stay with the family as a family guest and not a tourist and also reminded him clearly that he had been stealing from the kastom site owners and not paying them their due site fees. Kelson became very angry and shouted at me, standing and waving his arms, saying that I was treating him like an animal in his own house and that I had broken kastom law myself in declining island hospitality at his party (I knew that this would be brought up!).

Kelson said that he knew I would cause trouble for him and I was going to damage his business. I stood facing him and said to Kelson that, if he didn't pay the Chief 30,000 Vatu by the time I left for Vila, then I wouldn't just cause trouble for his business, I would do everything I could to close his business for good, since he was stealing from tourists, and that I would write to every Vanuatan tourist office and operator to inform them that he was a thief! He became extremely upset. We faced each other, literally nose to nose, eyeball to eyeball!

He then threatened me by saying he was going to call the police now and get me arrested. I replied, 'Please do it now so that I can also make a complaint about you stealing from foreigners.'

He then added he would have his men or the police waiting for me at Vila when I got off the plane to stop me flying back to England. 'Go ahead,' I said. We shook hands with each other, but it was the handshake of Judas and I knew more trouble would come. Moses and I then left.

On the walk back to Itabu village, Moses laughed, telling everybody he met how I stood up to Kelson. Everybody smiled and shook my hand. At the nakamal, Moses related the argument that I had had with Kelson, adding extra bits to enhance the drama, and said to everybody gathered, 'Iarueri is strong in mind.'

High Chief Wai Wai then said to me, 'Iarueri. I will take the problem of Kelson from you. If he causes you any trouble or gets the police involved, I will get my boys to kill him.'

Donald looked at me and smiled, nodding his head! The High Chief asked me to speak. I took my place as Chief beneath the banyan tree, speaking to the men, saying that only a peaceful solution must be found regarding the problem of Kelson and not to add to the violence. It wasn't the path of Spirit. The men who gathered listened to the speeches from Moses, the Chief and myself and others added their voices to the debate. One thing was very clear: tension was high and the kastom men were looking for an excuse to kill Kelson and possibly his father Kahi also for the stealing of their rightful earnings. The men looked at me when Moses explained how I stood up to Kelson to defend them. Moses said to me that the men had never had anyone speak up for them before and thanked me for this. Some of the men just looked at me and talked amongst themselves, others nodded and smiled and some waved.

Moses said to me, 'Iarueri. You have earned much respect by the men today. You are strong in mind, for they are uneducated and don't know how to fight against the likes of Kelson and the trouble with the church.'

I knew there were some men who didn't approve of my being initiated as a chief. These men either avoided me or turned away when I approached. The same men now treated me differently, as an equal. It was at this point I knew I had passed the tests and trials of being a chief. I hoped the outcome for all would be peaceful.

I was under armed protection at all times now. All Kelson had to do was pay the Chief what he was owed, 30,000 Vatu for my keep – problem over and finished – it was as simple as that. There was a risk now that Kelson might get his men to attack me either here at Itabu or in Port Vila. My safety, as always, was in the hands of Spirit.

Nikwei's people seemed more at peace and happier now that Nikwei had agreed to return to the kastom path. Nikwei came to sit next to me again and said, 'They wanted to kill me,' making a sign across his throat, indicating a knife cut.

'Nikwei,' I replied, 'You are a good man that walks with Spirit. The ancestors have protected you.'

He smiled and we embraced. Moses said to me that the old lady who had given me healing at Nikwei's village was traditionally a kastom doctor, but her medicine was taken from her because she left the kastom path for the church. Moses continued and explained that the Chief would kill a pig for her and drink kava so the ancestors would return her healing powers.

The afternoon was filled with debate on all sides, the Chief presiding like a High Court Judge. This was the first time I had seen women at the nakamal, all sitting at the perimeter, none spoke. When dusk came they all left, leaving the nakamal to the men for the kava ritual. I was asked for healing by one man who before had avoided me. We looked at each other, understanding the unique bond of brotherhood irrespective of colour, creed or race.

12th April 2004 – Easter Monday
Tribal myth connecting Isle of Man   Clubbed to death

I had an early start today. Moses and I walked to Port Resolution to see the Head Teacher of the school, to collect the letters from him and the children that are to be presented to my MHK, Andrew Douglas, in the hopes that the Manx Government can give the school some sort of educational aid. When we got there, we found that he was at Lenakel and would not be back until tomorrow. This was because of the Easter holidays, but also because the school was closed due to the tribal fighting, which was now in that area.

I saw Jerry and Ealise and spoke to Chief Noar, who wanted to talk to me urgently, so it seemed. The Chief, who spoke beautiful English, had seen one of the small Manx flags and books that were given to the children by Andrew Douglas as a gift from the Manx nation to the Port Resolution school. The Chief wanted to know as much as he could about the Triskele, the Loaghton sheep, which is a particular breed of sheep peculiar to the Isle of Man, and the Isle of Man itself.

I told him what I thought would be appropriate and he went on to tell me of a story that his grandfather had passed on to his father. This story is local myth now, but its telling by him left me stunned and in disbelief and wonder at such a bizarre coincidence! The Chief is himself a very old man, so this myth would have originated in the 1800s, if not earlier.

The Myth

Chief Noar reminded me of the Maruki creation myth of Majikjiki, continuing with the story to say that off the coast of England was a very powerful island and from this island the white twin, the white serpent, shall return to reunite the islands together again (Mann and Tanna) and you would know him by the sign he carried with him. (When I showed the Manx flag to the High Chief and Nikwei some time ago, they were very excited and I didn't know why.) Chief Noar went on to explain that the Triskele, or the three legs of Man, was the sacred symbol that they were looking for, it represented the three tidal waves that were created in the original myth, one of which carried the white twin (Majikjiki) to the west, from where the locals have been waiting for his return. The Chief became so excited and so did I. I couldn't believe what I was hearing. How fantastic!

On the way back to Itabu village, we went via the old colonial road, which followed the coast more and had many swamp areas and coconut plantations. Moses showed me two more missionary graves. Moses said that Kelson had already started more trouble, in that he was no longer letting his tourists see the kastom dancing at Itabu and was trying to get another village to start kastom dancing. Each village had its own traditional dances so, if the other villages tried to copy the dances or songs of Itabu, there would be more trouble. Kelson was doing his best to set the kastom people against each other.

After lunch, I had a rest and a brief vision was given to me by Spirit. I saw the river and waterfall and both lakes, Isiwi upper and lower, filled with blood. The waterfall was flowing backwards and it and the river were all blood red. I did not understand what this meant. I spoke to High Chief Wai Wai and told him the story that Chief Noar had told me and he said that he had heard the same myth from his father also, who had been told it by his father, the then High Chief Iarueri! The Chief was furious that Noar had told me this part of the story as he said he wanted to tell me himself when the time was right.

Chief Wai Wai called over a thin old man with white hair called Kahi, who also said his grandfather told him the same myth. Apparently, this part of the Maruki myth is only known in the southeast area of Tanna island, not anywhere else. The Chief also went on to talk to me about Prince Philip, who everyone here refers to as Queen Philip.

Legend

Long ago a tribesman from the New Hebrides (now Vanuatu) emigrated to America and married. He had many children and they had many children until eventually one lived in Europe and settled in England. This person was Queen Philip. When the Royal Yacht visited the New Hebrides many years ago, Wai Wai and Kahi had to perform a spear dance before the Queen and Philip, connecting the link between England and what is now Vanuatu. The Chief said it was no coincidence that he had met Queen Philip, for he was originally of this land.

Kelson was now playing dirty. He stopped four tourists who were coming to Itabu to see the kastom dancing and turned them away. He sent a message to the Chief to say that he would stop all tourists coming to Itabu and would stop the Chief from starting his own business. The kastom men were angry and didn't know what to do. They wanted to kill Kelson. The tourists believed the money they gave to Kelson for the dancing would be given to the Chief. Kelson kept it all.

Moses said that he has now heard that the leader of the breakaway John Frum Sect, Fred, had been killed. He said his arms were broken and then hacked off and he was then clubbed to death, front and back of the head. His body was taken away somewhere. Houses had been burned to the ground in some villages the previous night. Maybe this is what the vision meant – everything is returning to the way it was before, but at the cost of much spilt blood?

Moses disappeared for several hours, so the Chief and I couldn't tell each other our stories. I went to the nakamal, where the men had killed a pig to feed the refugees in Itabu. I was given some pig flesh, a piece of fat and skin and rubbery lung. It was definitely an acquired taste!

13th April 2004
Cyclone stone stolen   Limbs hacked off   Wading through bat guano

I felt ill for most of the night and couldn't sleep. I thought it was because I had eaten tinned tuna. The fresh fish was unavailable this far inland from the coast but tinned fish was available, sweating on hot shelves in the sun for months, probably with a very good bacteria count.

I asked Moses a variety of questions I had gathered up, such as facial painting protocols. Marking the face with charcoal or coloured paint or pigment for ceremony follows kastom law. Only persons of the rank of chief can use certain marks or patterns, either facial or upon the body, since these symbols call the guardians of the mark to the wearer who should be strong enough in spirit to accept the power. To mark your face without the authority or understanding of what the marks mean was breaking kastom law and the consequences would follow – sickness probably, as linked with tattoos. There are marks for different sacred ceremonies, as well as for war. They all have meanings and link you to a particular guardian spirit.

Moses explained that the main reasons why the tribal fighting started was due to the inappropriate planting and harvesting of the yams, but also the kastom cyclone stone had been stolen from its nakamal by the John Frum Sect members for some reason. Once the cyclone stone had been taken from its sacred nakamal, the power and forces of the storm were unleashed onto Tanna island and southern Vanuatu by the great guardian of the stone, whereas before the power was controlled with honour and respect by the chief of the nakamal, who was the guardian of the cyclone consciousness. The stone had been found and was now back in its rightful place, so the Chief told me there would be no more cyclones until the proper season commences.

The chief and kastom owner of a different bat cave near Itabu took me to see these caves after a good walk through the rain forest, which included traversing the top of a slippery waterfall on the cliff face. The origin of this water flow came out of the darkness of the cave. At the front of the cave entrance was deep silt, so I had to take off my boots and socks and, with the others, waded into the mire, having to bend low to get into the cave entrance. Once inside, I could stand easily, but the problem was that I was calf deep in bat guano and could feel the maggots, cockroaches and other creepy crawlies moving between my toes and around my legs, feet and ankles. It felt really weird! After my eyes had adjusted to the darkness, a torch was shone at the bat roost and I took a few flash photos. Hundreds, if not thousands, of small bats – absolutely fantastic. I had no idea what species they were. After emerging into the daylight, the chief insisted on washing my feet and legs in the small stream.

Once again, Kelson had coerced these kastom cave owners to make a path to the caves from the road and, when they had spent many weeks doing this, he refused to send any tourists. All the kastom people hated the Hoseas and they looked for any excuse to kill them both.

After lunch, Jerry came to see me to say goodbye. He brought with him the letters from the Head Teacher and pupils at Port Resolution school. He also asked me for some help for Ealise and his eldest son, David, to continue his education. I said I would pass his request on to my MHK.

The High Chief asked me about my family, so I told him about my twin brother, Barry, and my nephew, Aaron. The High Chief said that he would like to meet them and extended an invitation for them both to return with me next year, 2005. The Chief also asked me to write a letter to the authorities in Vila informing them about what Kelson was doing. I said that I would do this for him.

Moses turned up much later in the day and explained that he had got the early truck to Lenakel to ring Air Vanuatu in Vila to confirm my return flight to Brisbane. He had also arranged for his father, a taxi driver in Vila, to pick me up from the airport. I was greatly relieved about this because Kelson said he would get his father, the bogus High Chief Kahi, and his men to meet me at the airport and to talk to me "severely". Moses read a rough draft of the letter to the tourist authorities, which I had written on his behalf. The Chief approved its contents, so I rewrote it neatly for him to sign by oil lamp, since it was now dark.

The Head Teacher of Port Resolution school arrived to say goodbye. I went to the nakamal for the last time. I was asked to drink kava to honour the ancestors. Nikwei made me a small tam tam carving. We embraced. I said goodbye to the men, several speeches were made to thank me for the healing and the acceptance of their kastom tradition. Moses said that he had to visit the hospital in Lenakel with his baby yesterday for a routine check. Whilst he was there, he said the hospital was full of injured men from the tribal fighting. Some had their bellies slashed open and their guts were hanging out. Others had their arms, legs, feet or hands hacked off. Fighting was still continuing by the northern tribes around the White Sands area. Kidnapping was also very common. Moses said 16 men came in whilst he was there; most had their bellies slit open.

After we had left the nakamal, the Chief's family had prepared, at great work and cost to themselves, a tribal or island feast to honour me. I was deeply touched by such generosity and kindness. Before we sat down to eat, the High Chief was the first to be given a garland of leaves and flowers around his neck. I followed, then Nikwei. It was wonderful that, after being the pariah, he was now publicly given a place of honour at our feast. He had lost face in having to surrender to the High Chief, so by this gesture Nikwei resumed his place of authority and status in the community.

I was formally presented to all gathered by the High Chief who spoke at great length about he and I being brothers. I could understand the basics of what he said. The Chief suddenly stopped talking and began to cry. He couldn't stop, so I held his arm to support him. I felt a real feeling of brotherhood between us. I then had to give a speech to thank them all for accepting me as a member of their family, their tribe and as a chief. One by one they gave me their gifts. I gave a machete to Rachael and she gave me a grass skirt which she had made. I also gave a machete to Nahu but she was too shy to speak. She gave me some feather sticks for my hair which she had made. Donald made me a nambas, tusk necklaces and a stone axe, plus armbands. He bowed gracefully to receive his long-handled axe, holding it as if it were his baby. Moses was then called to receive his axe. He stared in disbelief as I handed it to him and touched him on the arm and smiled. He handed me some feather sticks. Afterwards Moses said to me, 'Nobody has ever given me a present before.' He had tears in his eyes.

The hut was bedecked with flowers and leaves; the flickering oil lamps cast eerie shadows across the room with the pungent smell of paraffin. Upon the floor on pandanus and coconut leaf mats was a spread of island food, lap lap, fruit, chicken, bat and a suckling piglet, including the head, which I was told, as guest of honour, I had to take the first piece of by cutting a slice. As usual, it was burnt black on the outside and raw on the inside. After the men had eaten their fill, the left overs were given to the women folk to eat, who had spent the entire day preparing and cooking it. I felt very uneasy about this but this is their culture; this is their tradition. It is not for me to judge or condemn in any way or even to compare. Speeches followed the meal again. Kelson still hadn't paid the Chief the money that he owed him.

14th April 2004
Road block   Prepare to die!   Second death
This was the day of my departure from Itabu village. I managed to find some extra Australian dollars in my money pouch to pay the Chief for my stay, board and lodgings. I had very little Vatu left. The truck, organised a few days ago to take me to the airport, couldn't get through from the north due to the road blocks and more fighting. Runners were sent to Port Resolution area to try and find another truck for me so, as we waited anxiously, I said my goodbyes to the High Chief, his family and all who had gathered to see me go. The Chief wept again. I felt very emotional also, so we stood in silence, side by side. Moses explained to me that Chief Wai Wai could not come with us since he was now a wanted man by the warring tribe because of his refusal to hand over Nikwei. The armed men at the road blocks ahead would capture him and would probably kill him. This would mean Donald as well.

I was pleased to see a truck arrive from the south. The driver pulled up and spoke at length to the Chief. The Chief looked uneasy and spoke softly to me, 'Iarueri, the driver won't take you unless you pay him 10,000 Vatu. I have just given him 5,000 Vatu. Do you have enough Vatu left?'

Luckily, I had about 6,000 Vatu left, so I had no option but to pay this price (normally the fare was only 2,000 Vatu). The reason he wanted so much was because the journey to the airport was through bandit country and was extremely dangerous. Very few other drivers would take on board this sort of trip. In fact all others had refused. That left me with exactly 1,000 Vatu for when I arrived eventually at the airport in Vila (the equivalent of five pounds).

My bags were put in the back of the truck, along with the other travellers' belongings, including a bound, squealing piglet, which had been given to one of the chiefs who had stayed at the village during my initiation. Moses, Tom and Roy from Nikwei's village went as guards for me. All stashed their weapons – machetes, bows and arrows and spears – under the seats and covered them over with bags and tarpaulins so that none of these things could be seen. I was told by Moses to sit in the front with the driver.

We left Itabu to waves, shouts and tears soon travelling across the ash plain leaving the volcano behind. We forded the river and continued upon our way. Each truck or vehicle we saw we stopped and exchanged news on the fighting and road blocks. Some vehicles changed their route; others turned back; others continued as planned. Everybody seemed very anxious and nervous. We then reached a major road junction leading to White Sands; this was where the rebel tribe had set up their road blocks, controlling three major roads, one south and the others north and east. Two trucks were parked across the road and an armed party of men converged upon our vehicle as we were flagged down. We pulled into the side of the road. I suddenly thought that it maybe wasn't a good idea for a man from Nikwei's village to be with us at this time but it was too late to worry about that now.

As the vehicles are all left hand drive, I came eyeball to eyeball with the tribal leader as he stood at my open window talking across me to the driver. Everyone in the back remained silent. I tried to make eye contact with this man who had a surly, pock-marked face of a yellow hue; he looked like there was a fair bit of oriental blood in him. All the men of the other tribe surrounded our vehicle. They all looked very different to the people of the Maruki tribe and those of the surrounding areas, since the tribes of the areas that I was used to all had very refined faces. These bandits, however, looked like pirates. Their facial features were markedly different and it was obvious that they were a breed apart, a tribe or even a race apart. All the men around our vehicle carried axes, machetes, spears, bows and arrows and some had clubs.

The bandit leader would not make eye contact with me and spoke animatedly to the driver who returned his conversation animatedly and said he had to get the white man, pointing his thumb at me, to the airport to catch his plane. I could understand enough words being spoken. After a very tense moment of silence and staring, the bandit leader waved us through the barrier and the armed men dispersed slowly as we sped away. The bandit leader laughed, pulling his thumb across his throat. I wondered why he did that.

As we pulled away, beads of sweat dribbled down the driver's face as he spoke to me in broken English. He said he was told to turn back but he had refused and said he had to get me to the airport. The bandit apparently said he wasn't really bothered whether we got through or not because there was another armed road block ahead at another junction and these men would be less willing to talk. The bandit leader said with a smile, 'Be prepared to fight and die.'

I sat silently in my seat. I felt sick. I had never known fear like this before. I thought of my brother and I as boys walking upon the green rolling hills and the purple mountains of home. I thought of the sweet yellow gorse rolling down to the blue sea, white quartz pebbles tumbling in the surf. I grew sad. I really believed that this would be the last day I would walk upon this earth and, if I were killed, would my body ever be found to be returned home to Manannan's Isle? I managed to control the fear rising in my belly. I could feel the vomit rising in my throat and I knew, as a chief, that I would have to fight with the men if it came to that. I would have to cut and slash and be cut and slashed, for I knew that the men in the back of the truck would defend me with their lives and I now had to prepare for my death, to fight and die with them. As we drove I pondered silently on our fate. I had had similar experiences in the past and, for some reason, a few came flashing to mind with vivid clarity. Was this some sort of subconscious survival ploy that enabled me to recall cellular memory of similar incidents, thereby providing the necessary chemicals and energy to be directed for the appropriate response? Maybe it was a mind diversion to prevent panic.

As soon as I had managed within my heart and soul to accept that this day I was going to die in battle and had become grounded, centred and at peace with this, I sighed a deep sigh and looked down at the handle of the machete under my seat.

Suddenly the driver pulled in to the side of the road. He got out and spoke to the men in the back. They spoke for a few minutes and the driver got back in and we continued upon our way. He looked very worried and I guessed what the conversation was about. As we proceeded, we spoke to the other truck drivers we passed who had got through the barrier, most of whom had told us to turn back. They said that the road block was ahead and there were men there that were prepared to kill. The driver spoke to me and said he had asked the men in the back what we should do. Should we go on and fight and die or should we return to Itabu? All the men in the back said, 'No, we have to get Iarueri to the airport. We will fight.'

So the men in the back of the truck were prepared to fight and die for me, just to get me to the airport, to get me to safety. I have never known such an amazing gesture of solidarity and bravery. There was no way that I could have abandoned them if the truck was attacked. I withdrew the machete from beneath my seat. The driver looked at me. He smiled and nodded.

The driver explained to me that around the next bend would be the road block. I wiped the sweat from my brow and ran my sweaty palm down my trousers to enable me to get a better grip on the machete handle. He banged on the window behind the cab to alert the men. I saw them withdrawing their weapons from beneath the seats and bags. I felt sick; I felt frightened; I wanted to cry but I would not. I refused to let my emotions or my weakness control me. I was going to make sure I would go into battle with the men who were with me as a warrior and, if I was going to die on this day, then I asked and prayed to Majikjiki to take my spirit to wherever it was meant to be, as well as those who may die with me. I was ready.

I couldn't see because of the stinging sweat in my eyes and then we rounded the bend. Suddenly we realised that the road was clear. There had obviously been a recent camp there, the remains of a fire smouldering. The driver looked at me and raised his eyebrows. He changed down a gear and put his foot to the floor. We drove off as quickly as we could. Everybody looked back. There was no-one there! The driver started to laugh in a very nervous way and I think, had I not been in company, I would probably have needed a change of underwear.

We eventually got to Lenakel and then, on to the airport. We sat down on the grass outside to await the arrival of my plane. We were told that everything was delayed because air traffic control was prioritising all military aircraft to come in to quell the fighting. We found out from a man that the road block had been cleared since the bandits were called away to fight elsewhere minutes before we had passed through.

As we waited for the military flights to come in and for the soldiers to disembark and collect their weapons, equipment and bags, Moses spoke to me, 'Iarueri, the truck driver is a very brave man. He was told by the men at the road block to turn back, but refused because he said he had to get you to the airport. The men only let us go through because they said that, at the next road block, they would certainly kill us all, so they really didn't care what we did. The driver stopped when he got over the mountain range and asked us the question, "Do you want to go back or do you want to go on and fight?" We said, "We go on and we fight, for we have to take Iarueri to the airport." The problem now is that, when we return, we may all be killed because we defied the men at the road block. The truck driver has risked his life for you, Iarueri.'

I stared at the grass, suddenly realising that the men who brought me this far now have to run the gauntlet again. I felt sick for them. All I wanted to do was take off in the plane and get back to Port Vila. We sat in silence in the hot sun. I thought of the enormity of what Moses had explained and realised that, as a chief of the tribe, I would have been expected to lead the men in battle with hand to hand fighting, hacking each other to bits. I shuddered and prayed that the plane would come and leave on time.

Ironically, I recognised a man walking towards me. It was Kelson – the last person I wanted to see. He came over and shook my hand and said that, when he had the money, he would pay the Chief. I knew he was lying so I just ignored him as best I could.

After the military plane had disembarked the soldiers, our plane arrived but was delayed because a woman was being loaded on a stretcher with an intravenous drip, accompanied by a doctor and relative. The seats had to be adjusted to get her in on a stretcher so she was then able to lie across the back seats of the plane. Moses said that the woman was a victim of the fighting and was going to the hospital in Vila. Two more small military planes landed, full of soldiers again and white officers to sort out the tribal fighting.

The final goodbyes were briefer than predicted, since we had to load quickly when the call came, as the weather was turning. Moses and I embraced. The plane was full. Another plane had landed while we were waiting, still carrying tourists, which surprised me. They would obviously be going somewhere well away from the tribal fighting. It was a very turbulent flight back to Port Vila.

After landing and retrieving my bags, I couldn't find the taxi that Moses said would be waiting for me. Eventually I approached a young lad who turned out to be a cousin of Moses, who had been waiting for me all the time but never said as much. I got to my hotel, cashed some traveller's cheques and phoned home to let everyone know I was all right.

After having a meal, I went to the travel firm who were agents for Jungle Oasis Lodge to make a complaint about Kelson and, as I looked through the window, I saw Kahi, David Hosea, sitting inside reading a newspaper. He was obviously waiting for me, tipped off by Kelson. Moses had given me his father's contact number and I rang him. He was called Mr Chack. He and his brother, Ben, came to my hotel to see me. I invited them into my room and we spoke at length about the situation of Kelson and Kahi, stealing and lying to the tourists and the kastom people. Ben told me that David Hosea had stolen a lot of money from people and even tried to steal money from Iaqurimano Primary School. Moses's father then said that Ben jabbed a pen into the forehead of Hosea and said, 'If you steal the school's money, you are a dead man.' Ben added that he would have killed him!

Both Kelson and David Hosea are hated, but Jerry is different. Both men said he was a good kastom man. Ben said he would call a meeting of the tribal chiefs in Vila because the Hoseas were also hated there and they would discuss the situation about them. It appears also that another white man had had money stolen by Kelson, so they had good reason to act. There would be trouble now. I gave them Chief Wai Wai's letter and they assured me they would hand it personally to the Minister of Tourism.

After the Chacks had left, I lay on the bed. I had been functioning on adrenalin and nervous energy. I now felt exhausted – emotionally, mentally and physically drained. I worried about my friends going back to Itabu. Luckily there was a nice deep bath in the hotel with plenty of hot water and I had a long hot soak until I fell asleep. I couldn't get the picture out of my head of the men returning back home safely and I prayed they would be protected. There was a news blackout on the fighting.

15th April 2004
Confiscation by Australian Customs

I was up at 4:50 am and left the hotel at 5 o'clock for an early flight back to Brisbane. After boarding the aircraft, I sat by the window next to a middle-aged couple. I felt sick because of the overpowering smell of aftershave and perfume; their petty conversation of the contents of their glossy magazines irritated me.

I was relieved and glad to be back on Australian soil. I declared all the gifts and items to quarantine officials who unfortunately confiscated the boar's tusk necklaces because they were seed beads. I was permitted to keep my boar tusks. Other items, including the binding rope, were fumigated. As the officials scrutinised these items, they knocked them on their benches and several small cockroaches and ants fell out; I could understand why they are so paranoid about keeping pests and diseases out of the country.

16th April 2004
Flashbacks of attacks in Africa

I changed more traveller's cheques. I felt very ill with lots of stomach cramps. In fact, whilst I was in the city, I had to return to my hotel because I was near to vomiting and collapse. I didn't know why I was feeling that way. I later collected my photographs from the processing laboratory and decided to leave the city for a few days and go by train to Beenleigh to get away from the noise, pollution and hassle. I just needed to be quiet, to meditate, I still felt very emotional and confused. I worried about my companions.

I was in Beenleigh for a few days but after every meal I felt sick and

1. High Chief Wai Wai Rawi.

2. Nikwei and Kwaramu preparing the Chief and God belts.

3. Chief Iarueri receiving the first tattoo by Isul.

4. Dancing in the nakamal after ceremony.

5. High Woman Mitac preparing to dance.

6. Mt Yasur volcano.

7. Maggie and Nahu receiving their tribal names from the High Chief.

8. High Woman Natu Elin and High Chief Iarueri after their marriage.

9. Natu and Nahu preparing lap lap for the earth oven.

10. Coast at Lenakel.

wanted to vomit. I felt exhausted through lack of sleep. I had feelings of being unable to cope with Western life style again and simply felt like screaming. I just wanted to be alone to communicate with Spirit, to connect with nature. I spent most of my time in this part of the state walking in the parks, walking in the bush, simply trying to come to terms with experiences I had had and the adjustments that would now take place.

The fear of the prospect of my imminent death had a deep and profound effect upon me. I no longer took things for granted anymore. The flashbacks of the other incidents in my life that I had experienced at the time of the tribal warfare haunted me day and night; I didn't know why. I needed the silence to enable me to face them again, to scream them clear I suppose. I began recalling them one by one, moving my awareness into each situation to relive them. I knew the physical experiences were unimportant. What was important was how I felt or related to the stimulus.

I spent the next few days isolated, nursing each experience like a vulnerable baby, until I had processed them all clear. The pursuit and attack by armed tribesmen in the jungle of Zaire; the military coup in Ouagadougou, Upper Volta where, under threat of execution, I had to dodge flying bullets to get evacuated by the American Embassy; armed arrest and interrogation as a spy, Ivory Coast; threat of execution by tribesmen by catapult, Ivory Coast; spreadeagled against the side of our vehicle by armed paratroops, Algeria; attacked by large mob who tried to overturn our vehicle and smash the windows, Algeria; trapped in a bush fire, Australia; fist fight to escape being thrown over a cliff at an isolated orphanage, Algeria; riots and attack of hostel, barricaded myself into my room, Papua, New Guinea; attempted decapitation in Sahara, Algeria; threatened by armed camel smugglers, Algeria ………. but the most frightening of all was sitting as a passenger when my elderly mother drove her car!

Interestingly and unexpectedly, this grieving process also highlighted the emotional trauma I received as a child at primary school by a teacher who was a sadistic bully. This man taught spelling and maths. Because of his emotional and physical abuse, I am unable to spell and do basic sums. At the time of the indoctrination, I withdrew deeper within myself, my salvation being my dog, "Mickey", who taught me to be still and listen to nature. We sought out the remote, secluded places where I felt safe and where, together, we sat in silence for hours at a time.

I thought about what the Chief said before, that I had to experience three deaths. I understood this to mean that, after every initiation, there would come a time to face a different death. I had just experienced my second death, realising that, once I was prepared and committed to face the situation, I had no need to experience the physical aspect. Had I allowed fear to take control, I believe that we would all be dead now.

22nd April 2004

I eventually arrived home on the Isle of Man. I felt exhausted. The first thing I did was take out the Chief's coconut rope and tie it to the apple tree outside the farmhouse where I lived to remind me of our binding ritual. I felt closer to him.

17th June 2004
Despair

Feelings of loneliness and despair filled my senses daily, heightened after the initiations and ceremonies in the tribal lands. I hadn't received or had any spiritual communications or visions which left me feeling bereft. I called constantly to the Goddess, Lord Manannan and Lord Majikjiki to help me make contact with Spirit. All I could hope and pray for was the strength to endure the dark night of the soul upon its journey into the light to a higher level of consciousness and awakening. I felt I was moving through a period of energetic transition within and perhaps Spirit had removed conscious communications for a while enabling me to go through this change.

My heart grew heavy each day when I could no longer communicate with the ancestors, guardians and enlightened ones. I prayed that the inner pain of confusion, irritability and despair would ease when the period of perceived abandonment passed and Spirit reconnected with me again.

My heart was torn in two also because I didn't know what to do to help High Chief Wai Wai against the betrayal of Kelson Hosea. One part of me hoped that he would be seriously and suitably punished, yet another part of me hoped that both men could be amicably reconciled in peace. I didn't know what to do in case I made the situation worse by interfering in some way; yet, if I did nothing, Kelson would continue to steal and cheat and the Chief would have no-one to stand with him to fight side by side.

My feelings and the dislike for the Western life style continued and the narrowmindedness and triviality of other people seemed to be magnified somehow. Yet my empathy with the Earth Mother and Mother Nature were as deep and emotional as ever.

23rd June 2004

I received a letter from High Chief Wai Wai saying that no help had been received in any way and that Kelson Hosea was preventing the tourists from coming to see the kastom dancing. The Chief went on to say that he had performed a chicken and kava ceremony to Tamaffa to send the God Majikjiki to help me. I was to write back to him with any questions, dreams or experiences I had. The following day I had a clear vision of Majikjiki and myself inside the volcano. It was very powerful. I gave thanks for this reconnection. All of the men were safe.

31st August 2005
Time for courage

I received another letter from High Chief Wai Wai. He wrote in very simple English that he wanted me to return for sacred ceremony around the time of September or October. I had mixed feelings when I read this, as a part of me recognised the unique opportunity of completing the third part of these ancient ceremonies as a chief. Yet another part of me was concerned about the many financial and travelling problems, plus the lack of encouragement from my friends, who believed I was being used by the tribe for a quick rip-off. One thing I believed was that this was my last and only chance of experiencing such a privilege that no other Westerner had gone through. Now was the time for courage, to live that way and to be that person. Now was the time for me to be the chief. This I recognised was another one of my tests.

8th October 2005
Financial help

I planned to depart for Vanuatu, possibly for the last time, so had rather mixed feelings emotionally. There would be many dangers to face and at times I had wondered if I were doing the right thing or not, as the financial outlay was ridiculous. Fortunately, I received generous help financially from a wise old friend, Steve Ellis, but even so it was a very long way to go. Another test! The opportunity may never arise again, so I had to go to experience these ceremonies. (Steve passed into the Ancestral Realms in October, 2009.)

A week tomorrow I would leave, so I hoped that High Chief Wai Wai had received my letter, which was posted several weeks ago to confirm my visit, and had not gone on walkabout.

13th October 2005
Attitude of Manx Government

I was out for the day and, when I came back, I found three letters pushed through my letterbox from Captain Andrew Douglas MHK. Andrew had been trying to get help for the two local schools on Tanna Island from the Manx Government without much success. In the letter addressed to me, he enclosed a personal cheque from himself and his wife for £200 for the tribe. Two other letters, each containing financial assistance to Mr Willie Lingkai of Iaqurimano school and Mr Lakin Laham of Port Resolution school. As both envelopes were sealed, I had no idea what sort of financial help Andrew had offered to both of these Head Teachers, but I was struck by his absolute generosity in doing this to help the tribal people. I felt saddened by the attitude of the Manx Government.

I saw my mother the night before I left and she gave me £200 for the tribe. I had been so very fortunate in so many ways of people helping me on this quest, and this again was proof that I was meant to be doing this work, otherwise this help would not have been offered. Everything was flowing as it was meant to be; all I had to do now was trust in Spirit and know everything would be fine.

PART 3

YERAMANU

18th October 2005

Emergency landing, Calcutta

Eventually, after delays in London, I boarded the QANTAS Jumbo Jet en route to Brisbane. As we were flying over India, the Captain spoke over the PA system that a fire warning light had come on in the cockpit, so he would have to make a full emergency landing, diverting us to the nearest airport, which was Calcutta. As we made our approach, the runway was lined with fire engines, ambulances, police and military vehicles. This reminded me of an Air France emergency landing at Algiers when we were informed that a bomb was on board the aircraft. Another Air France aircraft had been blown out of the sky over Chad. We landed safely but, as QANTAS has no jurisdiction in Calcutta, we were not allowed off the aircraft, so we had to sit for four hours in stifling heat until a temporary fix could take place by a British Airways engineer.

Eventually we arrived in Singapore, about five hours late, which meant all onward connecting flights had been missed by everybody.

19th October 2005

I arrived in Brisbane eight hours late. I booked into the hotel and went straight away to the Air Vanuatu office to pay for my air fare. I did some preparatory shopping ready for the journey out to Vanuatu. I felt exhausted.

23rd October 2005

I arrived in Port Vila, Vanuatu. It was very hot and humid but at least there was no rain. The contact number which the Chief had given me was for Philip, one of his cousins. I rang him and asked him to get a message to Chief Wai Wai to have a truck waiting for me tomorrow on my arrival on Tanna Island.

24th October 2005

Arrested as a spy   End of mourning

I went shopping, buying a long-handled axe for Nikwei, penknives, lighters, cigarette papers and tobacco for the men, and a large cigar for the Chief which I knew would give him status before the men as smoking is an important social ritual. The man with tobacco earns grade points. Remembering the mistake I had made in Africa, I chose an unwrapped cigar this time.

Previously, on a trip to the Ivory Coast I had arrived by bus at Nambonkaha village to stay with the Senoufo tribe. The Chief called everyone together before a huge fire in the village square to welcome me. I presented the Chief with a penknife, lighter and a packet of cigars which were individually wrapped in cellophane. The Chief took one from the packet and clearly had never seen cellophane before so couldn't work out how to remove it. He began to look frustrated and I knew he was losing face before the assembled crowd. I asked him if I could try. He handed the cigar back to me, a look of desperation in his eyes. I dramatically scratched my head, pulled my beard, pushed it, pulled it, then secretly pulled the cellophane tab, handing it back to the Chief. I held up my hands in surrender to the crowd. Everybody groaned. All eyes fixed on their Chief. He, of course, realising what I had done, removed the cellophane wrapper with a flourish to wild cheers and applause. I bowed to him. He smiled at me and invited me to stay in his mud brick house. The lesson I learnt from this experience was: never let a Chief lose face. The following day, I was arrested by police at gunpoint as a spy and interrogated for two hours!

Air Vanuatu had now taken over from Van Air, so the plane was bigger and cleaner and they flew on schedule. I arrived on Tanna Island, where Chief Wai Wai and some of the men were waiting for me. We were both absolutely delighted to see each other, holding each other tightly. The Chief cried and couldn't stop gripping my arm and looking into my eyes. We all piled into the truck and went to Lenakel where we stopped at the market to get some provisions, where unfortunately, I saw Kelson. He came over to the truck and shook my hand, saying, 'Welcome home!'

The other men knew about our situation and laughed. They said afterwards that, when he heard I was returning, he was not pleased. We stopped at various other country market stalls en route to Itabu village. I was put in the front seat with the driver, the rest of the men travelled in the back of the truck. It was hot and dry in comparison to the last two visits. The volcano was very noisy and active and lots of different sub-tropical flowers were blooming that I hadn't seen on previous visits. In the north of Tanna Island, kava does not grow because of the hot dry conditions, so it has to be bought at the market or from the stalls in the south of the island, where the growing conditions are more moist. Chief Wai Wai bought kava locally for the nakamal tonight to greet Tamaffa and the ancestors and to give thanks for the safe return of Chief Iarueri.

Itabu village had been changed. On my arrival, all the children gathered round me, patting and holding me. It was wonderful to have this reunion. My last hut was now being used by the Chief's family and was getting to the end of its natural life. Everything rots here quickly. A new smaller hut had been built for me and a new kitchen, as the old one was about to collapse due to the effects of Cyclone Ivy last year. Regarding the ablutions, a Western style toilet had now been installed and a shower, although there were no water facilities yet to be able to use them, so another squat toilet had to be used. A new water tank and rolls of water pipe were lying in the village, donated by World Vision, which has cost about one million Vatu. Part of this agreement was that those who were educated had to teach the women and younger children to read and write at the basic level.

I unpacked my bags in my hut and we had lunch – an omelette and rice with tomatoes. It was very nice. I had a rest and later Chief Wai Wai tapped on the door frame to tell me it was time to go to the nakamal. I was given the kava roots to carry and the Chief carried the water container. A few men had gathered to greet me, including Donald. I was instructed to take my seat beneath the banyan tree as chief, next to the sacred fire. Kava was prepared and my cup was reverently handed to me by Donald, who bowed gracefully. High Chief Wai Wai and myself drank simultaneously. We sprayed out the dregs of the kava on the ground, with a shout calling upon Tamaffa to give thanks for my safe return home. The men fell silent and called upon their ancestors before praying.

I ate some manioc and some fresh bread bought in the market today. A small pig was sacrificed to honour my return and was butchered near where I was sitting. I was then instructed to return to my hut with Michael to have my dinner. Fortunately, there were no mosquitoes in the dry season. My meal was rice and some sort of red meat, with a mixture of vegetables. It was very difficult to see, as the light from the oil lamp was not very good.

Before I left the nakamal, Chief Wai Wai said he would pray to Tamaffa and to Majikjiki that he may answer all my questions correctly. He also spoke about my receiving my tribal mark as Yeramanu and the possibility of both of us having our ears pierced for the traditional grade stick. He would call upon the ancestors that night to find out when the ceremony should take place. Now that the High Chief had ended his period of official mourning for his father's death (the former High Chief), he could now receive the mark of the Yeramanu and the High Chief. Indeed, this was why he invited me to join him so that we could both receive the mark at the same time.

25th October 2005
Installation of new water tank

I had a poor night due to the nausea and headache from the kava. As the kitchen and "restaurant" areas were damaged from previous storms, my meals were brought to my hut. Nakhu (Michael) appeared to be assigned as my guide and interpreter on this visit; he was 14 years old and a nephew of the Chief. There was something about him that I felt I could not trust, but I didn't know why this was.

Now that the new community water tank and pipes had arrived, every available person was preparing for its installation. This, I was informed, was an historic day for the community, to have fresh, clean running water for the first time in history. Everyone was so excited. People had been cutting roads through the bush to enable the men to manually carry the tank up to the ridge overlooking the valley. The men had made a coconut fibre rope net and, with bamboo poles threaded through the netting, had lifted the tank upon their shoulders. The tank holds 6,000 litres. The men stumbled but carried the bulky tank from Itabu, down the road, turning up a newly cleared pathway after about quarter of a mile. The ascent was tricky, as men were stumbling over roots and caught the tank occasionally on overhanging branches, which caused problems. I helped by putting my shoulder to the back, lifting and pushing with the rest of them. After a while, the Chief tapped me on my shoulder and asked me not to help as he was worried in case I fell and hurt myself. I smiled and laughed. He then fell and hurt his leg, causing him to limp for several days.

The men shouted, strained and pulled, some pulling in different directions. It was really quite hilarious and they were followed by the laughing women, barking dogs and shouting children. It was certainly a major occurrence for the community and everybody helped in so many ways. Eventually they reached the summit of the ridge and the tank was placed down on a flat surface, previously prepared. A local engineer from World Vision had decided where the site for the foundation of the tank was to be situated and he was overseeing the project.

As we returned back down through the bush, Absalom, a short stocky man, showed me strange holes cut into the base of palm trees, which had been trained horizontally initially, then allowed to straighten up. He explained that these were the traditional water holes that the community used to catch rain water in and that they were all over the bush. I had wondered what they were when I saw them previously. The problem was that there were health risks involved, such as breeding mosquitoes and decaying matter, causing stagnation. Wounds were washed in these holes also, which might explain why so many minor wounds became infected.

We diverted from our trek home for me to see where the source of the water was coming from to fill the tank. The men had cleared land where a small stream had been flowing out of the ground on a steep side of the ridge. A cement and timber box had been constructed rather like a miniature dam, but this was leaking in several places. A tap at the top was to connect to the water pipe leading to the tank and a tap at the base was to drain the sump. I felt the next heavy rains would fill the little dam with silt, as they had removed all surrounding plants and there were now no roots to hold the earth in place.

The men brought over a bag of cement and black grit that had been covered by a plastic sheet nearby and mixed the sand and cement with their bare hands. The World Vision engineer arrived, a man called Tom. He was from one of the northern islands and brought his toolkit with him and wore oversized boots, a status symbol in these parts. He made up a cement wash in a small plastic bag and, by using the beaten stem of a certain plant that had frayed out, he applied the cement to the small wall with his "brush".

We left the workers hard at it and returned to Itabu. We had lunch, which was rice, red meat of some sort and mixed vegetables. After lunch the Chief explained about the water and the water pipes. He was hoping to get everything connected up within two weeks and later that year for the water system to work in all of the surrounding communities. Running the pipes out through the bush to all the small villages was a huge undertaking, leaving standpipes at small settlements.

I had a rest after lunch, then the Chief called for me to see Willie, the Head Teacher at Iaqurimano Primary School to present to him the two letters from Andrew Douglas, one on behalf of the Manx government and the other one personal. I didn't go to the nakamal that night.

26th October 2005
Fire walking   Prepare for tattoo ceremony
After breakfast, the Chief, Michael and a couple of other youths walked with me to the outskirts of Port Resolution to watch a native firewalker. On arrival, a garland of flowers was placed around my neck; they were yellow French marigolds. Other Westerners were expected from yachts moored in the bay. The three lots of yachties turned up to see weaving, archery demonstrations and what was described as the magic leaves. These pumpkin sized leaves were laid on the earth, overlapping each other. A small boy then lay upon them and two men lifted him off the ground without the leaves separating. This was a traditional method of carrying injured people as a makeshift stretcher. The leaves just fell apart afterwards.

Before this demonstration took place, a bed of volcanic stones had been prepared with heaps of burning wood laid on top of them, so that the red hot embers would fall between the stones. The stones soon got very hot; we could see the heat haze rising from them. After the wood had burnt, the burning residues were swept away, just leaving the glowing embers and hot stones. At this point, the kastom firewalker went off into the bush to pray to the ancestors and to get himself into the correct frame of mind. He came to the stones then, raising his hands into the air, wiped his feet on the bare earth and slowly walked across the hot stones. This he repeated twice more. Water was then poured from a hollow bamboo container on to the stones, which created impressive amounts of steam.

On our return to Itabu, we stopped off at another village to buy some paraffin for the oil lamps. On the way back, the Chief explained to me about the tattoo ceremony and that we would do it later that day. The chief explained that Absalom is one of the tribal hereditary tattooists for the Maruki tribe and his firstborn son would take this position at his death. The ear piercing would also take place at the same time! As far as I could make out, Absalom was Michael's father. The men stressed to me with some relish that the tattoo was very painful and very bloody!

I had lunch on our return to Itabu. The Chief said I had to prepare myself for this ordeal, probably the most difficult test of all, that of enduring pain. From the moment I receive my tribal mark, the mark of the Yeramanu, I would no longer be a Chief, but a High Chief. The Chief added that the tattoo would be done on the right upper arm. This is the most powerful arm, the one that is most used and the most seen and the reason why the tattoo is on the right upper arm is that, when you are facing your enemy in tribal warfare, he can see your mark of power, your status.

4:00 pm – nakamal time. The plan had changed! Absalom was still working on the water pipes so it was now too late to do the tattoo ceremony, since it would take one and a half hours in total. Chief Wai Wai said the ceremony would take place the next morning. The Chief had gathered the appropriate sacred leaves for the coronets and necklaces and the aromatic plants of the Majikjiki shrub.

The Chief and Michael spent some time with me to explain about the sacred mark and the process. 'The mark that we shall receive is universal throughout Tanna Island. Other islands have different marks, representing their particular customs and culture. The further north you go,' the Chief explained, 'the more similar the traditions are to Papua, New Guinea and the Solomon Islands.'

The Chief brought a piece of paper with him upon which he had drawn the two marks that would be given tomorrow. The tattoo represents the Yeramanu belt, or office, or, as the Chief kept calling it, the "strap". Each mark represents initiations of the High Chief's life from circumcision, taking part in a sacred tokka dance, kava, spiritual attainment, understanding kastom, tribal myth and legend, grade-taking ceremonies, marriage and various other ceremonies, even tribal warfare and head hunting. On a higher representation, the markings represent the symbology of Majikjiki, the Serpent God. Only black and white colours are permitted for the tattoo and belt, no other. Majikjiki is sometimes spelled Mashishiki and is the God of creation and nature and is often represented with long hair and a beard. The traditional hair style is long hair which is braided. Chief Wai Wai said that his father and grandfather had their hair down to their waists. (I have seen early photographs of chiefs with this length of hair in the museum in Vila.) Majikjiki is also depicted upon the national currency, holding a spear as the warrior God. He is venerated as the God throughout Vanuatu and all islands.

As a newly established Yeramanu and High Chief, my tattoo was to run vertically up on the right arm. The outer edges were large black triangles, which gave the impression of paler or whiter diamonds on the inside. Within the centre of these diamonds were black spots. The Chief explained that this was the mark of a newly created High Chief and Yeramanu, whereas, because he was an established, hereditary Yeramanu and High Chief, his tattoo markings were different, in that they were small triangles on the outside, as opposed to large.

The Chief went on to explain very clearly and said, 'Your twin brother is not permitted to wear this mark. Your nephew, Aaron, is authorised to wear it as your next bloodline relative upon your death, but, upon your death, he must wear the mark of the established High Chief, not the newly created one. Both the tattoos or marks are the same grade and convey the same meaning – the God mark. Both are hereditary.'

I was told again that the process would be bloody and painful. They kept telling me this. Whether they were saying this to try to wind me up, I didn't know. I expect they had a laugh at my expense and good luck to them! So only the tattoo would be done the next day, not the ear piercing. Only the Yeramanu could authorise the collection of the special sacred leaves and herbs for this ceremony.

Since it was now time for High Chief Wai Wai to receive his grade mark, he had invited me to return to Itabu to participate in this ceremony and to receive the same privilege, never before given to an outsider let alone a white man. I was reminded that this was a sacred gift that nobody else had experienced.

The Chief instructed me not to go to the nakamal that night but to rest and pray to Majikjiki. The High Chief was to prepare himself tonight spiritually by calling to the ancestors and to Tamaffa to aid our ceremony. I was glad because it gave me the time I needed to prepare myself physically, emotionally, mentally and spiritually. It had been very cold that day because there were lots of clouds; I hoped it would be warm and sunny the next day. I had my dinner, more rice and tuna.

27th October 2005
Receiving High Chief tattoo   Opening skulls

Every morning at 4 o'clock a rooster sat outside my hut crowing which set off all the other roosters in the neighbourhood. At 5:30 each morning the tam tam drums were beaten, which echoed through the ranges, valleys and the gorges, and, when I listened carefully, I could hear a response from other tam tam drums and the men shouting and calling to each other with a peculiar type of yodel. These morning calls were hauntingly beautiful. There was heavy rain this morning.

At 7:15 am Chief Wai Wai came to my hut to inform me he was going to summon the men for the ceremony with a particular type of beat on the tam tam drum. He said this ceremony was to be secret so there would be no observers. The kava had been paid for the night before the ceremony and a pig would be obtained that morning for the sacred sacrifice. I asked the Chief how much was the cost of the kava and the pig and he reluctantly said 5,000 Vatu. As a proud man, he wasn't going to ask for any financial help but I explained to him that, as we were participating in this ceremony together, I would like to share the cost as his brother. He accepted this explanation so it didn't make him feel inadequate or lose face that he could not provide.

In a strange way that I cannot explain I felt like I was the condemned man having his last meal at the breakfast table – a combination of apprehension and excitement at such a rare honour and privilege that I have been fortunate to experience. The Chief said by the time the preparation was in place, that involved collecting the pig, preparing the nakamal and organising the participating men, it would be about 10 o'clock before the ceremony could start. The tribal people are great orators, actors and performers who love a celebration, feast or ceremony.

At 8:30 in the morning I heard more tam tam drums beating in the local area calling the men to ceremony. I had seen and heard a squealing pig being carried, slung from a pole over the shoulders of the Chief's two daughters. Both were shy girls and, when they saw I had spotted them, they rushed off giggling. I hoped and prayed that I didn't have to kill the pig and I could pass the right and privilege to another man. The rain started again.

10:15 – it was time! The High Chief sounded the tam tam then came into my hut to prepare me for the ceremony. I stripped naked, my nambas was tied into position and a woven armband which held the Majikjiki leaves was placed around my arm, around my head was placed a circlet of knotted green shoots and the same around my neck. Around each ankle was tied a string of cut seed pods, which had the effect of rattling when I walked and danced. The Chief wore exactly the same.

We both walked to the nakamal nearest the village and the men trooped out of the hole in the centre of the banyan tree. We all danced, clapped and sang to begin the ceremony. This was a really special moment for me, for my first secret ceremony was held in this very same place and the public ceremonies were held at the other nakamal. The pig and kava were brought and laid in the centre of the nakamal. Only the participants in the ceremony were present. It was a quiet affair, one of the reasons being that everybody else was busy working on the installation of the water pipes, yet everybody knew what was taking place. I was glad that there were no onlookers for I felt very self-conscious being the only white man amongst the Ni-Vans.

I was instructed by the Chief to take the club and to symbolically place it upon the forehead of the pig to make the sacred contact and to honour the spirit of the pig. I then handed the club to Donald who swiftly dispatched the pig with one sharp blow, splitting the skull, allowing the blood to flow upon and into the black volcanic earth. I was reminded that it was essential that the blood flowed into the earth. I never found out why. The High Chief gave a speech in his native tongue but, by his mannerisms and body language, I knew he was introducing me to the ancestors and asking for a blessing from Majikjiki. I had to respond with a speech in which I thanked the High Chief and the people of the tribe for accepting me and allowing me to become a part of their family and to do this sacred ceremony. They all clapped.

Absalom could not participate in the ceremony for some reason. I think he had to oversee the laying of the water pipes as the Chief's brother. Note: The tribal term of brother does not necessarily indicate a blood relative, but a trusted friend. I found this very confusing initially. However, another hereditary tattooist from a different tribe had been summoned to Itabu so he was called upon to perform the ceremony. I was the first victim! I sat on a plank of wood beneath the banyan tree (the symbol of the chief) and Sam, the tattooist, produced his arsenal of tools of the trade – three blunt sewing needles tied together with red thread and a small pouch of charcoal and lamp soot. He also produced two leaves, one a large, heart-shaped leaf, which the Chief told me was a particular type of pumpkin leaf, and the other a purple leaf and stem, which looked to me like a purple coleus of some sort. I asked the Chief what Sam's tribal name was and he said it was Isul.

Sam then produced a sea shell and put the soot and charcoal into this, adding a little water to make a sloppy paste. He then began drawing a rough outline of the tattoo on my arm with a pen. Then, with the needles, he punctured my skin rhythmically until the blood started to ooze out; it was indeed painful as the men had predicted!. He then applied the soot mixture on to the wound, rubbing it in gently, followed by more puncturing with the needles, adding more charcoal to the blend. As Sam worked, the Chief said that traditionally they used orange spines but occasionally the point would break off into the wound and cause infection. Needles are now used. After more soot and charcoal paste was applied, the two leaves were rolled together into a ball about the same size of a golf ball and the juice squeezed over the wound. Job done! This process took about half an hour.

It was then the High Chief's turn to receive his mark. Wai Wai sat on the seat and looked at me with a wry smile and said, 'Maybe I cry now!' We laughed.

The process was repeated to the Chief who was clearly in pain, grimacing often. There appeared to be more blood seepage from his arm than mine. I got the impression that, as the tattooist had never performed his art upon a white man before, he was holding back a little and not stabbing me quite so deeply as normal.

The weather was kind to us, sunny and warm, for the ceremony. At the conclusion of the ceremony, High Chief Wai Wai turned to me and said, 'You will carry this mark until the day you die.'

Sam told me not to wash for two days to allow the soot and charcoal mixture to be absorbed into the skin and not to wear a shirt, as it could rub off the scab and interfere with the healing. I remembered Sam saying that in some countries they use electricity to perform a tattoo. This process had no connection with God or the ancestors and was not sacred, he stressed.

After a final dance to honour Spirit, we passed through the banyan tree to the fire beyond and changed into our Western clothing. The Chief had someone collect my trousers from my hut. As Sam had provided a ceremony for me, it was customary for me to present him a gift, so I gave to him a good quality penknife, which he was delighted with. Right on cue, Yasur roared into action the moment we finished.

I returned to my hut where I had rice and tuna again. Later in the afternoon we would return to the nakamal to take kava and to butcher the pig to celebrate this very important day. Hopefully more men could join with us for the celebration after working on the water pipes. By 12:30 my arm was beginning to throb and ache. I took some homoeopathic medicine and wondered if I had any remedy for gangrene!

I had a rest. Afterwards I found the ground was far too hot to walk on in bare feet. I could not keep the flies away from my tattoo wound, and the insect bites were driving me mad. At 3:00 pm I went into meditation and linked with Spirit at the nakamal.

At around 4:00 pm the Chief called for me and we returned to the nakamal where I put on nambas and the other sacred ornamentation. We led a procession of men serpent-like through the banyan tree, filing through the opening, forming a spiral, then circle to sing, dance, clap and stamp our feet to honour Spirit, returning back through the tree after our performance. The pig was butchered and the meat skewered upon sticks over the fire. The sticks were turned occasionally to stop the meat burning. We drank more kava followed by a piece of manioc. One of the men stood and gave the traditional yodel across the valley signifying that a special ceremony had been performed at Itabu village. It was very beautiful and I found the pitch of his call in the twilight very moving and sacred. A similar call was heard from another village nearby in reply.

We sat around the fire listening to the sound of the volcano and the flying foxes calling to each other far above the tree canopy overhead. A dog barked as the smoke from the fire filled our nostrils and stung our eyes. The Chief completely astounded me. Tapping his head, he said, 'Tell the men what you did to heads.'

I looked at him in amazement, for I knew exactly what the Chief meant but I knew that I had never told him I had trained as a post-mortem assistant and mortuary attendant at a hospital in Australia and I specialised in opening the skull for brain removal. The Chief looked at me and nodded, instructing me to begin. The men gathered around me as though I was a school teacher telling them a fairy story. All remained silent except for the occasional stick poking the crackling fire, sparks flying through our hair, catching our beards and nambas. I explained the process with simple words, using sound effects and actions of what I used to do. The men were fascinated and it had clearly touched a subconscious memory in them of ancestral cannibalistic practices. After I had finished telling the men this story, the Chief just looked at me in his usual way, raising an eyebrow, and exclaimed, 'Yeramanu!'

I returned to the hut for a special meal, brought to me with reverence to mark an important ceremony. I was now High Chief. It was a traditional dish of a chicken cooked with lap lap and island cabbage steamed in leaves, tied at the neck and decorated with orange bougainvillea flowers. The family had gone to a lot of trouble to prepare this meal for me to celebrate my ceremony.

28ᵗʰ October 2005

Chief's staff   Volcano Spirit angry

I was confined to my leaf hut today as I had to be shirtless because of the tattoo wound. I would have to be careful as I could get badly sunburnt. I couldn't sleep again, due to the effect of the kava and also because I was restricted in my sleeping pattern, having to sleep on my left side as best I could, as the tattoo wound was becoming very painful and was seeping. The confused rooster started to crow at 11:00 pm the night before and full bellows at 4 o'clock in the morning.

After breakfast the Chief asked me to do some healing for his family. Nikwei arrived from Sulphur Bay so there was a wonderful reunion and greeting and I gave him his long-handled axe, a pair of shorts and some tobacco. I was told that the kava we had last night was made extra strong due to the importance of the tattoo ceremony. The Chief and Sam asked me questions about the perennial problem of the church and the kastom way. The Chief was no longer limping after the healing and said that his leg felt much lighter.

I took more homoeopathic remedies for the tattoo wound and swollen insect bites. I felt they were from the bedding, since I had a mosquito net around me each night.

When speaking to the Chief, it appeared that there were to be no tests or trials this visit at all. These were successfully passed last year. The first year (2003) was a secret ceremony but in 2004 all ceremonies, tests and trials were very public.

Nikwei left returning in two hours with a new nambas and a carved grading staff for me. This staff is the representation of the chief's status and authority. It shows a tribal man at the top, with an entwined snake around the shaft. Nikwei also brought a freshly cooked chicken for me in a plastic bowl, covered in leaves and wrapped in a cloth.

Michael took the two letters from Andrew Douglas to Lakin Laham, the Head Teacher at Port Resolution school, as I could see no way of getting there myself at the time. I wanted to make sure the letters were handed personally to him.

I had lunch of rice and mixed vegetables with a strange, tough, white meat which was full of grit. I had no idea what it was.

Most men have been kept very busy in dragging and fitting water pipes and getting them joined and installed to the different communities and villages. The women were even more delighted with this system than the men, for it is they who have to carry the water containers for many miles from the jungle springs.

I went to the latrine, which was a roofless hut of woven pandanus palm leaves with a cloth hanging down in front of the opening. The wind had a habit of blowing open the cloth in mid squat. The latrine had a cement base with a hole in the centre over a deep pit. A huge cockroach the size of a mouse seemed to live in the pit and scuttled to and fro over the contents. It was a bit disconcerting knowing it could fly upwards at any time I decided to squat. I hoped it didn't come out at mealtimes!

Since I had been coming to Itabu and the area for the last three years, I had noticed a marked Western influence creeping in to change the daily routine or traditional ways. In one way it was sad, yet in another way it was nice to see them have some of their daily burden lifted or eased, especially for the women who work so hard. The ancient tribal customs were beginning to fade away, I feared, even at this place. I noticed at yesterday's tattoo ceremony that the nambas were held in place with synthetic belts not the natural fibre ones, as the year before. The tattooist would normally have had to wear nambas also and sacred leaves, yet he wore a shirt and shorts. He also used a ballpoint pen to outline the mark on the skin, whereas before it would have been in a traditional method of some sort. Small things perhaps, but significant nonetheless I felt, for each year tradition was being eroded away and forever lost. In a few years time, this way of life will be on display as a tourist's gimmick. I had been very fortunate in experiencing this way of life at the end of its traditional, cultural heritage. I felt that the Chief would be the last true kastom chief. Donald, I feared, had too much peer pressure to perform in the Western influence. However, there was Enoch, the Chief's youngest son who was ignored by the other boys in the village. He was very humble, quiet and shy and loved nature. His eyes were clear and beautiful. He had the spirit of the Yeramanu and I felt personally that Enoch had the spirit to become a High Chief.

At 4:00 pm High Chief Wai Wai called me to go to Yasur volcano with Sam and Michael to connect with the spirit. It was rainy and cold. I wore my shirt hoping it wouldn't knock off any scabs from the tattoo wound. Yasur was impressive, as always, projecting molten lava bombs high into the air. Because of low cloud and wind, vent fumes and smoke shrouded the summit so it became dangerous to remain on the ridge, as we could no longer see where the lava bombs were going to fall. I felt clearly that the volcano spirit was very angry. The energy was aggressive and hostile. I was uneasy.

When some tourists arrived in their 4 x 4 vehicles from different resorts around the island, I suggested that we should leave. Sadly, Vanuatu Post had erected three very large and unsightly signs and a postbox to denote "the only volcanic postbox in the world". I felt sick when I saw this disrespectful, tacky disregard of the sanctity of the spirit guardian of Yasur. No wonder he was angry.

As we returned along the track in the darkness to Itabu, glowing fire sticks could be seen bobbing to and fro as people carried them on their night journeys. When we met anyone on the road, only whispering was permitted. Hands were gently touched in a reverent greeting. On our return, the cicada's choirs hit the high notes all together as usual. This was truly an amazing experience. Flying foxes were now foraging. Usually one landed on the thatch of my hut each night with a thud and a scream. This started the dogs barking. If a pig strayed into the village at night time, a pack of dogs would attack it, filling the still night with bloodthirsty screams and howls.

Skull keeper   Taking heads   Feast of rats

I had a bucket wash for the first time in a couple of days to clean the dried blood, soot and charcoal from my tattoo wound. It made me feel more human. It looked like it hadn't taken very well and nothing like the Yeramanu strap design the Chief drew for me. The tattoo mark looked rather like a prehistoric slug! I decided to get it correctly redone in Brisbane, as this sign or mark is very important to me and links me to Majikjiki and the lineage of the Yeramanu. Sam had never tattooed a white man before so some parts of the mark were very light, some were deep and dark. The Chief's mark was not so easy to see with his black skin. His also was not very clear, yet he appeared to be pleased with it. For some reason, the Chief had decided not to do the ear piercing ceremony this time.

The Chief came to my hut at breakfast to let me know he had organised the kava and the pig for the next day's ceremony. The Chief sat across the table from me and offered to answer any of my questions. Those he could not understand, he would get Michael to help him with. I was glad of this long-awaited opportunity, as the weather was overcast and humid. I enjoyed these sessions with the Chief for I learnt much from him.

Chief Wai Wai is Chief over three nakamals, he explained. There are about 50 High Chiefs on Tanna Island. All the High Chiefs meet occasionally in council to discuss major events or changes, such as roads going through tribal lands. Each year a High Chief is voted to be leader; all take a turn of this office.

The Chief explained to me more about the offering of the pig and kava during ceremony. The blood of the pig upon the earth is very important, sacred, and finishes trouble between tribes or individuals. Legend states that the pig is used in this way for sacred ritual and sacrifice to Majikjiki. Majikjiki also told the ancestors that kava was to be used in sacred ceremony. I asked the Chief why the pig and kava was used this way, but he didn't know. He said, 'It just is!

During all ceremonies one pig is killed and kava drunk, no more than this, but for festivals and feasts it is different. The Chief also explained that there was a particular bird called the queria and this can only be shot with a bow and arrow by a chief. If a boy shoots this bird, he can be killed.

When I began to ask questions about any myths or legends of a crystal skull, the Chief could not understand what crystal was. I was informed some years ago that an ancient crystal skull came from these islands. He changed the subject saying, 'Iarueri. I am going to tell you secret information which is not permitted to be told to anyone else except your nephew, Aaron.'

He dismissed Michael, the interpreter. The Chief continued, 'The Yeramanu is the tribal skull keeper. The Yeramanu speaks to the ancestors of the skulls. There is a secret, sacred place where the skulls are kept, which is taboo for all men. Skulls hold sacred power. There are still secret places in this area which only I am allowed to visit. In olden days, anyone transgressing tribal law would be killed and then eaten.'

Chief Wai Wai went on to explain in detail the secret tribal protocol of taking heads and how to care for them and the ritual butchering of the body for feasting, including the correct way to carry a man who was to be eaten for the feast. Information was given on the procedure of attending to the body of one who died of natural causes and all funerary rites. It was truly fascinating.

At regular intervals throughout our talk, the Chief stressed that this was secret information he was giving to me and that, as I had now received the mark of the Yeramanu, I was now allowed to know this. I scrubbed out my notes in my journal, later burning the pages, just in case I lost them and somebody read them. I gave my word to the Chief that I would never reveal this knowledge. Interestingly, I had already done this work in another form as a mortuary attendant, post-mortem assistant and trainee funeral director. The Chief said ruefully, 'In the olden days, we were strong because we ate meat. Now that we eat rice, our bodies are weak.' (This information is now in the public domain from various sources.)

It is interesting that all of my life I have been fascinated by skulls and mortuary practices, collecting skulls as a boy from nature. For my final exams at school, I painted a crystal skull and created a skull from clay.

The Chief said to me that, at the final ceremony the next day, he would pass to me the spirit of Majikjiki, the spirit of the Yeramanu. It is one of the most important ceremonies next to the tattoo ceremony and one of the highest sacred rites that can be performed by any man. Chief Wai Wai told me, in the early days of the Christian missionaries, anybody who refused to give up their tribal kastom beliefs had their right hand cut off. The Chief said, if ever that situation arose again, he would never ever join the church and would allow his hand to be cut off because the church is built upon lies. The missionaries forced the local people to submit at gunpoint or through organised barrages from ship's guns that destroyed their villages and the issuing of diseased blankets, knowingly, to weaken the strong. The local people were forced to go to church because they were afraid of being killed or maimed. Many local people managed to keep their traditions alive under the severest of persecution and many ceremonies were done secretly in the remotest areas of the island. Where missionary interference took hold, the ceremonies that were permitted were altered accordingly, so not all have an ancient heritage now.

The Chief called for me after lunch to go to the nakamal with him, as a discussion was being held, and he wanted me to take my place beneath the banyan tree alongside him. The men were discussing problems with the water pipe since an airlock had occurred preventing the water flowing to certain villages and surrounding areas. The worry was that the World Vision engineer had only a few days to get the job finished, so everyone had lost a whole day in trying to rectify this situation and tempers were being frayed.

A man would stand and speak, all others sitting in silence until the orator had finished. Another man or the Chief would then stand and say their piece. It was very diplomatic and fair and what impressed me was that everybody actually listened to what was being said. Moses was there and Absalom came later carrying a live chicken. As Absalom came up to where the Chief and I sat by the fire, he snapped both legs of the chicken in two with a loud crack. I was absolutely horrified and felt physically sick, as the chicken screamed in agony. The bird could no longer escape so was put on the ground. I had to keep reminding myself that it was their culture and way of life and it was not my right to interfere or say anything. It transpired that Moses and Absalom had quarrelled whilst they were laying the water pipe in the hills so the traditional kastom way to overcome any animosity was for one man to give a gift to the other. Kava could not be drunk if two men had a bad spirit between them. Bearing in mind that these people had very little, a chicken was a large payment as a peace offering. Moses took the bird and plucked it near to me after killing it. Its feathers drifted upon the breeze and fell into the fire. The smell of burning feathers was nauseatingly awful.

The men put root vegetables and corn on the cob into the embers of the fire to roast. As the speeches drew to a close, the kava had been prepared and was ready for drinking. All the men called upon Tamaffa to help them with the problem of the water pipe. Roasted taro was picked out of the fire and its charred skin scraped clean with a piece of broken glass. The chicken was butchered and bits skewered on sticks which were stuck into the ground over the flames. The liver was placed upon a hot smouldering log. After drinking kava, I was given some taro and a chicken leg to eat. Willie wanted the head and neck, which he put into the glowing embers to cook. The men then asked me to speak after deciding to dismantle the pipes and relay them.

I stood next to the High Chief beneath the banyan tree, explaining to the gathered men about my displeasure regarding the tourists going up to Yasur volcano and the signs and postbox erected by the government, informing them that the guardian of Yasur was not being respected and honoured and the government was turning the sacred place into a tourist site to make money. I told them I sensed that on my last visit Yasur was very angry. The men fully understood and agreed with me wholeheartedly. Nikwei, through Moses interpreting, explained the traditional method was that you had to cover your entire body with coconut oil prior to going up to the volcano. The volcano does not like Western standards such as the lack of respect, strong deodorants and Western clothing.

As the twilight drew darker the men, as ever, were very helpful, kind and courteous, placing me on a log nearest to the fire to keep warm and gave to me the best bits of meat.

I returned to the hut at 6:00 pm, with Sam, for my dinner – more rice and the other chicken leg. It was very difficult to see what was on my plate at night because the light from the hurricane lamp was not very bright. This reminded me of a time when I was living with the Attié tribe in the Ivory Coast. I had arranged to live with the chief of the village of South Danguira through the British Ambassador to collect seeds for a local Manx school project and to study ornithology. I was given scientific status so I would not be troubled as a tourist. My escort and I arrived in the village by bus late at night, where I was introduced to the chief and the council of elders. I was then seated at a table to eat. I could not see what the food was and it tasted peculiar so, when I enquired, the hurricane lamp was pushed nearer to enable me to see a bowl full of cooked rats, all of their staring heads hanging out over the rim, their bulging eyes looking at me. I just managed to retain the meal. The next day, after a coconut shell of Bangui (locally distilled palm alcohol) with the chief and council of elders, I was invited to partake in a ritual where a large rat was killed and cooked, then split open. The liver, kidneys, heart, tongue and testicles were then given to me to eat, followed by jungle snails. I lived on rats and snails for a month!

30th October 2005
Skewered   Yeramanu lineage   Rack of skulls

I had no sleep. The dogs barked the entire night outside my hut and a rooster crowed from the early hours of the morning. Kava had a stimulating effect upon me but had a relaxing and calming effect upon the locals. They always seemed to sleep well. My whole body was aching, especially my kidneys and my joints, for some reason. I couldn't get comfortable at all and was very hot with my hips, back and ribs aching. I had paw paw and cucumber for breakfast with some dry crackers. It was overcast but humid.

At 10 o'clock Chief Wai Wai called for me to go to Sulphur Bay with a party of men. I had never been to Sulphur Bay before and knew it was connected to the John Frum Cult. The Chief explained he was told of a twin stainless steel sink that was for sale so he wanted it for his "restaurant". As much as I wanted to see Sulphur Bay, I wanted even more to lie on my bed, for I felt really ill in a manner I hadn't experienced before. My whole body was racked with a nauseating ache and I had a bad headache.

I went along to Sulphur Bay, which was a tidal estuary, the waters steaming from hot volcanic springs. We found the sink lying in a pile of rubbish. It was in poor condition and I would have advised the Chief not to buy it, for it was also filthy, but I felt too ill to talk to him. We walked across the sands of the estuary, as the tide was out. I felt much better after breathing in the sea ozone and prayed to Manannan and Majikjiki to help me, to give me strength and healing, especially for the ceremony later.

Several outrigger canoes were beached upon the sands. I couldn't be bothered to take photos. I had a guided tour around the hot thermal springs. The men showed me one spring in particular that was boiling. Pigs were often plunged into it to cook. In the past, it was used to cook human flesh. Other areas of the springs were different temperatures, women sat washing clothing in some and children bathed in the warmer pools. The men bathed in the hotter pools. One pool was actually very cold.

When we returned to Itabu, a plate of food was placed before me but I felt so ill I could hardly eat any. I apologised, explaining that I felt sick from the kava the night before, but this puzzled me because the effects of kava had never lasted for this length of time. I wondered – had I got some bug or tropical disease?

I returned to my hut and lay upon my bed, praying that the last ceremony would be cancelled for today, as I was not up to it at all. I could not get comfortable and was in agony; every part of my body ached. I was burning up with fever. Then I experienced a peculiar sensation which took my breath away and made me cry out in agony. An energetic spear was thrust through my body from my right side to my left side. I could see this psychic weapon. It was a spear, banded black and white. It was the spear of Majikjiki.

I became alarmed at my condition and, with great difficulty, managed to sit up gasping in agony to ease the intense pain. The feeling was exactly that of being skewered. I managed to get off the bed and stumbled to a chair and I prayed for help. Sweat dripped from my forehead; I could hardly breathe; I felt sick and faint. I thought I was going to die.

About 3:00 pm Chief Wai Wai called for me to see the two belts or straps of office that were being made for the ceremony for the Chief and myself. Nikwei and Willie had been preparing for this ceremony all afternoon. I was not permitted to see this sacred ritual wearing Western clothing so I had to strip and put on nambas. I was allowed to photograph the process, which surprised me.

The two grade belts that were being made were a High Chief belt and a God belt, the Majikjiki belt. The bark of the female banyan tree was being used and two strips about three inches wide and a yard long were soaking in a container of water. The outer skin was removed, leaving the inner bark which was virtually white. It was explained to me that the belts were not allowed to touch the earth or even a man's leg. Special leaves were gathered, like ferns, and laid upon the ground for the belts to lie upon. The strips of bark were then pounded upon a smooth log with a small club to soften the fibres. Sticks were then cut and had their ends beaten to create a fibrous end, which had the effect of becoming a coarse paint brush.

In a coconut shell, powdered charcoal and coconut oil were blended and the stick dipped into the mixture. The belt was then painted with a stippling motion. The God belt was done first and a serpent design was created, very similar to the tribal tattoo of the Yeramanu. The High Chief's belt had more triangles and dots than the Majikjiki belt. These belts were then frayed at the ends to enable the wearer to tie them on, rather like shoe laces. The belts were then hung from a banyan tree to dry. I was told that only black and white were permitted, no other colour (the black and white serpents).

Shortly afterwards, the ceremony of divine alignment and blessing began – the highest ceremony in their culture and one very rarely done. It was another secret occasion. The High Chief, suitably attired, waited in the centre of the nakamal, as the other men and I prepared ourselves with the ornamental leaves, bangles, nambas, etc. Kava roots and a small pig were then brought to the nakamal. Donald carried the pig and I was asked to carry the kava. I also brought my gifts to present to the High Chief in the traditional gift sharing after the ceremony. In procession, we filed through the hole in the banyan tree to form a circle, like a coiled serpent, placing our gifts in the centre, and then began to sing, dance, clap and stamp our feet. I did my best to keep up but what was important I was told was that I was to participate, adding and sharing my energies with the local men and the guardian spirit of the nakamal.

After the dancing, several speeches were made by the High Chief and myself. I then had to hold a club against the pig's forehead in symbolic sacrifice. I passed this right and privilege to Donald, who swiftly despatched the pig, allowing the blood to flow into the dark earth, the most important part of the ceremony. It seemed fortuitous if the splattered blood sprayed on your feet and legs. I had to stand next to the pig and kava, holding a bow and arrow (these and a spear are the symbols of the warrior God).

As I held the bow and arrow, High Chief Wai Wai Rawi called to the ancestors and to Majikjiki, invoking divinity to be as one with me as he placed his right hand upon my crown, invoking and passing to me the lineage of the Yeramanau. I and Majikjiki were now one in spirit, he said. In their kastom I had become the Chief embodying Majikjiki, the God man, the greatest honour that any man can receive in their culture. Unfortunately, as I felt so ill, I couldn't appreciate fully all that was or had happened, which was disappointing.

It was my turn to give another speech and I presented to the High Chief a gift of my Celtic culture, a pewter chalice called the "Glastonbury goblet", and a friendship cup engraved with both our names. Inside the chalice was a small amethyst crystal skull. The Chief and men were delighted with these gifts.

Strangely, immediately after the ceremony had concluded, I felt strong and healthy. All joint pains had disappeared and the general aches, fever and headache had vanished. I began to wonder if some final energetic adjustment had taken place to me prior to the ceremony.

We filed back through the banyan tree and to the fire, which was rekindled. The pig's body was strung up with a rope through its lower jaw and duly fired to singe off its hair, then butchered and its meat stuck on sticks to cook over the fire. Kava was prepared and, as usual for all important ceremonies, it was made extra strong. I felt ill just by smelling it! I managed not to vomit and a piece of burnt pig was given to me to eat. A pot was suspended over the fire and rice added for the feast.

As we sat in prayerful silence around the campfire, a clear vision of a crystal skull came to me. For several days now I had been having visions of crystal skulls, not understanding why. This crystal skull was very clear, spinning clockwise, with a black background. This morning I noticed the skull had stopped spinning and the black background had changed to a crystal blue one. Something had happened; a change had occurred. When I gave the Glastonbury chalice containing the amethyst skull to the High Chief, I became aware of a crystal skull sitting on a quartz pedestal in a cave high in a mountain range, somewhere similar to those around Itabu. It was obviously a very powerful sacred site, the crystal skull looking out across the valley below – a guardian perhaps. To the right of this skull and pedestal was an alcove in the cave containing the remains of past Yeramanus, the skulls of the ancestors. What was fascinating about this alcove was there were twelve skulls in total on three shelves, four skulls on each shelf. The top left-hand skull was clearly recent and of human bone. As the skulls aged in time in their magical alcove, a transformation was taking place so that each skull was at various levels of crystalisation. The skull at the bottom right-hand corner was virtually pure crystal and this would replace the crystal skull on the pedestal when it had completed its task. I was also told that, when this took place, all the other skulls would be moved along and when High Chief Wai Wai Rawi died his skull would be placed at the top left-hand.

I became aware of a pair of black hands, turning the crystal skull on the pedestal, slightly to the right, realigning it for some reason at this time. A shaft of crystal blue light, like a laser beam, was projected from the third eye of the skull to a distant cave further down the mountain range. A sound was emitted from the crystal skull, which I cannot describe except to say it was similar in fashion to a woman holding a high pitched singing note, which seemed to travel within the beam of blue light. From this cave in the distance, another shaft of light was projected and I could see another chain reaction occurring, gridding the area, seen and unseen, with a web of light. Were there other crystal skulls in these other caves, I wondered? Spirit told me clearly that I was now a Guardian of the Ancestral Skulls.

I became very emotional and a feeling of completeness came over me, a feeling of fulfilling destiny in some strange way. It became clear to me that, when High Chief Wai Wai Rawi held the energized amethyst skull in the sacred space of the most high ceremony of their culture, invoking the presence of Majikjiki, something magical had begun (see Appendix C). I felt a great sense of privilege that I had played a small part in something that was larger than my understanding.

I returned to my hut with Sam.

31st October 2005

God belt   Ancestral wounds

I slept well until 1:00 am when the dogs started barking again outside my hut with the rooster joining in. I was badly bitten again with mosquitoes all over, the bites coming up in red swollen weals with a clear centre, rather like cigarette burns. My bed was uncomfortable since the base was constructed of bamboo poles lashed together with a thin mattress on top. I did some laundry before breakfast.

The Chief then came to my hut to tell me that he was going to get the two chief's belts which were still hanging on the banyan tree. He returned shortly with the belts folded neatly, both still damp. The Chief presented to me the God belt, the belt of Majikjiki. He also wanted to give to me a bow and arrow or spear to take home as a symbol of my status of the warrior God, but I explained that sadly I would not be permitted to carry weapons on the plane. Chief Wai Wai said that, now I was a Yeramanu, I must wear my nambas in public places at all times. I explained to him I would not be permitted to do this, otherwise I would be arrested and probably put in prison. The Chief could not comprehend this.

At 9 o'clock, Chief Wai Wai and Sam called for me to go to Nikwei's village to listen to the villagers sing their songs and to watch the people dancing. When we arrived, the Chief and I were given fragrant necklaces of red and white flowers. The village had not been burnt to the ground during the tribal warfare because of army intervention. Speeches were given by the Chief, Nikwei and myself. A line of villagers shook our hands and we sat in a place of honour to enjoy the entertainment. It was very beautiful, even though the guitars kept breaking strings and going out of tune. Singing is an important way of life to reach God for these people. Nikwei asked me for a new guitar but the local people have no awareness of how expensive these things are, for to buy a guitar in Port Vila would cost three times the price of one bought in Australia. The likes of guitars are classed as luxury goods and therefore taxed accordingly. Many of the songs that the local people sang were about Majikjiki. Nikwei then showed me their nakamal and the massive banyan tree that stood nearby. He presented to me another one of his amazing carvings.

It was hot and sunny today; I felt much better. I had lunch on our return to my hut – more tinned tuna and rice. I rested for the afternoon. The men were still busy connecting and repairing the water pipes.

At 4:00 pm the Chief called for me to do some healing on himself and four others. During the healing, the ancestral spirits opened my inner vision to assist me. I sensed the lineage of the Yeramanu working through me. I felt very excited. On one man, who had a knee problem, I saw a yellow arrow through the knee. The arrow was removed with the permission of Spirit; then it was broken in half and buried. Another man had a broken spear shaft in his third eye area, which was obviously old, probably a manifestation of a carry over of an ancestral condition. He had head pains. The spear was removed. The same man had stomach problems and I saw a black psychic unsavoury manifestation. Recognising that this was beyond my present capabilities and experience, I called on the ancestors to deal with and remove it. Surprisingly, I found out later that this man was a Seventh Day Adventist Christian. I was surprised that he had come at all.

Another man had back ache. I saw a round black stone lodged up under the back of his skull, touching the lower jaw. This was removed. I was able to sense, feel and intuit a range of psychic or energetic intrusions or manifestations within the energy counterpart of the physical body. This experience would have been much harder at home in our Western life style but in this traditional tribal culture these kastom manifestations were very clear and it was great experience and practice for me.

After the healing session, the Chief explained that, in this part of Tanna, the tam tam slit drum was never used traditionally rather a conch shell to call the men to war or dance. On a still night it was possible to hear the ocean from Itabu village.

There was no nakamal tonight since the Chief said his father told him to abstain occasionally, as too much kava made you sluggish. A break should be taken every few days. The Chief was expected to take a half cup, not a full one, and should take one drink only.

I returned to my hut for dinner, rice and tuna. As I sat in the eerie light of the hurricane lamp, I pondered back on the three years of my initiations. I felt a great inner peace and stillness.

1st November 2005
Spirit of the waterfall   Penis sheath on fire

The local people were up and about at 4 o'clock. I had my bucket wash and went for breakfast. Most people were in the forest near to the village to watch a huge hardwood tree being felled by a man with a chainsaw. I was told about this yesterday, as the timber was to be used for building accommodation and for repair to existing homesteads. Even so, I felt sick when this magnificent old tree crashed to the ground. Something was missing. The environment felt empty and sad.

The Chief and I went to see a man called Joseph at Iaqurimano village; he is a cousin of Kelson and is a Seventh Day Adventist preacher. I recognised him as the man I gave healing to last night. Joseph wanted me to take some photographs of his horse riding business which he had just started, with the approval of the Chief. He wanted me to get on to one of the two horses but I refused. I told the Chief it was a long way to fall. The Chief laughed! We went for a walk with his men through the bush to a waterfall site. Now, in the dry season, it was just a trickle. Joseph asked me for my advice on how he could improve the area for tourists. I asked Spirit to advise me and I connected to a ledge three-quarters of the way up the waterfall site that was green and lush and sensed the presence of a female guardian. This guardian told me clearly that the ledge was sacred to her. She would permit the tourists to visit if a beautiful garden was created to honour and respect her and, as long as the tribesmen educated the tourists in the kastom way, that each may be touched by local divinity.

I thought this information would not go down very well to a programmed Seventh Day Adventist (SDA) Christian but I told Joseph and the men exactly what she had asked me to convey to him. I received interesting remarks and excitement and continued to advise them to keep the area free from litter, pointing to two items at the base of the waterfall, to clean out the silt to construct a pool for the dragonflies and to grow flowering plants to bring in butterflies and birds, insects and reptiles. I picked up the litter and stressed the point to the men that, even if you are Christian, you must still honour the environment in all its forms.

We returned to Joseph's "restaurant" to have lunch, a local dish of manioc and island cabbage. Joseph, the Chief and I spoke for over two hours about Christianity, kastom beliefs and the ancestors. When I first met Joseph, he was aggressive with a superiority complex over the kastom people and their beliefs, but, by the time the Chief and I had left, his energies were open, clear and gentle.

On our return to Itabu village I had more people waiting for healing. Another lunch was also waiting for me! I asked the Chief more questions.

I then had a rest and at 4:00 pm the Chief called me to go to the nakamal. I changed into nambas and helped to light the fire. The Chief was horrified to see the bite marks all over my body, so I told him that white meat was more tender for mosquitoes. He laughed!

Before the other men arrived, the Chief asked me to explain to him the story of my ancestors. I explained how the prehistoric people lived, as best I knew, wearing animal skins to keep warm and how they hunted with spears, stone axes, bows and arrows. They hunted big animals like elephants, bears, lions, bulls, stags, wolves and boars and I gave a demonstration of how a group of hunters would creep up to a mammoth to spear it, some men distracting it while others would move in to throw their spears. I'm afraid I got carried away with the drama at times, much to the delight of the Chief as his eyes were wide and shining. He laughed loudly, clapping his hands like a child. As I danced around the fire imitating spearing a wild animal, my nambas caught alight and smoke rose from the area of my crotch and then flames started to creep up to my belly. The Chief shrieked with laughter and started to beat the flames out. That didn't feel too good! We rolled about in the damp soil, hugging each other, laughing and crying.

After I had finished my story and acting, the Chief looked at me and said, 'Iaureri. We are from the same culture!' I had to agree.

Donald, Willie and Sam came to prepare kava. Nikwei and Jack came later but disappeared. The Chief and I drank kava, which was very strong tonight for some reason. I was given a piece of manioc to eat afterwards. The Chief spoke to the men about our visit to Joseph's house and to the waterfall. Prior to our departure, he said that he and Joseph talked intimately for some time and that Joseph had told him that, at the end of the discussion with Iarueri, he had understood everything I had explained and wanted permission to return to the kastom way of life again, to regain his heritage and to leave the church! The men roared with laughter and called me the first kastom missionary! They slapped me on the back.

In the stillness of prayer time I saw Majikjiki appear from the banyan tree and come to the fire. He held a black and white ringed spear and behind the spear head were tied two feathers, one black and one white. Majikjiki thrust the spear deep into the centre of the fire, which we all sat around, and said quietly, 'I am pleased.'

I whispered this to the Chief who excitedly informed the gathered men who were also clearly excited. The Chief spoke softly to me as the other men prayed explaining that he hoped that the next tokka dance at Itabu would be in 2008 and I should attend. He explained the dancing and singing went on for three days and three nights with 200 pigs slaughtered for a massive feast. 'In the olden days,' he said, 'the local people either went about naked or used the bark of a certain tree to cover their genitals. The missionaries forced them to wear clothes. If they refused, they were beaten and tortured.' Later, Sam took me back to the hut for my meal.

2nd November 2005
High Chiefs are twins   Phoenix

Up at 5:30. We had planned to go to Lenakel today to get some shopping. The truck arrived early to take us at 8 o'clock. The Chief spoke to the driver who said, because it was a special trip, I had to pay twice the fare. The Chief was clearly upset and angry. By the time 8 o'clock had arrived, the truck was laden with people wanting to go to Lenakel to sell their goods at the market. Some were from Itabu, others from further afield. Despite this, I still had to pay twice the fare.

When we arrived at Lenakel, I tried to reconfirm my flight to Port Vila but the man in the office said the phone wasn't working so he couldn't do it. We went from store to store buying supplies such as axes, machetes and a saw. Nahu, the Chief's daughter, had been looking after me, collecting fresh drinking water and water for my daily wash. I asked the Chief what I could buy for her and he said a bowl for doing the laundry and for washing the infants. I was hoping to get her something personal but, because of native culture, women are seemingly classed as second-class citizens. I asked the Chief for permission to buy her a sharp kitchen knife. He agreed.

On the way back to Itabu the Chief saw a sign outside a native "restaurant" by the sea advertising fresh fish, rice and cabbage for 200 Vatu per head. He asked me if we could stop. Everybody had to have a meal and I felt I had paid for most of it! As fresh fish is a treat for the men, it was too much of a temptation, consequently, I couldn't eat my lunch when we arrived back at Itabu, so I asked the Chief to explain to his daughter why I didn't want her cooking. By a great coincidence, we met Lakin, the Head Teacher of Port Resolution school, who was coming to Itabu to give to me two letters in response to Andrew Douglas's letters from the Manx government.

I sorted out the gifts which I had planned for everybody and put them under my bed. I was hoping to buy more axes but could only find a few of good quality. There were a few bush knives, or machetes, and axes and bowls left over from my personal list, so I asked the Chief if he would distribute these to those in need. I had a rest.

The Chief then called for me to go to another village to do healing for a sick woman, who was too ill to walk to Itabu to see me. Martha, the Chief's wife, came along also but never walked with us, always a few yards behind. She remained silent. I found this unsettling but it is their culture. As we walked side by side, I asked the Chief many questions. I asked him if he would confirm that the name of the tribe was the Maruki tribe, expecting him to say yes. He said no. I was startled. He said that the correct name for the tribe is Nasipmane. I said that I didn't understand because, every time I had asked in the past, I was told that the name of the tribe was Maruki. The Chief explained that the tribe is Maruki's tribe, but the name of the tribe is Nasipmane. I felt confused.

I then asked what the name Iarueri actually meant and he said, 'God, but especially God of pigs, kava, chicken, sacred stones and fruits, the God of nature.' He said that the name Majikjiki means God of Vanuatu, God of our land. He went on to explain that the kastom name in his language for Tanna Island is Nhak. The Chief also said that, in his tribal language, the kastom name of nambas is ninam and this was given to people to wear by the instructions of Majikjiki in his myths.

I asked the Chief how old he was. The Chief said he remembered his father telling him that he must remember the date of his birth because it was very important. Very few people can remember this so, when I asked him how old he was and when he was born, he said he was born on 12th July 1954. I stopped dead in my tracks and I stared; my jaw dropped open looking at him. He raised his eyebrows. I said to him that my birthday was on 11th July 1954. This is remarkable because it signifies the twinning of the creation myth. It is absolutely amazing to think that we were both born within the same 24 hours on different sides of the globe. We are twins. The Chief smiled and nodded. He knew! I had mistakenly believed that Chief Wai Wai was the firstborn son of his father. In fact, Chief Wai Wai was the second born son to the former High Chief.

Originally, the first pregnancy to his parents were twins – a boy, the firstborn, and a girl. Unfortunately, the boy died so, as the hereditary lineage goes through the male bloodline, Wai Wai automatically became the next High Chief in waiting.

I asked him what the significance was of the beard and the Chief said to me that his father had told him he was never to cut his hair, otherwise he would become weak. The kastom way is for the chief in particular to have long hair down to the waist, if possible, and to have a long beard. The Chief said his grandfather, Iarueri, had waist length hair. Apparently in this part of Tanna Island the bigger the beard indicates the higher the status of the chief.

As we walked up the steep mountain track I saw a tree which appeared to be dead, yet it was full of strange puncture marks, as though somebody had been using a brace and bit to drill holes in it. These, the Chief explained, were the boreholes of a large grub. When the tree finally died, it would be cut down and these grubs extracted to eat. He showed me the size of the grub by expanding his fingers to about four inches in length.

When we arrived at the village I was introduced to the husband of the sick woman. I could tell by his face she was clearly very ill. I went into the hut to meet her. I shook her hand and knelt by the side of her bed. I placed my hand on her brow. She wanted to come outside into the sunshine to receive the healing so we helped her into the centre of the clearing in the village. Everybody stood around the perimeter to watch. I tried to cut out everybody's stares and I attuned to the ancestral spirits, asking for help. I saw a blue psychic dart piercing her left wrist. A torrent of hot, steaming, black fluid "vented" from her solar plexus area. During the process of the healing a bird of fire, like a Phoenix, left her body from her bowels, up through her mouth and up to the ancestors. I was told later she had bad stomach problems and was passing blood when going to the toilet. A dog (bitch) persisted in sitting next to where the woman stood, not leaving her right side despite people calling it and throwing pebbles at it to move. I indicated for them to stop, to leave the dog alone.

After the healing, her husband, the Chief and I sat for over an hour discussing the usual topic – Christianity versus the kastom tradition. This man was another Seventh Day Adventist Christian. He asked very pertinent questions about the kastom way of life. I answered to the best of my ability, including that Spirit also required the dog to be present for the healing of his wife, for some reason. This is how the kastom tradition works; we are all one Spirit. The Chief and the man spoke together before our departure and, on the way home, the Chief began to laugh explaining to me that the "kastom missionary" had struck again, converting another sinner!

As we returned to Itabu, I asked the Chief more questions. I asked him to clarify what he meant about the Maruki name and who can be called such. He said that, in the tribal kastom, the High Chief's first name, not the family name of Rawi is used. This enables the different bloodlines of the same family to be recognised, as all are Rawi. He said that I have the right to call myself Maruki, or Rawi. He said that it is all the same.

As an ornithologist, I asked the Chief if he had ever seen, found or shot any birds that had metal rings on their legs, but the Chief could not understand what I was asking. The idea of a bird wearing a metal ring was clearly nonsense to him. In Papua, New Guinea and Africa, I have seen tribesmen wearing metal birds' identification rings around their necks as necklaces, and this would have been an ideal opportunity to make a note of the ring numbers of the different birds that had been caught for research on migration.

3rd November 2005
Snake dancers   Dragon of Volcanic Fire

My last full day at Itabu. Since the vision in the parallel universe of the beam of light and the crystal skull upon the pedestal in the cave, this had become more etherealised and had metamorphosed into pure light until there was nothing left of a physical nature. Each day I had tuned into this process to watch the changes. The pedestal now stood empty at the cave entrance. As I tuned again into the crystal cave, I became aware of a force of energy building up in some way.

To the physical sounds of the tribal singing, clapping and stamping in the nakamal below where I sat in my hut in meditation, I could hear and see similar activities taking place inside the crystal cave in a deeper section from where the pedestal stood (the physical chanting seemed to act as a catalyst to aid my meditation in some strange way to connect to the crystal skull). Inside the crystal cave, the male dancers were all painted with white rings around their dark bodies and limbs. All had black and white feathers in their hair. I knew these men were performing a snake dance, raising the power of the serpent consciousness. Not only that, the symbology of the black and white rings was representing Majikjiki as the sea serpent and his two twins, one white, one black, which both Wai Wai and myself symbolise. It was deeply moving to witness such a marvellous sacred dance. All the dancers were of the highest grade in tribal society. This seemed to be the dance of the Yeramanu. The acoustics within the crystal cave were indescribable; an echo resonance seemed to harmonise with a consciousness of its own. Maybe the guardians of the cave were manifesting through sacred ritual and sound?

Then, without warning, one of the dancers broke away from the group and indicated for me to follow him. As we journeyed deeper into the back of the cave, the snake dancers began a peculiar serpent weaving dance in a similar motion to how a snake would move through water. The deeper we progressed into the cave structure, the darker it became, yet plenty of light was in evidence to allow us to see clearly where we were stepping, as light seemed to be stored in the crystal formations of which the cave was created. These crystalline growths appeared to give off a blue or white light, which made them look like blocks of ice. We then reached a point where I could see over the edge into a deep abyss, into a pool of crystal light that seemed suspended in an ethereal manner, giving difficulty in assessing how far I could see. I could still hear the snake dancers' chants, which seemed to get deeper and further in as we journeyed.

As my eyes adjusted to these magical sights in the dim light, I could see long ladders leading down to what appeared to be three levels deeper into a volcanic haze. I was instructed to follow my guide, who I sensed was a

Yeramanu, slowly climbing down each of the long ladders to a level, and then the process repeated itself three times until we reached the lower level that was hot, yet of pure crystal which appeared clear and black.

Inside a large alcove was another crystal skull of light upon another pedestal. This was "living" in an energetic way and its energy was phenomenal. The Yeramanu picked up a small sliver of crystal from the floor and tossed it through the alcove opening towards the skull. Instantly the fragment of crystal was incinerated by a force field that I can only describe as being like a high voltage electric barrier. The Yeramanu moved a small stone in a niche in the wall and the force field disengaged, allowing us to enter into the sacred alcove. I was not permitted to touch the skull or get close to it. This was for my own safety, I was told. The Yeramanu then instructed me to ask the spirit of the skull a question.

I thought for a moment, 'I ask that the true nature of the guardian of the crystal skull may be revealed to me in a way I can understand.'

Immediately a passage opened at the back of the alcove which was long, dark and seemingly wet with a jagged path and sides. The substance that appeared to be water was something different that I couldn't identify. I don't know what it was, as there was no odour, taste or feel to it. It was just "wet". As the passage was roughly hewn out, care had to be taken where we trod. The passage was very hot and I could sense volcanic energy. As we passed through, a mist-like light or pressure waves passed us at regular intervals, altering my energy frequency and making me feel lighter and more cleansed at a deeper level. I suddenly realised that we were becoming one with the serpent consciousness; the dark passage and the light pressure waves made me feel like a snake.

At the end of the passage I stood in awe and wonder at what I could only describe as being at the centre of the earth! Below in a deep abyss was swirling, molten magma and a rugged terrain of crystal that would do justice to the most heroic of the Nordic myths and legends. The light of the combined glowing magma and rough, clear crystal blocks gave a surreal landscape of immense energy, raw, primeval, creative power in action.

Then the Dragon rose before me in its frightening, magnificent glory, a fire serpent so powerful it could have snuffed out my life instantly had it chosen to do so. Fire and crystal, liquid fire and liquid crystal at the centre of the earth. Now I understood what the dragon consciousness was!

At this point I felt strongly impressed to call forth and invoke the Dragon Sword into my hands before me and the shield of Manannan behind me, bearing the Triskele. I was instructed by the Yeramanu to ask the Dragon a question.

'Great and powerful Dragon of Volcanic Fire, thank you for the privilege of being allowed to visit this sacred place, the most sacred I feel within the earth. I ask that you reveal your true identity to me.' The abyss was filled with a sea of molten light. 'I ask that you may manifest through me and around me to enable me to fulfil my destiny within this incarnation in accordance with the will of the Great Spirit.'

The look the dragon gave to me was indescribable. Its huge, red serpent head was put to one side so that its right eye stared piercingly at me, or rather through me – an eye of red and yellow liquid fire. I raised the Dragon Sword with both hands in tribute, honour and respect and immediately I, and the sword, were engulfed in swirling flames for a split second until I and the dragon consciousness were one. I felt powerful; my body tingled all over. The fire serpent then metamorphosed back into its previous form.

The Yeramanu and I returned back to the crystal skull in the alcove, where we gave thanks. The passage was then sealed and we left, reactivating the force field.

Upon our arrival on the upper level of the cave entrance, the other snake dancers had removed the most crystalline skull from the skull rack and had carried it to the thermal pool of azure blue light where they had bathed it with great reverence. Then, once clean, the skull was carried back to the cave entrance and placed on the pedestal looking out across the mist-shrouded mountain range and the valley far below.

Suddenly the clouds gathered momentum and what was once a clear blue sky became dark and stormy. Within seconds powerful electrical storms had erupted and a thunderbolt slammed into the third eye of the crystal skull, creating a force field of some sort. The skull began to glow with light. It had been dormant; now it was activated and energised. The sky cleared. The men then carefully moved each of the remaining skulls along to develop their crystalline deposits. A vacant place remained that was reserved for the skull of the former High Chief to begin its magical journey. There are always twelve skulls on the rack, the thirteenth on the pedestal.

———————————

Most of the day was spent healing either at Itabu or in the village in the mountains that I went to yesterday. We took the native path to the village this time, not the easy way, which was virtually perpendicular and slippery, but it was a short cut.

On our return to Itabu, the Chief spoke of my leaving tomorrow and that tonight was my last night in the village. He became very emotional with tears welling up in his eyes. We went to the nakamal to have our last kava together. One boy called Angelo had caught a small bird called a "white eye". The bird had been stunned by a stone from a catapult and then a long length of fine vine had been tied to its leg so it couldn't fly away. Angelo played with it like a toy. It was very cruel to see; yet, by the lack of attention paid to him by the men, it was obviously a normal thing for a boy to do.

A sick puppy was lying in the ashes at edge of the fire trying to keep warm. It was shivering and looked as if it were dying. After the kava somebody had brought a fresh fish, ready cooked, so I had a small portion which I "accidentally" dropped in front of the puppy. The pup managed to eat it.

I returned to my hut where the Chief's family had gone to a lot of trouble to prepare an Island feast for me to celebrate my stay. The Chief asked me to tell the story again of my experiences in opening the skulls for brain removal to his family. I put on a good performance of sound effects with animated drama which had the daughters of the Chief gasping in horror. The men laughed.

After the meal, the women removed the dishes from the floor where we all sat and the men that remained gathered in the hut to talk. Before Donald left, he offered to me a boar's tusk necklace, a chief's armband and a pandanus leaf hat, bowing to me.

4th November 2005
Letter   Chief crying

I was up at 5 o'clock, had a wash in the bucket and then breakfast. I gave all of my gifts away this morning, as planned. Everybody was very pleased. I wished that I could have given others something, those who went without.

At 8 o'clock we left for Lenakel with a truck load of villagers to see me off. It rained sporadically so those in the back got wet and muddy. We stopped at the market place on the way to the airport at Lenakel. Michael asked to borrow my pen to write an address on an envelope on the truck bonnet. The Chief saw him too so, curious, he moved closer to see what he was doing. He and I were horrified. It was an application form for a correspondence course on Bible study for the Seventh Day Adventist Church. The Chief was clearly furious, as children and young people were not permitted to go to the church from Itabu. He said nothing, not there and then anyway. Michael duly posted his letter. Now I understood why I couldn't take to this young man. I was told later that he had worked for Kelson.

We arrived at the airport for 10 o'clock and had to wait two and a half hours for the plane to arrive. When it was time for me to leave I hugged everybody but Chief Wai Wai sat in the corner weeping. I held him close to me, speaking softly to my brother. He couldn't look up into my face, he was clearly struggling to keep himself from crying out loud. I felt for him. I knew that he loved me as his twin brother, as I did him and now we didn't know when we would see each other again.

The other departing travellers obviously wondered who the happy band of waving and cheering pilgrims seeing me off were. I felt a little embarrassed at their enthusiasm, yet delighted that I had made good friends who respected me. The Chief sat silently, his head lowered, tears streaming down his face.

I arrived at Port Vila on schedule. I checked into the hotel, then had a walk around the town; I bought a boar's tusk necklace from the market and some bananas. After a meal, I had a long soak in a hot bath, pondering what the next trigger would be thrusting me into my third "death".

5th November 2005
Tribal survival   Grade sticks

Through the day, I pondered back to my recent experiences at Itabu and the overall three year plan laid out by the spiritual ancestors of the tribe.

People in the West tend to view tribal communities through rose-tinted glasses simply because, deeply within their own psyche, they are searching for a path of deeper spiritual fulfilment which the church and state has virtually destroyed. Make no mistake about it, tribal peoples, whether they live in the Arctic tundra, temperate rain forest, mountains, deserts or tropical rain forests, are living to survive by honouring their local Genii, the spirit of place, Gods and Goddesses of their homelands. Each environment is breathtakingly beautiful in its own individual way, yet each has its hardships, dangers and joys. I have, therefore, compiled these notes as firsthand observations and experiences of how the local people live in southeast Tanna. No foreigner, no matter how long he or she lives within a different cultural heritage can ever come to fully understand the kastom way, for it is within the DNA, within the suckling babe-in-arms, the very consciousness inherited within the auric field for many generations. Some things you cannot explain; you just know. For many generations, the ancestral bloodline and spiritual lineage of the ancestors have shaped the tribal consciousness to build a foundation that reaches back to the dawn of humanity.

I have been accepted into the Nasipmane tribe as a member of the family, for the ancestors have willed it so and the people accept me as Chief Iarueri, an honour and privilege greater than the highest bauble or trinket that any Western head of state could confer. Western glitter is not earned. Tribal rewards must be earned and are marked usually by a suitable body mark – tattoo, scarification or piercings. Those who mark themselves thus without earning the right are banished or killed. I have earned my hereditary position, my boar's tusks, tattoo and chief's grade belt through the grace of Spirit and the generosity and gentleness, patience and trust of a culture battling against an ever-increasingly hostile church and Western society. Why does the white man have to destroy everything he doesn't understand?

I was awake for most of the night in the hotel in Vila. I couldn't sleep due to the drunken locals shouting and singing all night outside my window, so I decided to write up my notes in my journal. I felt smug that I had coped with my second "death" so well after the initiations in 2004. I didn't realise that time and space have no meaning with these things. When the time is right, that is when you are vulnerable, you will get it!

I decided to go to the National Museum of Vanuatu to look at their native artifacts and various collections. Here I found some volcanic rock from Yasur volcano on Tanna Island. The label described the specimen as "scoriaceous lava – a very vesicular and asitic lava containing white crystals of feldspar". Looking at the section on Tanna Island, I noticed with interest that Erromango Island, which is next to Tanna, is the traditional enemy of the Tannese and the people who live on this island still have sacred caves where they hold the skulls of their ancestors. It was good to have this and other information confirmed officially. I also saw examples of the grade sticks that are pushed through the ears of the high chiefs. They are the size of a small pencil traditionally made of cane and intricately carved or marked. These are the grading sticks that Chief Wai Wai and I were meant to receive.

After leaving the museum, I was walking back through the main street of Vila when a man shouted to me. I stopped and turned around to see the Yeramanu from Ipeukel Village near Sulphur Bay who treated my cut chest on Tanna last year. I was amazed. He was walking with a friend who interpreted. We shook hands and he said to his friend when he saw me, 'I know that man.'

He asked me through miming how my bad shoulder was. I said it was good. He smiled.

6th November 2005
Death of a friend

No sleep again because of the noisy drunks outside the hotel. A battered taxi arrived just before 5:00 am to take me to the airport to catch my flight to Australia. The driver asked me how long I had been in Vanuatu and where I had been staying, so I explained that I had been at Itabu Village on Tanna Island doing sacred ceremony with High Chief Wai Wai Rawi. The taxi driver laughed; then he amazed me by saying that he was a cousin of the High Chief and that his house is near the entrance to Yasur volcano.

I eventually arrived at Brisbane on schedule. The quarantine officials confiscated the seed necklace from the boar's tusks that Donald had given to me.

When I arrived at the hotel, I rang home to let my family know I was still breathing and was shocked and devastated to learn that a very close friend of mine had died whilst I was in Vanuatu. Over the following weeks, I went through all the stages of grief from sorrow, anger, denial and then, finally, acceptance. I realised that most of the experiences I was having were not connected to the death of my friend but to the effects of the initiations from the tribe. When I realised that the bereavement process was the trigger to face my third "death", I relaxed into it and the bereavement process simply faded away. I didn't fight it any longer. I believed I had passed the test of what the Chief described as the ordeal of my third "death". I was wrong!

9th November 2005

I went to a tattoo studio in Brisbane explaining about my Yeramanu mark and showed the tattooist the drawing the Chief had made of what the tribal mark should be like. He said to return in half an hour as he had to redraw it on a special piece of paper. I duly returned and had my tattoo redone neatly and clearly. I was very pleased with it. I got some antiseptic cream to apply as directed and I went off to the Botanic Gardens. When I returned to the hotel, I removed the paper towel bandage and I was surprised at the amount of bleeding that had occurred.

10th November 2005

When I awoke I was horrified to find that my pillow was marked with the tattoo ink and lots of blood. I told the hotel receptionist who seemed not too bothered about it. She simply said that it was the laundry people's problem. That was my last day in Australia.

11th November 2005

After 40 hours of travelling and waiting for connections I felt exhausted and miserable. I eventually arrived on the Isle of Man late at night and was met by Barry and Aaron.

30th November 2005
Reactivate grade mark

In sleep state I received a message from the ancestors, 'Invite the spirit of the Yeramanu to be one with you, to reactivate and re-energise your grade mark that it may identify you through your auric field to those who walk with you in spirit.'

The message clearly stressed the word "invite". I did as instructed and saw the Yeramanu mark light up like a beacon of fire and light, shining through my energy body and altering my auric resonance, or signature. I knew that a lot of my emotional trauma was part of this process.

During the following months, I kept in touch with Andrew Douglas who was trying his utmost to get government aid for the two schools on Tanna Island but, unfortunately, the Minister and Committee for Overseas Aid denied our application. Andrew was very upset about this. He was a rare breed of man – a politician with morals and scruples. He was a decent human being. Sadly, he passed to the ancestors in January 2010.

I continued to receive visions of the tribal people of Vanuatu and Majikjiki.

26th December 2005

Recovering lost skulls

When I connected to Spirit in meditation, I clearly saw a tribesman in native attire standing at the base of a volcano. I was not sure if it was Yasur in Vanuatu or not, but it was certainly in that part of the world. He was very anxious and he came to me and examined the tattoo of the Yeramanau. He then beckoned to me urgently to follow him. After walking through the soft, volcanic ash and silt, he stopped and looked up at the spewing volcano and pointed with his bow and arrow to a rocky outcrop upon the shoulder of the volcano. It was an area covered in tropical foliage and honeycombed with crevices and holes. As I looked at the area, I could see a recent eruption had caused a landslide and caused much damage to this area covering it in fine volcanic ash and debris.

He then beckoned me to follow him to what appeared to be an ash sand-dune. Here he became very agitated and upset, pointing at the ground. As I looked amongst the debris, I saw a human skull, then another and another. Clearly a sacred skull cave had been breached and damaged, sweeping the contents into the ash plain below. He indicated to me that he had no authority to touch the ancestral skulls but he pointed to the tattoo on my arm and indicated he needed urgent help from me to recover the skulls. I asked him where the other Yeramanus were in spirit and why they could not be called on, since they would be more suitably aware of the situation than myself. He pointed up to the sky and waved, as if to say that they had gone on to a higher level of consciousness and could not return to help him.

I began the process of recovering the skulls, asking how many were lost from the cliff face. I received the answer – three. Fortunately, all three were lying near to each other and appeared undamaged. I gathered the skulls into my arms and followed him up to the volcanic ash and debris slope, which was like climbing a sand hill. He was anxious, urging me on as if there was a time limit of some sort upon their recovery. At a point at a deep crevice high up the cliff face, large enough to squat in but not to stand, I was led to where other ancestral skulls lay. Some lay scattered upon the cave floor, whilst others appeared intact upon a stone ledge looking out across the plain below. Inside the darkness, I saw another tribesman squatting on his haunches, wide-eyed and tearful. One side of the cave had collapsed because of the volcanic activity and the ceiling caved in, spilling the contents. There appeared no possibility of moving all of the skulls to another place and I received the strong impression they must stay where they were.

I began to clean the debris out of the cave with the men and, with fallen stones, we rebuilt a retaining wall to support the weakened ceiling. The cave was much smaller now but possibly stronger after our work. We placed long stones up like pit props and called on the ancestral guardians to protect the place. Then we rebuilt a stone table and I was instructed by Spirit to place the skulls, seven in all, in a particular way that each one looked out over the plain and villages below at a precise angle, so every area of the community was being watched over by a skull. When we had finished, both men touched my feet and cried, holding up their hands to my heart. It was very emotional. I came out of meditation. The lesson I learnt from this experience was, once you commit your life in service to Spirit, much of your work is metaphysical.

15th January 2006

Keeper of the Ancestral Skulls

I connected with Spirit in meditation and I found myself in an emerald cave. The dragon who lived in this cave took me to a special place high amongst the emerald crystals where a huge crystal skull looked out over an emerald sea. Then I heard somebody calling me, 'Yeramanu. Yeramanu! Consider this, Yeramanu, that you will find skulls in every crystalline manifestation of light connected to your world. Each has its individual energetic signature and matrix consciousness for specific roles and functions. All are connected, as a spider's web is connected to the creative manifestation at its centre. Each is separate, yet integrated.

'Now that you have fulfilled your initiations in the tribal lands as "Keeper of the Ancestral Skulls", this is only the beginning of a new phase for you. Now you must learn to become more sensitive to the emanations of the crystalline web of light and the temple and eternal flame at its centre. The physical appearance of the crystal skull is unimportant. What is crucial is the awareness of how to access, understand and use the latent power contained within this matrix for, make no mistake, when you reconnect, for this is what you are doing – reconnecting – with the crystalline, cosmic web of life, you are plugging into a force of such unimaginable power that you must be very disciplined, focused, prepared and attuned in utilising this energy within and around you, then to understand what this is and the capacity of what it can do. Then you may actively redirect this cosmic force under divine supervision, a little at a time.

'If you receive too much power, you are in danger, since it will "blow your circuits" within your nervous system. You need to diffuse the static power that will accumulate around you, as the intense electromagnetic fields may switch your polarity. You need to actively ground yourself on a regular basis and direct this energy into the earth. You are now connected to the crystal skull consciousness.'

26th March 2006
Crystal throne

Again I had a deep sense of wanting to connect to Spirit. I easily found myself back in Vanuatu at the sacred pool of Itabu where I saw Majikjiki and High Chief Wai Wai Rawi who were waiting for me. I saw the water spider at the pool and Nuie, who I gave thanks to as guardian. Then Majikjiki, who was arrayed in his cloak of scarlet and black feathers, raised his spear high. I recognised the spear which I had seen before, alternating rings of black and white with two feathers behind the point, also one black and one white. This represented the black and white serpents.

Majikjiki thrust the spear deep into the sacred pool of Itabu, whereupon a vortex of black and white light carried us up into a higher level of consciousness to a realm of crystal-like light. We had arrived, as far as I could determine, at an exact replica of the geographical layout of the sacred pool, with the kava stone at the top and the volcano stone at the bottom. The water course, as upon earth, was formed into a Y shape. Majikjiki instructed Chief Wai Wai to take the left path and I was to take the right. We climbed a crystal walkway and this converged at the top to reveal a crystal platform which had upon it two crystal, throne-like chairs, sharing a single central armrest. Behind the thrones was a low table or platform which had upon it a large, clear crystal skull.

Majikjiki brought Chief Wai Wai Rawi and myself together before the crystal throne. Majikjiki now wore a cloak of gold and white feathers. He then bound our arms symbolically as one, as twins, then instructed us to take our places on the dual throne, side by side. Majikjiki raised his spear and, with lightning quick movements, pierced our skulls at the brow with the spear tip. At this point there was a physical lightning-like thud at my head, as though some sort of power transformation had taken place. I felt a little dizzy; I could tell the Chief felt that way also.

Majikjiki then spoke to us, 'It is now time. The transferring of the spiritual lineage of the Yeramanu consciousness has taken place jointly to you both. Your roles will be revealed in due course but do not expect an easy journey. Further energetic adjustments are to be made to enable you both to manifest the highest levels of the Yeramanu consciousness. You will receive support.'

We were then instructed to stand and our arms unbound – Chief Wai Wai's left to my right. We then walked back our separate pathways returning to the sacred pool of Itabu.

1st April 2006
Goddess of the dance

On a shamanic training course in Avalon, our group, for the last night, decided to do some dancing and I felt compelled to join them. I had never danced socially before, so to join in was a big deal for me. However, I felt safe in this environment amongst the group of like-minded souls.

The Goddess of the dance took me and I allowed myself to let go and became, for a few moments, one with the Goddess energy. In fact, she danced through me. I had never felt such an exhilarating experience before. Then a strange thing happened. Everyone else sat down except one particular girl. Our eyes met with intent for the first time. At a soul level we touched and began to dance together – a dance of inner beauty and soul consciousness. I had never experienced this feeling before and now, holding me, was the Goddess manifest through and around this young woman. For a moment, I was aware of nothing else or nobody else except her. I was in a place between time and space; her form, her scent, her touch were those of the Goddess. I fell in love with her.

Then suddenly, as it had all begun, it was all over. We both stood silently, awkwardly, a little embarrassed, for everyone was watching us. They too had felt Her presence. I became very emotional and needed so very much to hold this young woman, to be one with her, but I found out that she had a partner and two children. I had never fallen in love so deeply before. It was so amazing, so wonderful.

I spent a few days alone in Glastonbury and I couldn't stop crying. I don't know why I was crying, but I couldn't stop. This woman, through Spirit, had opened something within my heart and my soul. I felt that the Goddess had touched me and opened my heart. I felt very vulnerable, alone and frightened. Then I went to see a Tarot reader to see if she could make any sense of what was happening to me, because I felt so very confused. The Tarot reader cast her deck of cards and said to me that in a few months time I would meet my true love. I could not comprehend what she was saying, for I knew that I was in love right now. The problem was that this young woman lived in the south of England and I lived on the Isle of Man. I knew that she felt the same way about me. We both loved each other. It was totally beyond our control.

11th July 2006
Third death

We had an intense relationship that lasted one month then, after a very difficult conversation, this young woman admitted to me that she no longer loved me and wanted to end our relationship. I was devastated and heartbroken and, once again, I fell into the grief process. I went into denial; I knew that this could not happen to me, for I thought that I had found my true love, the woman whom I wanted to marry, but this was not to be. I fell fully into the ordeal of the second phase of my third "death". I felt broken spiritually.

In the bleak, dark despair of the weeks following the loss of this woman, I managed to do a shamanic journey to ask for guidance as to why I felt so devastated that I felt like ending my life. What came was remarkable and helped me to understand what I was going through, although it did not take away the soul pain.

In Vanuatu, the High Chief spoke of my initiations and of how I must "die" three times. I assumed he meant symbolically but I now knew that he meant literally, for since my first initiation I had reached the point of total despair three times and had stood at the portal of death three times. I now understood that the sacred, magical encounter with this young woman was the final catalyst for my third "death", for I had dropped like a lead weight into the blackest of holes and had thought of my own suicide to ease my soul pain, my bereavement of the most important thing that had ever come into my life. This beautiful soul was everything I had prayed for. She was the most amazing woman yet, for some reason that I could not understand, she no longer felt the same way about me. I had never known such terrible, cruel torment and pain. I loved her so very much; I adored her and now I had nothing. I was alone again.

I couldn't stop crying for her for weeks. This truly was a cruel death for me and I struggled to keep going, not to give in. It was so hard to function and cope with everyday life. Everything was so very difficult.

10th September 2006

Suspected skull fracture   Maggie

Today I did a fire ritual at the hearth to ask Spirit that all past connections no longer serving my highest good were closed and that I could move on and find a lady companion and to fulfil my spiritual vocation. I wrote my request with intent on to a piece of paper and then burnt it in the fire. I then stood up and began to call in the ancestors as taught to me by High Chief Wai Wai Rawi. I felt dizzy; then I fell unconscious.

The next thing I knew, I was lying on the edge of the stone hearth, spitting blood and bleeding profusely from both nostrils and my head. I had fallen face down on to the edge of the stone hearth, gashing open my forehead down to the bone. I staggered to a mirror. I had never seen my own skull before; I was fascinated, yet horrified. I began to fall into unconsciousness again and, when I came to, I managed to get to the phone and rang Susan, my sister-in-law, who came down immediately with Aaron. Sue phoned the ambulance and I was taken into hospital with a suspected fractured skull and nose. My neck had received a whiplash injury and was very painful, as were the misaligned vertebrae between my shoulders and a possible misaligned jaw. One of my front teeth had been knocked loose and the others had been rearranged. I had a cut nose, lip and chin with a possible fracture of a rib and a grazed knee and cut finger. I was generally very sore!

After several tests at the hospital, I had a couple of X-rays and the wound on my skull was cleaned and stitched. No fractures were found. I was discharged into the care of my family and sent home.

I made an appointment to see an osteopath who advised me to see Maggie, a craniosacral therapist and physiotherapist. As soon as I heard her name, my heart sang. I felt exhilarated in a way that was new for me. I had known Maggie some years ago when we were both external tutors for an aromatherapy school on the island. I thought she was the most delightful creature I had ever seen.

I felt a shiver of excitement in my heart as I met her after so many years. She was still slim, tall and beautiful. After the treatment, we had a meal together to "catch up". I felt elated to be in her company. After several more treatments with Maggie, I wrote her a poem, explaining how I had fallen in love with her. After posting it, I felt stupid and foolish and began to worry in case it may have offended her.

At my next and last appointment with her, she acknowledged the poem and said she thought it was beautiful. We arranged to meet socially the next time for a walk.

18th October 2006
Falling in love

We climbed to the top of a hill called Cronk Sumark in the north of the island, a place venerated by our ancestors which has two high points, one male, the other female. We sat at the female side of the hill and Maggie opened her heart to me to explain that she felt the same way for me. I was overwhelmed, ecstatic! Tentatively, I held her hand, then hugged her and we kissed. At that point, I knew that my burden of loneliness was banished forever and I was free. I felt great peace within me. I had known what it felt like to be turned "inside out". Now I felt complete, fulfilled, whole and happy.

In the weeks, months and years that followed, my love for Maggie has become deeper and more profound. She is the greatest gift the Goddess has ever given to me and I now realise that the other woman I had fallen in love with was part of the process to enable me to release my frustration and emotional baggage, to clear the way for my beloved (I recalled what the Tarot reader had said in Glastonbury).

Eventually, when the time was right, I asked Maggie to marry me whilst we were again at the top of Cronk Sumark, in the moonlight. (I'm an incurable romantic!) She said, 'Yes.' We moved in together and became a couple.

I wrote to the Chief in Vanuatu asking if he would perform a traditional tribal wedding ceremony for us. I received a letter back after many weeks from him saying that he would be delighted to do this. He had taken kava with the men at the nakamal and spoken to Tamaffa asking for a blessing for us. The Chief said that Majikjiki had given him a secret name for Maggie, which he could not reveal until her grading ceremony prior to the wedding. Maggie told me that the Chief often came to her in her dreams and talked to her.

PART 4

NATU ELIN

18th December 2007
Tribal wedding requirements
	I received a letter from the High Chief which tells of the tribal wedding requirements, copied as written:
	'My brother, what I want to make you know about our traditional ways of custom married is I am asking you for these following items and goods, only for cooking for the people to come and support you as a High Chief and there is their food to eat like two cow? 10 bags of rice (25 kgs) relating to goods of cooking food or soup. Reason for why, we take two cows because the traditional way of kastom married man and woman should take cow both sides and inside the kastom married that will held inside our nakamal is need to take two pigs and 15 kava. Why is that, because kastom married is the biggest married that people come and see and dance and most interesting and that why the most people in our area wanted to support you as a High Chief and they respect you and know that they have another friend chief that he is the most High Chief with Chief Wai Wai and is from England. My brother, I have already found the two cow, the 15 kava and the two pigs.' He then gave the price for these.
	The Chief then went on to say that his wife Martha was very sick and asked me to connect to Tamaffa to help her and send healing, which I did.
May 2008
High Woman dead
	I received another letter from the Chief dated 25th April 2008. He said that Martha had died on 24th March from cancer. He was distraught. He spent the last four months in Port Vila hospital, then came back to Itabu with her to look after her and to allow her to die in her own home.
	He continued that the marriage ceremony for Maggie and me would still continue and that the ancestors had told him specifically that our wedding was to take place on Friday 19th September 2008. There were many parts to the kastom marriage ceremony that he would explain when we arrived. We could take part in other ceremonies and Maggie could do ceremonies with the women. 'The women,' he said, 'are already preparing her native dress.'
	We now began to make our travel arrangements and preparations.
1st September 2008
	We left the Isle of Man on schedule, spending the night in a hotel in Manchester Airport ready for our departure to Australia. I felt apprehensive, yet excited.
4th September 2008
Incompetent Travel Agent
	We arrived in Australia and went straight to our hotel. We went into the city to reconfirm our onward flight with Air Vanuatu but found that their office was empty. We went to a travel agent and asked them to look at our travel tickets and they informed us that the tickets we were given were not valid. We tried to ring several flight agents to get correct tickets and eventually we had to buy a complete set of new tickets ourselves, ringing a friend in the Isle of Man to put sufficient cash into our account to pay for the credit card transaction. It turned

out that the travel agent we had gone to in Ramsey was so incompetent that hardly any of our tickets or schedules were correct.

We spent the next few days trying to arrange our onward flights to Vanuatu and then Tanna Island. We had found that the flights which we had booked on Air Vanuatu were now on "Pacific Blue" and we couldn't reach them on the telephone. Frustrations built up as what should have been a wonderful preparatory wedding trip turned into a nightmare of reorganisation.

7th September 2008
Wedding ring

On the bright side, we found a jeweller that stocked real Australian gold. To have had a wedding ring custom-made for me from the gold of Australia was very important to me because it was reconnecting me to the lands of the South Pacific and to my first incarnation upon earth.

We bought some clothing and some gifts for the Chief and the tribe. I bought a large Bowie knife for the High Chief as a gift after the wedding.

8th September 2008
Island dress

We left Brisbane and arrived in Vanuatu on time. By the time we reached Vanuatu I was a nervous wreck. I was amazed to find that all the taxis were smart, clean and respectable. There were no more taxis that were battered, tattered and torn. It was such a disappointment, especially after I had told Maggie how exciting they were. We arrived at the hotel which we had booked only to find that we had no reservation. Every part of the journey from the Isle of Man to Vanuatu had been fraught with difficulty – none of the tickets had been honoured in any way, shape or form. We felt tired, drained and exhausted, but so glad to have at long last arrived.

The weather was very hot, humid and sticky. After leaving our bags at the hotel, we went quickly into town, where we looked for a suitable dress for Maggie to wear on her arrival in Tanna Island. I wanted her to arrive wearing the traditional "island dress" so that she would appear as equal to the women of the tribe. Eventually we found a nice dress in purple, blue and white, with hanging ribbons of purple. Maggie looked really beautiful in it.

9th September 2008
Prepare for grading ceremony   Martha's grave

We got a taxi to the airport to find that our flights to Tanna Island were still not booked after all the preparations that we had made and paid for in Brisbane. I felt we were never going to arrive at our final destination! Maggie had to go to an ATM machine and draw out some cash to pay for a second set of new tickets. I changed more money just in case we needed some cash when we got to Tanna Island.

As we arrived on Tanna Island, the Chief was waiting for us. We embraced tightly and he wept openly. Maggie wore the island dress and I introduced her proudly to the Chief and they embraced. The Chief looked a little embarrassed. Sam and Donald were waiting for us also. I saw Kelson at the airport. I was pleasant but diffident to him. He actually thanked me for coming home!

The Chief had hired David Hosea's truck and his driver, a young man called William, who was very gentle and spoke very good English. He had bad scars on his body from a fire in his house in Port Vila where he lost one of his children. We went into Lenakel to get some supplies. We met David Hosea, alias Chief Kahi, who said to Maggie that I was his son! I had already told her about the story of his lies. Maggie offered her hand to shake it and he made a point of squeezing her hand so hard that her fingers were bruised.

The rough roads were slippery from recent heavy rain. We both squeezed into the front of the truck with William. After a two hour drive we arrived at Itabu village, where I paid David Hosea for the truck and the Chief introduced Maggie to Jean who was to be her guide and interpreter. The Chief's wife, Martha who had died earlier in the year, left a vacant space within the Chief's life and community, since there was now no "Big Woman". The Chief explained that when Maggie went through her grading ceremony to receive her tribal name and tattoo, Donald's wife, Namu, would also receive the same mark and change her name.

It was also made clear to us that, without Maggie going through her grading ceremony to enable her to marry me, the wedding could not go ahead. No pressure there for her!

The Chief told us that she was to receive a tattoo, the grade mark of the tokka stick, an ancient symbol of the tribe representing many aspects of life, such as fertility, dancing and harvesting. It seems it was a multi-use tool for survival prior to the influx of the white man's tools. As Namu was now technically Big Woman, she would take her grading mark at the same time as Maggie so both are equal in rank, as I am equal in rank to the High Chief. When Maggie had undertaken the grading ceremony, she would no longer be known as Maggie but Natu Elin. The Chief explained what this meant – Natu means high and Elin means good woman. Natu was the name Maggie would be known by after the grading ceremony.

Maggie stayed with Jean and the other women whilst I went with the Chief and others to the nakamal with kava roots. At the nakamal, the old hut had disappeared that we used to shelter in and to change into our nambas, and most people, especially the men, now seemed to have mobile phones which absolutely horrified me. I felt sad that these people had succumbed to the Western plague of constant noise and nuisance value, yet to them it was an exciting new toy and a wonderful tool. When a phone rang, everybody ran to see what the excitement was about and to share in the conversation, writing given numbers in the earth with the point of a stick or a bush knife, hoping that somebody's foot wouldn't scuff it out. The elders did not seem to approve, especially at the nakamal, where a phone rang during the rite of preparation for the kava and prayers.

Since Martha had died, the children seemed less disciplined and more noisy at nights. I asked the Chief why his hair was still short, since he had told me that he would grow it as long as he could after the last time we spoke. He said he had to cut it short to honour the memory of Martha, which is a bereavement process that lasts for at least one year. It also meant that we couldn't do many of the ceremonies as planned because of this mourning period. The Chief was not happy with my short beard, saying, 'Not good,' patting my face. The higher the grade, the bigger the beard!

On the way to the nakamal, we passed through the homestead of Donald and his family, where the Chief now lived. His old home with Martha was abandoned and had been taken back by the encroaching jungle.

We stopped at the site of a fresh grave. A few golden marigolds were in flower in stark contrast to the black volcanic earth. The grave was fenced off at the end of a leaf hut, which I presumed was where the Chief now lived? The two of us stood in silence and I then spoke a few words of how I remembered her. This seemed important to the Chief. I saw tears rolling down his face.

At the nakamal he explained to me that the body is put into the earth a distance from the actual grave site because it is seen as taboo to look upon the dead. Burial rites in Tanna are different to some places, such as Papua, New Guinea and the Solomon Islands, where the skulls of the dead, especially the higher grades, are put in caves to look over the village to ward off evil. The Chief said that in Tanna the body must be buried deeply and concealed, one of the reasons being to stop the pigs digging it up to eat. The Chief explained that, now I had returned home and had spoken to Martha, it was very important that a pig was killed in ceremony to honour her spirit and the homecoming of Iarueri.

The boys and dogs were despatched after a small black pig into the jungle to the sounds of serious grunts and screams from the pig's angry mother! The dogs and boys leapt back into the safety of the nakamal pursued by the angry sow. They were looking back over their shoulders as they fled. I had a job to stop laughing! Eventually more boys and dogs were rounded up and put on the job and the small pig was captured and brought for the ceremony.

The small pig was brought to Martha's graveside and clubbed to death, allowing the blood to seep into the dark earth. The pig was then taken to the nakamal to be butchered, its organs and meat impaled on sticks pushed into the ground to cook over the fire. The blood and fat crackled and spat as they dripped into the flames.

Other men were gathering at the nakamal and greeted me as long lost brothers. It was so good to see them again – my old friends. Many had moved on, the Chief had explained, to Vila or to their villages in other parts of the island or to Lenakel. Sam and the Chief explained more about the wedding ceremony which, I thought, would now take place earlier than planned? The date seemed to be variable depending upon circumstances. I hoped it would be on the full moon on the 15th.

The Chief said that the word was being spread to the different chiefs in the area to assist in the preparations and for the people to come to the feast. We would all have our faces painted. Maggie's face would be painted differently to show her grade; no-one else was entitled to have these markings, or mine.

When the kava was prepared it was offered to the Chief and me together. We stood facing west as usual, left hand by our sides, holding the coconut cup to our lips with the right hand. We quaffed the contents, throwing the sediment to the ground and spraying out the last mouthful, shouting Tamaffa. Then we prayed aloud for a blessing for Martha and the forthcoming ceremonies. I drank water afterwards; then we had a portion of the cooked meat from the fire. I was given some of the liver, burnt on the outside, raw on the inside. I was called for my second cup of kava. This time, when all were still and quiet, we drank and sprayed but remained silent.

I returned to my log by the fire, rubbing my bare feet in the warm ashes, as I was cold. I was given some pig heart and island cabbage to eat.

10th September 2008

Lap lap   Bull for the feast   Spirit pig stone

It rained heavily during the night. The drumming of the rain on the palm frond thatch mingled with the cicadas singing and the volcano booming made my heart sing. It rained in the day also. I gave the Chief the necessary money to buy the beasts and other provisions for the feast. Before he and the men went off to Lenakel to buy what was needed, the Chief arranged for us to go to Nikwei's village to see the trance dancing and healing. Nikwei had returned to his old ways in defiance of the Chief's instructions. Nikwei's mother was the principal trance dancer and healer. After the singing and dancing, Nikwei gave Maggie a boar's tusk necklace and he gave me another carving of a man wearing nambas. We walked back to Itabu in the rain. Jean explained that Nikwei was stubborn.

The Chief had organised that Jean and Namu would show Maggie how to prepare and make their traditional dish of lap lap in an earth oven. The women were not quite ready so we both had a rest for a short time.

Jean called for Maggie and they went off to do women's work. I was called some time afterwards to see how they were getting on and we were shown a miniature version of preparing the small earth oven, using volcanic stones heated in the fire. The women used split sticks to move the hot, smouldering, tennis ball sized stones and Maggie and Jean finished off their lap lap, then wrapped it in banana leaves.

After lunch, the Chief and men arrived from their spending spree and told us that, instead of buying two small cows which is their tradition, one each from the groom and bride, he had decided to buy a young bull of superior quality, which was a better buy. Jack and the others walked the bull back to Itabu, a journey that took all afternoon and all night.

After lunch, Maggie and I returned to participate in the cooking of the lap lap and covering the earth oven with soil. At 4:00 pm I went to the nakamal with the Chief to take kava with the men. It poured down with rain so the Chief and I sprinted the last hundred yards, sheltering under the banyan tree. The men and boys sat around preparing the kava root, as usual. Then a package arrived from the kitchen containing the lap lap that Maggie had made. The Chief was very proud of this and made a point of letting everybody know who had made it.

The rain eased and, as usual, the Chief and I drank the kava first but this time, instead of facing west, we faced north to the volcano. I was reminded again that the reason the people do not talk after dark, or at least whisper, is to honour the spirit of the night. Tonight, prior to the kava ritual, the Chief took me to the place by the banyan tree, containing the sacred stones for the flying fox.

This area is taboo for all others to go into. The Chief wanted me to repay my respects to this place as a guardian of these stones.

Also, something I had not known about before was that amongst the small rugby ball sized stones for the flying fox was a flat stone I had never seen before, which the Chief explained was a sacred spirit stone for the pig. I asked the Chief if he was also the guardian of the pig and he said that he was, but I was not. The pig is the most important animal in their culture so whoever holds the pig stone is the most important chief. The Chief explained that the pig stone he held was the highest grade and that other chiefs also can sometimes have a pig stone. The Chief further explained the way to contact the spirit of the pig is that you get a certain magical leaf and roll it between your palms, then place it on to the pig stone. Then you drink kava and call Tamaffa. The pig spirit then comes out of the forest into the nakamal. The Chief reminded me that the things he was telling me were secret and that no other white man had been shown these stones or told their mystery and magic. What I am revealing is permitted.

11th September 2008

Volcano ceremony   Rooster sacrifice   Injured child

I woke early and heard the bull calling, which had arrived in the early hours from its marathon hike overnight from Lenakel. We both heard it calling near our leaf hut where it was tethered and we both felt sad, since we knew it was to be slaughtered for our wedding feast.

We had a breakfast of bread, tomatoes and coffee which were fresh from Lenakel the day before. The Chief came to talk to us and explained that, as soon as the smoke from the volcano could be seen from the village, the weather would be suitable for us to go up to the volcano crater to speak to Yasur. The Chief and others were constructing a new kitchen for the wedding feast to enable the cooks, both men and women, to have shelter.

A young man climbed a palm tree and cut down palm leaves for the women to weave into mats, baskets and plates. We watched the women prepare taro and weave the palm leaves into thatching for the kitchen roof.

The Chief informed me he wanted me to do a public ceremony to connect Maggie to the volcano which the Chief explained was part of the marriage process. The Chief wanted to be a participant also, so the villagers who were preparing for the feast were invited to observe. Women are allowed at the nakamal during the day only. I instructed a boy to fetch wood and constructed a medicine wheel in the Celtic style, placing the elements in the four quarters, plus four quartz stones from the previous ceremonies, which the Chief had given to me after getting a small fire burning in the north. A smoking fire stick was placed in the east, a stone in the south and a coconut bowl of water in the west. I smudged the Chief and Maggie as they entered the circle and Maggie smudged me. I asked permission to sing to Yasur and to connect to him, which was given. Maggie felt the connection to Yasur in her heart, she said, and went into a magical space. We thanked the guardians and closed the circle.

The rain and low cloud remained for the rest of the morning so we had lunch, which was green beans, tuna, onions, sweet potato and taro. I was still confused as to when the ceremony would take place, as different dates had been suggested. It must have depended on circumstances and the logistics of getting everything organised or the Chief knew that the time was not right for whatever reason?

So many people were preparing and helping for the feasts and celebrations, it was awesome to know that these folk were doing all this for our wedding ceremony. Everybody seemed happy and they were talking about the forthcoming event as word spread. I think it had given the local people something to talk about.

We still could not see the smoke from the volcano because of low cloud so Maggie went off with the women to make more lap lap in the earth oven. I was called later by Jean to witness their hard work!

We returned to the hut and soon afterwards the Chief appeared with a big rooster under his arm. I went out to talk to him and he explained it was very important that Maggie touched or caressed the rooster before it was killed as an offering to Yasur, or rather the guardian of the volcano. Nahu was called and given the rooster and she and Maggie went off to the kitchens to do the necessary, while the Chief and I went off to the nakamal to meet the other men and to take kava.

Maggie told me afterwards that it was very difficult to eyeball a chicken and then see its head chopped off.

A boy came into the nakamal with a leaf package which he gave to the Chief. The Chief smiled and unwrapped it, offering it to the men with obvious pride that this was the lap lap Maggie had cooked again. The men had erected a temporary wooden framework at the nakamal, which had a blue tarpaulin tied over it. During the heavy rain, it gave temporary relief from being soaked as long as you were not sitting directly under the myriad of holes. At least it kept us out of the wind and sheltered the fire.

Again after the kava ritual, I returned to our hut. Sam, who escorted me, left with the usual cheery, 'Good night, Chief.' Jean came to the hut and called us to have dinner. She had her small son with her, who had a cut face across the nose and cheek; he had been pushed down the steepest slope of the volcano's ear pit hitting his face on a large outcrop of stone. Donald's son, Wai Wai, was the culprit. It seemed that Wai Wai, the young lad whom I helped to heal as a toddler, was a bully and a mischief in the village. He had now become the naughty boy of the family. Jean's son's face was swollen and I thought he might have a broken nose. Maggie brought out the medication we had purchased in Brisbane and tended to the child, who sat on Jean's lap.

12th September 2008
Volcano Guardian   Forgot knickers   Lava bombs

We washed some clothes at dawn in a bowl of water and had breakfast. Jean brought her son back to see Maggie again for some more treatment on his face. Maggie did some craniosacral work to release any compression in his skull.

The weather was suitable today to go up to the volcano so Donald, Enoch and a small boy set off with us. We paid our entrance fee at the gate and began the ascent. Maggie struggled at times; it was hot, humid and a steep climb at almost midday. We stood at the side of the track about three-quarters of the way up to let a truck carrying tourists pass. It was driven by William, who stopped the vehicle and offered us a lift. We declined but thanked him for his courteousness. Interestingly, as the truck began to set off up the steep track, its wheels began to spin in the earth and the whole stretch of road for some time afterwards began to give off volcanic steam and gases which were definitely not apparent prior to the truck's arrival. We realised that the road was a thin crust covering the magma beneath our feet!

As we climbed, Donald explained to us that his father, the High Chief, was in charge of 13 to 15 villages and many people. He said that Yasur volcano is actually owned by his father and Donald emphasised to me that, as his father was my "brother", I was also the volcano's kastom guardian with him. He explained that many generations ago a group of greedy chiefs from the other side of the volcano at Sulphur Bay told officials the volcano belonged to them and sold it to the government, thereby cutting out the rightful kastom lineage of the Chief's descendants and his family now. The Chief receives no income whatsoever from the tourists that climb to its crater. In fact, the guardian of the volcano told the Chief that it does not like or want tourists coming up to its face. The kastom men do not like it at all, feeling that it is disrespectful. Traditionally ceremony was carried out to get permission to go up to the volcano for any specific reason.

Donald showed us some kastom medicine plants on our journey. One in particular was good for the runs. I thought that we must remember that one.

A volcanologist was monitoring the volcano for a few days and he had his equipment at its base and elsewhere. About three-quarters of the way up Maggie turned to speak and I expected some profound words of wisdom about how beautiful or powerful the volcano was, but all she said was, 'I do wish I had remembered to put my knickers on.' That's my girl! We arrived at the crater's rim, Maggie glowing seductively – or as she put it 'hotter than the crater and twice as red!'

The cycle of the volcano was quiet at that time of year but the Chief told me prior to our departure that he would do sacred ceremony to make the volcano active for us. This was one of the reasons the chicken was offered last night, he said. We were not disappointed. Yasur was active, throwing up lava bombs and giving a few very loud bangs unexpectedly that made us jump out of our skins. We connected to Yasur but were unable to go to the far side, where we could look directly into the crater, because the wind was too strong, blowing ash and smoke horizontally. This meant we could not see the lava bombs if they came in our direction, so it was deemed too dangerous. We stayed on the southern rim. Even so, as Maggie had never been to a volcano before, she was thrilled.

We returned to Itabu, Maggie striding ahead going downhill. Upon our arrival, Jean brought her son to us for some more treatment. We had a rest and then ate lunch.

The Chief went to Lenakel again with the men to get more supplies for the feast, especially kava, rice and taro. The women were preparing for the wedding feast for the whole day. Today they were still weaving mats from palm leaves, which were also used to create the walls of the kitchen.

At 4 o'clock I went to the nakamal with the men as usual. For some reason, the Chief, Nikwei and I have not worn nambas. The Chief seemed lost in a sense now his wife had died since she seemed to organise much for him. Maybe not wearing nambas was part of the bereavement process to honour her spirit? There were 12 of us at the nakamal tonight. I had specifically bought some pipes and tobacco as gifts, so now I gave Donald and Nikwei a pipe each and some tobacco. They shared them amongst the other men. One of the elders, who had an injured right ankle tied in a dirty bandage, took the pipe, turning it over and over in his hands slowly, his face lit and smiling at its beauty and symmetry. He shouted, 'Nambah One!' He savoured the fact that he was permitted to have the first smoke of a new pipe. This gave him great status.

The Chief was still not back from Lenakel so I drank kava alongside Nikwei, this time facing west. We had roasted banana and then my second cup of kava. In my meditative state, I saw Majikjiki at a tribal dance, which I presumed was the tokka but later found it to be the napen napen dance when I explained it to the Chief once he arrived.

13th September 2008
Jungle hike   Bat caves   Downpour

The dogs barked all night and kept us awake. At 6:30 in the morning, we heard a woman sobbing loudly in the village and other voices were consoling her. We went for a cold shower in the newly constructed bamboo hut before breakfast at 7:00. The Chief came to talk to us and I asked him what was wrong with the woman who was crying but he changed the subject. The Chief asked if there was any particular place we wanted to visit so I suggested Shark Bay, but the Chief said it was too cloudy and you needed bright sunshine to see the sharks in the bay below the cliff. The Chief suggested that we went to see the bat cave, which was good as we could see some huge banyan trees en route.

Jean and a young girl were our guides; the girl carried our bottle of water. Maggie asked Jean what the problem was with the woman who was sobbing earlier in the morning and Jean said that it was the Chief's sister who had been told by some men that she was not needed to help prepare the wedding feast. She was broken-hearted and came to the Chief to ask why. The Chief told her this was not the case and organised work for her to do.

I had been to the bat cave before so knew Maggie would love it. However, we passed the path leading to this cave and continued further up the road, turning off at a different track. Jean didn't know the path to the cave so it turned out she was taking us to a village for us to get a guide.

I recognised the track but knew we were not on the right road until I realised that we were going to a different cave, which was a long way away, not nearby as I had told Maggie. The hike became long and tiring, especially for Maggie, who struggled going up the steep, slippery jungle paths, but was fine on the flat and going down, although she wasn't happy on the equally steep descending paths as we traversed each ravine. Maggie realised afterwards, she told me, that even with her heart palpitations causing her to stop and rest, making her feel ashamed and inadequate before us all, it was actually another test for her which brought up feelings of anger at not being able to keep up. We kept waiting for her and Jean kept saying, 'Slow, Maggie, slow.' I kept reassuring and encouraging her.

Eventually we reached a village and I recognised the area, having travelled this path before but from the other direction. We had to pay for the guide, a woman who spoke only French. As Maggie spoke a little French, this gave her some status in the party as nobody else did. The two native women spoke Bislama with each other and it was interesting to hear Jean tell the other woman all about the wedding preparations and the cost of the bull, to the other woman's tut-tut of amazement. Even though we could not speak Bislama, we could understand what was conveyed.

The climb was long and arduous again, Maggie looking at me in total frustration and pain. She was angry with herself, more than me, for holding up the party by having to take rests. Some of the paths were dangerous and very slippery again, going down almost vertically in places. Some of these paths never even saw the sunlight; they were in total shade. I wanted to hold Maggie close and comfort her, but this would have been inappropriate before the other women, as they do not show affection openly in their culture. In fairness, I had told her that the bat cave was an hour's walk and, by this time, we had already been hiking straight up for two hours.

We descended eventually into a river bed with a few puddles in it. As it was the dry season, there was not much water running. In the wet season, a torrent would fill the gorge. The guide picked some fern leaves for us and instructed us to place them on a particular large stone, which had a ledge on it, as an offering to the spirit of the cave to let it know we were coming and to introduce ourselves with our intent. This was a tribal kastom stone. We then had a very steep climb up to the bat cave. The last time I was here, the cave entrance was full of tree debris from Cyclone Ivy. I had told the men to clear it out for the tourists, which they had obviously done. The cave had no bats in it then and seemed to be all silted up. It was not silted up now, the men had cleared it and it was now full of bats.

This was the original site where Yasur volcano erupted above the ground. We passed beneath an archway of solidified lava which had within its centre point a blow hole. This opened up into a womb-like area which led to the cave. This was the place of the feminine energy, whereas the volcano was male energy. We stooped to pass into the entrance of the cave and, with a couple of torches (their batteries almost spent), we saw the bats wheeling about and clinging to the cave roof.

We then returned to the guide's village, where we rested under a tree. Strangely, Maggie was able to climb back without any problems whatsoever. It seemed as though she had regained her strength with the grace of Spirit. The guide sent off three boys to find some coconuts for us to drink from. They returned after about 15 minutes with three coconuts, which the guide cut open at the top with a machete. We were thankful to drink the milk and eat the flesh. The guide sent one of the boys into the village to get a bamboo tube containing some feather sticks. We thought they were gifts but then realised she wanted payment for them. Not having the right amount of small change, she received a note far in excess of the value of the feather sticks, but they were beautiful.

The sky began to darken and raindrops began to fall so we decided to go, leaving the guide behind in the village. The rain soon became torrential, soaking us all to the skin. Maggie began to laugh and the reason was, she told me later, that she had asked the universe for a cold shower to cool her down, so she got what she asked for. How about that for manifestation! The young girl accompanying us slipped and fell as we descended down a steep track. She burst out laughing. Jean picked a taro leaf and covered her new mobile phone. This was a kastom phone cover!

We arrived back at Itabu like drowned rodents but had a cold shower and changed into dry clothes. Jean said she was glad the hike was over, as she was so tired. This heartened Maggie no end since, by the time we had arrived back at Itabu, Maggie was bouncing along at full speed. I knew that Jean would report back to the Chief.

We went for lunch, which was tuna, cabbage, onions, carrots and rice, with a hot drink. It continued to rain heavily for the rest of the day. Just before dusk, the Chief and I went to the nakamal, having to sprint the last leg of the way to get under shelter. It always amazed me that, no matter how heavy the rain was, the locals would stand or sit outside in their clothes getting absolutely soaked, yet not seemingly bothered about it at all. I found the rain to be very cold and uncomfortable. I sat by the fire at the edge of the tarpaulin with the elders, who spat into the flames as they turned roasting taro covered in red hot embers with their fingers. Smoke had the same effect to their eyes as mine, yet they seemed to recover from the stinging and watering far more quickly. The Chief saw I was getting nicely wet under the leaking tarpaulin so he called me over to the shelter of the banyan tree, where I cowered under the matted roots formed into a rough roof which was far more effective than the tarpaulin.

I watched the nightly ritual of preparing the kava unfold, which always fascinated me. The boys and men sat out in the open of the nakamal in the pouring rain. Donald, Jack and Enoch had earlier gone hunting in the forest with dogs for a wild boar which was now being prepared and cooked over the fire.

Again, during the kava ritual, the Chief and I faced north towards the volcano to drink; then he instructed me to return to the fire. As is customary after kava, I had a morsel to eat, never before. The Chief instructed the men to give me flesh, not offal, on this occasion and also water taro. After my second cup of kava, I felt nauseous, dizzy and ready to fall off my log. This time I was the only man having two cups of kava; I didn't know why. This meant I had to perform the drinking ritual alone in front of the Chief and the men. Another subtle test perhaps?

As I sat swaying on my log by the fire, the Chief ventured across the nakamal, holding a leaf in his palm. It contained salt and he gave it to me to sprinkle upon the meat. I had never seen this done before or been told to do it. After I had done this to a particular piece of meat pointed out to me, the Chief pulled at the meat in the flames and cut off a portion with his bush knife, wrapping a leaf around it for me to hold to prevent my fingers getting burnt. It was very hot, charred on the outside, raw in the middle. It was important to the Chief that I ate it there and then.

Sam then arrived from the village kitchen carrying a large, battered aluminium bowl on his head full of steaming, boiled manioc and this was put by the fire for the men to feast upon. They used small, sharp sticks to pierce the white root vegetable, as it was too hot to hold and it was the kastom way to eat, transferring the cooked food on to a leaf platter.

The Chief gave me more meat from the same leg I had sprinkled salt upon and he insisted I was to give it to Maggie, which she must eat. The Chief instructed Sam to see me safely back to our leaf hut. The Chief soon arrived after me and said we were not to go to the "restaurant" as normal but from now on we were to eat with the family. Sam guided us up to the newly constructed kitchen, made especially for the wedding feast, and we ate the same food as the family, although we did sit apart from the adults. We were placed with the children where the fire and the cooking pots were. Maybe we were babysitting by stealth?

The coconut leaf mats that had been woven during the day by the women were on the floor and made the sides of the kitchen. Plates were also made of woven leaves, stacked in a pile near the doorway. I suppose "baskets" would describe these better. Sam came to sit with us and explained that a large flat leaf would be placed in the bottom of these platters to put the food on, covering the holes.

We were in bed by 7:00 pm. Torrential rain all night, dripping through the thatch on to the bed. Ants had decided that Maggie's videorecorder was an ideal home so were using the inbuilt microphone and speaker as their exit and entry points. We put the camcorder into a sealed plastic bag hoping this would force the ants to come out of the inner workings of the camera.

14th September 2008
Mark of High Chief   Grading ceremony   Calling ancestors

Torrential rain caused flooding and erosion everywhere, washing away paths and roads. During breakfast, Donald brought in a conch shell to show us and explained how they cut off the end to blow it and, by using the voice, to create a "rise and fall" sound, indicating that a circumcision ceremony had been performed and that kava and pig were available to feast upon.

The Chief came to our leaf hut and informed us that the naming and tattoo ceremony would take place for Maggie and Namu in the afternoon. Maggie seemed concerned about performing the ceremony in the pouring rain but the Chief just smiled. I explained to Maggie that the Chief would do a ritual with the rain and sun stones to change the weather. She looked at me disbelievingly. The Chief went on to explain that he and I with the other men would take kava and speak to Tamaffa beforehand. Maggie was beginning to get apprehensive now!

After lunch, the women gathered up their colourful grass skirts and lengths of floral calico cloth, along with the pungent Majikjiki herb. The rain had stopped now and the earth steamed as the sun dried out the dampness.

Maggie was amazed and very impressed but mainly thinking of the wonder that indigenous people still retained the awareness and knowledge of how to communicate and work harmoniously with nature.

The Chief called to us and told us it was time to start the ceremony. He carried into the village square taro and kava. Nahu came with the other women to collect Maggie and prepare her for her initiation. For some reason, she was going through the ceremony with Maggie and not Namu. We asked the Chief about this and he said Namu would do the ceremony later. Sam asked Maggie for three sewing needles for the tattooing because he had forgotten his.

Maggie put on her "island dress" but the Chief asked her to change this into a long skirt and top. After Maggie had done this, she went off with the excited, chattering women to be prepared. The Chief said that this was women's secret work. I felt sad for him because I knew that, had Martha not died a few months ago, she would have overseen all these preparations and held a space as Big Woman. The impression I got was that Namu and Nahu were going to share the position of Big Woman until Donald finally took the position as High Chief.

After a while, Nahu and Maggie emerged with their faces painted, feather sticks in their hair and with grass skirts on, floral calico material draped over their chests and left arms, to leave the right upper arms bare, where the tattoos would be. Nahu wore the feather sticks we had bought from the guide at the bat caves. Both women wore the sacred leaves of Majikjiki on their left arms, with a coronet and necklace of sacred leaves. They both looked very beautiful. I felt so proud of Maggie.

The Chief told me to tell Maggie that, when the men arrived carrying the pig, it was time for the women to go to the lower nakamal for the ceremony. As he spoke, Donald and the men appeared out of the jungle carrying a sow, hanging from a pole, in the traditional manner, over their shoulders. The Chief told me to hurry and we both ran down the track, cutting through the forest to enable us to get to the men's shelter at the back of the banyan tree leading into the nakamal. Donald and the other men arrived soon afterwards. We all undressed, putting on our nambas. I felt apprehensive since this was the first time the Chief and men would see my tattoo, redone in Australia. The Chief studied the tattoo carefully and said, 'This is very good.' I felt so relieved. The men helped to prepare me. The Chief tied my nambas on around my waist, but it wasn't tight enough so Donald stepped in and, together, they tightened it more, catching my belly skin in the knot. I yelped! They didn't want it falling off in front of the women. They put on my sacred armbands to Majikjiki and my coronet and necklace. Then the men helped the Chief to prepare. Donald had the soot and charcoal powder prepared in a leaf, adding saliva to it to mix into a paste. This was rubbed across my brow with his thumb and the same mark upon the brow of his father, the Chief.

The Chief looked at me earnestly and spoke, 'Iarueri. I give you my power as High Chief.'

We then lined up, myself behind the Chief, Donald behind me, followed by the others, in a procession through the banyan tree into the centre of the nakamal, where Maggie and Nahu waited next to the pig, taro and kava. The women from the village sat around the perimeter on the far side, the men under the banyan tree. The Chief positioned Maggie and Nahu to one side of the pig, taro and kava and he and I stood on the other side. The Chief said this was a secret ceremony so I didn't bring my camera but, as we stood there, he said it was fine to take photos. So he despatched Sam to bring my camera from the shelter behind the banyan tree and I instructed Sam how to use it, hoping he wouldn't cut off too many legs or heads in the photos.

Then we stood, shoulder to shoulder, the women on our left, whilst the Chief picked up a club to kill the pig before us, as an offering. Maggie looked away. The blood spattered on the Chief's and my feet, as the life force of the pig drained into the dark earth. The dogs drank the hot blood as it gushed out of the pig's ears and skull.

The Chief spoke to the assembled villagers, saying that he gave his power to me and that, after the grading ceremony, Maggie would be known as Natu. The Chief invoked the God Majikjiki as he raised his right hand before Maggie and Nahu and spoke to the ancestors. He then formally gave Maggie her tribal name and a new tribal name to Nahu, which she confessed to Maggie afterwards she didn't like, so she would not use it. Women are women everywhere! The Chief asked me to speak to the assembled guests, which I did, thanking them for the privilege of accepting Natu and I into their family.

The Chief and I left the nakamal and passed through the banyan tree to the men's shelter, where we removed our tribal attire and got dressed in our Western clothing. We returned to fulfil the tattoo part of the ceremony. Natu and Nahu sat on bamboo poles at the edge of the nakamal, looking a little worried as Sam bound three needles together with red thread.

Maggie had asked me in the morning if the tattoo hurt, so I said, 'Not really.' However, when I had my tattoo done three years ago by Sam, the needles were blunt; these were now new, sharp needles. Natu was the first initiate and Sam drew the shape of the tokka stick upon her right upper arm, the sacred symbol of power, authority and fertility. He borrowed one of my ballpoint pens to do this. Sam had never tattooed a white woman before, so he was a bit nervous. He held Natu's arm tightly; then began to stab the skin with the needles, following the outline of the tokka stick until the blood oozed to the surface. Natu looked straight ahead and never flinched or complained. It was obviously painful and I felt extremely proud of her.

After the outline was made in oozing blood, Sam opened a leaf package containing a mixture of fine charcoal, lamp soot and the juices of the pumpkin leaf and a purple leaf, unidentified. He mixed this into a black paste and then rubbed this into the bleeding wound. Then he took up the needles again, puncturing the skin over the charcoal mix to push it further into the wound. This process was even worse. More charcoal mixture was added to seal the wound, with instructions to Natu that she was not to wash for three days and three nights.

Natu was now fully initiated as a kastom woman and upgraded to marry a High Chief. She looked at me as much as to say, 'Just you wait till I get you back to my hut.'

Sam then began the same process with Nahu but this time the blood trickled down her arm. The Chief wiped the blood away with his thumb.

During Nahu's grading the men had hung the pig up on a branch at the edge of the nakamal, next to the banyan tree, and started a fire from a fire stick. They were singeing the hair off the pig, burning the dead skin away with palm fronds. On one occasion, the pig caught alight, causing the men to step back and fall about laughing. The pig was then butchered and some taken to the kitchen and some to the upper nakamal.

After the ceremony, the women changed and Natu went to the kitchen with the other women and I went to the upper nakamal with the Chief and men for the conclusion of the grading ceremony. Kava had to be drunk to celebrate the ceremony and to honour the spirit of place, Tamaffa, and to the God Majikjiki. Meat from the pig was skewered onto pointed sticks, leaning over the fire to cook.

The Chief addressed the assembled men and boys, as they prepared the kava, telling them what had occurred during the grading ceremony and what was said by him and myself. When the kava was prepared, the Chief and I were called forward by Donald. We stood side by side, facing the volcano, to drink the kava. We said our prayers to Yasur and the ancestors to give thanks for the ceremony and for the blessings upon Natu and Nahu. Again, for some unknown reason, I was called forward to take a second cup of kava, to perform this rite alone before the men. This time it was very strong. I felt ill. The men told me that you drink strong kava after an important ceremony. I could hardly focus and staggered back to my log by the side of the fire, my head spinning, my bare feet in the ashes of the fire to keep warm in the chill evening air.

The flying foxes circled silently overhead; in the dusk, the cicadas sang in unison with such a loud piercing sound it almost hurt my ears. Yasur grumbled in the background. Again, I was given a particular spike of meat to look after and this, I was told, was for me and Natu to share. As we sat around the fire, dripping pig fat exploded in the crackling flames. An elder stood silently and went to the northern perimeter to face the volcano and began to call in the ancestors in their traditional way, a type of yodelling. It was hauntingly beautiful and usually only done after an important ceremony. I gazed into the night sky at the myriad of stars. Everyone was still and silent in prayer.

The Chief came to me and whispered, 'I give to you the power to call in the ancestors now.' This was a great privilege for me to be permitted to open the portal to the Spirit World using my voice.

Sam then arrived carrying a large, crumpled aluminium pot full of boiled taro and pig meat for all to feast. The Chief instructed Sam to escort me back to my leaf hut, carrying with him the spike of meat for Natu. The Chief said again that it was very important that Natu ate the meat, as it was cooked in ceremony for both of us to share. We left some of the meat on the earth for the spirit of place outside our hut as an offering to give thanks, which the dogs quickly found and consumed. Natu struggled with eating it, as she had become ill soon after the grading ceremony and felt nauseous, with diarrhoea.

Natu said that, after the grading ceremony, a bird of prey had circled the village three times very low where she had stood with Nahu, then flew off towards the volcano. This was very significant. I told the Chief about this the following day and he said he had called the eagles of the volcano during the Tamaffa kava rite the evening before for their presence to bless Natu and Nahu after the ceremony. Neither of us knew about this until afterwards. This again was proof of the work of Spirit.

We went to the "restaurant" for the usual meal. Natu was not well at all, so couldn't eat much. When we arrived back at our leaf hut, Natu had severe abdominal cramps and explosive diarrhoea. She was off to the toilet at regular intervals during the night with her trusty torch. It was a full moon and a clear sky.

15th September 2008
Natu sick

Natu was not well at all today. She still had abdominal cramps and the runs and couldn't eat anything so was fasting for 24 hours to clear out her system. Her tattoo wound looked inflamed and swollen. Natu said that she needed to sleep and rest. After one and a half hours, I began to get concerned, as Natu looked very ill. I called Donald and told him about Natu and her sickness. He came to see her and asked her if she wanted him to make some kastom medicine for her, to which she agreed since it was our wedding day tomorrow.

Donald returned after half an hour with a plastic bottle filled with a dark brown liquid with sediment at the bottom, which he gave to Natu to drink. Natu looked at it hesitatingly, so I tried some in front of Donald. It tasted like liquid mud. Natu drank some. I became sick later on. Both of us were ill for the remainder of the day and night – nausea, diarrhoea, headache, abdominal cramps and insomnia. I couldn't eat lunch so I knew I was going to have a problem at the nakamal in the evening at kava time.

I went to the nakamal at the appointed time. There were about 22 men present, so the Chief came round to each man with a fern leaf and gave each a piece of the frond as a counting aid. When you had your kava, you handed in your portion of leaf. This way, he knew that everybody had had their drink. I sat at my usual place at the fire, coconuts roasting in the embers which glowed in the dim light of the evening. After the kava ritual, I was given some roasted coconut flesh, which smelled and tasted like soap.

Again, for some reason I could not understand, I was the only man to have two cups of kava. I returned to the fire, feeling very nauseous and exceedingly dizzy. I had an empty stomach, because I had had no lunch, so had great difficulty in not falling off my log and projectile vomiting.

As I left the nakamal to return to my hut, I was aware that I was staggering behind Sam, as if I were drunk with alcohol. I felt wretched and sat on the edge of the bed wondering which end was going to explode first. Natu looked very sick. Neither of us could eat our evening meal. We were both very ill all night, Natu making several forays by torchlight to the latrine. I prayed to the Goddess and to Spirit, to Majikjiki, for help on the most important day of our lives tomorrow. In fact, to be honest, I swore at Spirit for allowing the sickness to spoil these rare days with the tribe.

16th September 2008

Tribal wedding   Spring dancing   Bull slaughtered

This was our wedding day. At 6:00 am, the tam tam was sounded in a particular rhythm to inform the people that the wedding ceremony was going to take place today. Both of us looked and felt dreadful. Natu had the runs badly. We were told to have our breakfast, which was crackers, a bit like dog biscuits, tomato and cucumber. Natu couldn't eat anything. I felt concerned that she was losing weight rapidly and getting weak.

The day was sunny with a cloudy sky. People bustled busily, preparing in a state of excitement. We were both moved deeply by the trouble and the hard work of the villagers over many weeks for our marriage ceremony. The women came for Natu to prepare her. Natu looked worried, as she needed the toilet at regular intervals.

Natu went off with the giggling women to get her face painted and dressed as my bride. I was called to go around the back of the hut with the men, where they helped me prepare. We were not permitted to see each other at this stage. The men wore traditional lava-lava, a kind of sarong. They put one around my waist and then Nikwei began to paint my face in the shape of a chalice. A large black triangle, point downward, was painted across my forehead and down the front of my nose. On either side of this was a line of red and then a line of blue; then across my upper lip, two black marks. The paint they used was a powder mix that was blended into a coconut oil base which they obtained from a store in Lenakel. They now tend to use this sort of paint for body art instead of using traditional herbal or clay pigments. Nikwei, the Chief and Donald had single lines across their brow. Nikwei's was blue. I had a coronet and necklace of leaves and a coconut shell bangle was placed on my right arm containing fresh Majikjiki's herbs. A red feather stick was put in my hair but, because my hair was fine and not tight and curly as the islanders, it would not stay upright so stuck out like a unicorn's horn.

We had to wait some time as word had come back that the women were not yet ready. I gave Sam my camera and he went off to the women's camp to take photos – brave soul! Meanwhile, in the centre of the village square, a mound of taro had been brought and, on top of that, a selection of hand-made woven pandanus leaf mats, symbolic of making a home. When the women were ready they came down the hill escorted by the warriors, carrying kava and a live pig slung from a pole over two men's shoulders. The pig was placed upon the ground by the pile of taro and mats, alongside the kava roots. Donald clubbed the pig to death before Natu and the women on the instructions of the High Chief.

In the meantime, I was escorted into a hut by Nikwei at the edge of the village square. Inside sat Chief Naknow. I sat next to him, then Nikwei sat on my right. These were our witnesses for the wedding ceremony.

In the village square, the Chief was explaining to Natu what he was going to do and what was expected of her. Then he took her by the hand, leading her around the pile of provisions for the home in an anti-clockwise direction. Then he led her to the leaf hut where I waited for her with the two witnesses. Natu looked so beautiful as she approached the hut with her bridesmaids. She wore a multi-coloured grass skirt over her brown skirt and, around her top, a red and white floral calico top that could be used as a lava-lava. Around her head, neck and waist and upon her right arm were various herbs. In her hair, she wore two multi-coloured feather sticks. Her face was beautifully painted. The other women looked magnificent also. Nahu and Namu had their faces painted red.

Natu was led to the hut, where we waited. Nikwei and I shuffled to the right to allow Natu to sit between me and Chief Naknow. To ease her abdominal cramps, Natu raised her knees but the High Chief indicated immediately for her to keep her legs flat on the floor. I think he thought it wasn't lady-like. The warriors stood outside the leaf hut in a guard of honour. All wore face paint and had leaves and ferns in their hair.

When the High Chief was satisfied that everything was correct and in order, he stood at the verandah of the hut to give us our marriage vows and looked at us lovingly, as a father would do to his own son and daughter. He was clearly touched. I wished Martha was with him. He spoke carefully before each of us and our witnesses. He looked at Natu first and spoke, 'Natu. If you have difficulties between you in your marriage, you are to go to your friends and tell them.'

Natu replied, 'I will.'

He continued, 'From this time on, Natu, you are to agree that you are no longer allowed to kill Iarueri.'

Natu replied, 'I do.'

The High Chief smiled and looked at me as though I were his dearest brother or son, 'Iarueri. Should you have difficulties with your marriage, you are to tell your friends.'

I replied, 'I will.'

The Chief continued, 'Iarueri. From this time on, you are to agree that you are no longer allowed to kill Natu Elin.'

I replied, 'I do.'

We were then instructed to stand together, side by side before the hut. The High Chief called Nahu and Namu and the bridesmaids to stand before us, between the ranks of warriors. The High Chief, Chief Naknow and Nikwei then followed the procession between the guard of honour, which led to the edge of the hole in the village square known as the Volcano's Ear, where we were invited to stand beneath a bower of tropical flowers. Hung from the centre of the archway was a bunch of small coconuts; beneath our feet, a heart-shaped mat of mauve and violet flowers, rather like streptocarpus.

We were then guided to the village square, where the men removed the mats which Natu and the women then rolled up. The taro was carried away and the area cleared to enable the men, including myself, to do the kastom dancing before the women. The ground was uneven and sloping. As we sang, danced, stamped and clapped, the women, including Natu, had to spring dance on the spot, rather like the Masai warriors do in East Africa. When I spoke to Natu afterwards, she said she felt weak and faint and was only able to do a little; she still had abdominal cramps and this was not a good dance to do if you have

173

severe diarrhoea!

The High Chief gave a speech to the assembled chiefs, elders and villagers and I had to respond. Natu had to leave quickly for the undergrowth. It was over! We were man and wife. I felt absolutely elated; my bride was sitting on the latrine.

We got changed but left our face paint on. Now the villagers began to prepare the final bits for the feast tomorrow. Natu spent the rest of the day resting. At 4:00 pm, I waited for the call to go to the nakamal and, on the way, I asked Sam if I could be spared the kava tonight as I felt really ill. He spoke to the High Chief about it. All the chiefs and others were at the nakamal waiting for the kava to be prepared. I needed urgently to go to the toilet, as I had the runs myself and abdominal cramps, so I made the excuse of getting tobacco from my hut as a wedding gift for the men.

I duly returned to the nakamal with the tobacco and saw a man sitting with a staff. I recognised his face, but could not place where I'd seen him before. He stood awkwardly and said to me, 'Iarueri. Do you not remember me? It is Samson.'

Then I recalled that, on my first visit to a different nakamal in 2003, it was Samson who gave me two cups of kava before the High Chief as "sport" to see the white man vomit and fall off his log. He asked for healing, so I took him to one side and laid him on the ground to massage his lower back, right buttock and thigh. His muscles were very tight and he was in severe pain (this was the only healing I did on this visit). As I worked on Samson, the Chief and the elders were closely watching me, so I had a little performance anxiety. After I had done what I could, the Chief asked me if I would take kava, as Sam had told him I wasn't well. I replied to him I felt sick and could I not take the kava this night. This was, I knew, a bad move for me on my wedding night, as I was expected to drink kava with the men to celebrate and connect to the ancestors. I knew that, had I done so, I would have rejected it! Reluctantly, the High Chief agreed. I could sense that he was disappointed in me. I knew it reflected upon him.

I returned to my hut and Natu. Not having the usual post-kava nausea enabled my system to get a good start on healing itself. The bull was slaughtered in the afternoon and butchered. A huge fire burnt at the side of the nakamal to heat up the large volcanic stones, to cook the beef and lap lap overnight in a large earth oven. The Chief had hired a portable generator with a video player for the children, as a treat for the wedding celebrations, but had no money for fuel, so he asked me for sufficient cash to get some. The generator was run all night, as the people cooked and prepared the food under its lights. Everybody was in high spirits. During the night, a truck arrived, bringing in large pots and cooking equipment for the feast tomorrow.

17th September 2008
Dancing and feasting

I felt better this morning. I had a cold shower. Natu was still very ill. We went up to the restaurant for breakfast – more hardtack and cucumber. The butchered bull was hanging up in bits around the kitchen which resembled a butcher shop. Men began to carry large timbers and branches to the nakamal,

I presumed to build another large earth oven. Women carried off large baskets of food, whilst the men returned to carry off large pieces of the beef on their shoulders. Some struggled, as the fat made the weight slide in odd directions. It looked bizarre that the men carried whole legs and shoulders of beef on their backs. It was gruesome in a way.

Everyone was in high spirits again. I heard distant tam tams sounding across the valley, probably letting others know of the wedding feast at Itabu. I gave Natu some healing and, during this process, I received two insights. One of the reasons we are both here at this time was to help to re-awaken the Goddess consciousness of this ancient land and culture. I was shown the image of the form of a sleeping woman in the mountains and was told that we had to go to the emerald centre. I asked where this centre was and was shown the area outside the bat cave, which manifested as a clear, emerald-coloured pool. So this was why we had to go to that particular cave! I was told that something had to be placed there but I couldn't tell if this was energetic or physical. If physical, then one of us would have to return again. I knew it wouldn't be Natu!

The second insight was that Natu was not sick until just after the grading ceremony, slowly progressing to a deeper level. The reason why she was so sick was because she was now adjusting to a different frequency after receiving the tribal mark associated with the power and energy of the guardian of the tokka. This was an indication that, in undertaking and even preparing for sacred ceremony, the physical body has to adjust to the higher, more refined frequency, so it throws off toxins and energetic sludge. This proved that Natu had undertaken a true initiation. Natu had been drinking the kastom medicine and was beginning to feel much better.

The Chief called us to go with him to the upper nakamal at about 8:00 am. We could already hear the singing in the distance and knew that the tribal people were dancing. The Chief wore a purple cloth around his head like a turban. As we arrived at the nakamal, we were ushered to sit on a banyan root, under the shade of the canopy of the tree, to watch in absolute fascination the local singing and dancing in our honour. This really uplifted us both and we felt much better.

Everyone was so colourfully attired, most in Western tops and shorts, some in the traditional garb with feather sticks and grass skirts. In the centre of the dancers was the kastom dance master and song leader, who led the process in military style. When a mistake was made, everybody fell about laughing. The dancing consisted of lots of clapping and stamping, jumping and running in an anti-clockwise circle; every so often the women would move from the back of the male dancers with their haunting singing and, in twos, would run round the group, almost as if they were containing the masculine energy. Sometimes the women would hop around the group in pairs, or singly. The women nearest the volcano sang and held their hands to their mouths and faces.

Jerry Hosea was invited as an official wedding guest by the Chief. We didn't recognise each other when we met. I was delighted to see him and he sat next to us and we chatted.

After some vigorous dancing, the participants had a break and the High

Chief stood up and spoke and the other chiefs and elders responded. I was not asked to speak. The older men and chiefs sat in the shade under the blue tarpaulin at the edge of the nakamal. We saw women picking lice or ticks from their children's heads and eating them. This was also a common practice in Africa. I never found out why they did this.

The dancing and singing continued at full pelt until lunch time when we were taken back to the village, where we waited for a while for the organisers to prepare the next stage of the proceedings. A man, whom I had never seen before, seemed to act as a sort of director of ceremonies, calling out names in order of the official wedding guests to assemble in the village square. There were several chiefs, some of whom I recognised, most I didn't. A local string band had begun to assemble, their instruments laid under a tree – battered guitars, drums and tambourines. They moved them out of the hot sun and formed into a band at the head of the wedding guests, playing. It was quite some time that we had to wait in the sun until all the official guests were located and placed in the correct order of seniority.

Natu and I stood at the head of the guests with the High Chief. Then word came through that everybody was assembled, so the band struck up more tunes and led us up the hill to the new kitchen for the feast. We passed between two wooden archways, decorated by split palm fronds and hibiscus flowers. We stopped at the entrance of the kitchen to allow the string band to re-assemble and to play and sing in Bislama and English. The bass player had a tea chest with a pole and a piece of string to pluck, a bit like the ones in skiffle groups in the 60's.

After the musical rendition, we were ushered into the kitchen to the official dining area, where a table and two chairs were positioned for us to sit on. The official guests sat behind us for their meal on the coconut leaf mats on the ground. Before we sat, the Chief gave a speech and I had to respond on behalf of us both. The Chief's brother, also a chief, spoke to the assembled crowds who sat on the ground outside. I asked the Chief earlier when we should offer our gifts to him and he said, 'At the feast.' We had brought these items from the leaf hut with us, offering them to him in public, the large Bowie knife in a leather sheath and a large-headed briar smoking pipe and tobacco, with a purple sarong, or lava-lava, that they were wrapped in. Everybody cheered and clapped. The men were very impressed with the Bowie knife.

We were then instructed to stand before the table, which had on it a large covered plate, which contained beef lap lap. It was decorated with hibiscus flowers. There was also a jug of pineapple cordial and two glasses, all newly purchased out of the wedding funds. We were instructed to put our hands together on the knife and cut the wedding "cake". Natu had to offer me some to eat and a drink of cordial. Under normal circumstances, had Natu been well, I would have also been expected to offer her some of the beef lap lap and cordial. I forced a mouthful down, but could not eat any more. I could tell that the women who cooked it were not very happy. Had Natu eaten any, she would have certainly brought it straight up again. We were expected to eat a huge meal together but neither of us was well enough to do so.

In the kitchen area, the beef was hung and butchered as needed. Large pots were cooking over the open fire, containing beef, pork, fish, rice and taro. As we sat, women handed out leaf plates to the long queue of guests, who passed along the line as the "dinner ladies" piled high their plates with whatever was in the bowls before them. Our wedding lap lap was used as well, fortunately. Everything and everyone reeked of beef fat. As one lot of people came to join the line, the Chief, who was also director of ceremonies, called more by name to join the queue in an orderly manner.

Nikwei and his band now sat outside and played to entertain the guests with singing and dancing. I estimated that there were approximately 500 guests. Everybody had such a good time! One very large woman danced suggestively, causing mirth and laughter. I saw her dancing behind me at one point, very suggestively with a stick which she threw down when I saw her. The other women were bent double with laughter. She rubbed her breast and smiled at me. I smiled back and winked at her. She blushed, then became more suggestive! She later had a scrap with another woman. Namu had to intervene. I think she was the tribe "character". Natu gave a performance of Arabic dancing, which went down well, but she felt too weak to continue too long. The men were fascinated by this. I felt so very proud of her. Everybody loved her.

We then moved our chairs outside to watch the guests having fun. Natu left for a brief rest so I remained with the Chief, which he was delighted with, squeezing my arm approvingly. It was amazing that all these festivities were for our benefit, for our wedding and all in the traditional kastom way – nothing that had been witnessed before by any Westerners. The Chief and the other chiefs danced. The Chief gave a direct signal with his hand for me to join him, which I did. I am not a natural dancer but, hey, I did my best even though I gave the locals plenty to laugh about.

Natu returned after an hour and looked and felt much better. The Chief was delighted to see her, as he felt responsible for her sickness. What really made the Chief pleased was that Natu had returned in island dress so that she was the same as all of the other women. She looked beautiful. Packs of dogs chased each other amongst the revellers. One bitch was alone; she had a broken lower jaw which hung horribly.

A second serving of food was now ready so others were called to line up and those who wanted more, of which there were many. After the food had been handed out, portions of beef were distributed to various people to take back to those who could not attend. People began to disperse in the late afternoon. Interestingly, I saw David Hosea arrive but, as he was the local SDA minister, he did not come to the kitchen to eat, as he would not touch pig flesh. He never came to speak to us or get involved with us in any way, so it was a mystery why he came in the first place, perhaps to be "seen" to have been invited?

At 4:30 pm, it was time for the kastom men to go to the nakamal. I gave Donald the rest of the tobacco to bring to the nakamal for the chiefs, thinking this would give him some street credibility, but instead he ran off up to the kitchen to give it to his friends who remained. At the nakamal, there were about ten chiefs and many elders. Many chiefs stood and gave speeches to thank the High Chief and to honour me for such a good day. I wasn't asked to respond.

We did the kava ritual and I was given lap lap. I knew I shouldn't refuse kava tonight. I returned to our leaf hut in the bright moonlight. I searched the clear sky for the "Southern Cross" and watched the shooting stars. Natu and I went for our evening meal of beef stew and rice. We both managed to get some food down thankfully. We returned to our leaf hut and sat on the plank outside, hand in hand, to look at the amazing night sky. The generator was started up as the Chief had hired another video for the family and children to watch, which played all night accompanied by peals of laughter long into the early hours of the morning. We both rested well for the first time in days.

18th September 2008
Curse on ants   Nightmare

There were lots of dog fights in the night. We both felt much better today. We went up for the hardtack biscuits for breakfast; there were only a few left. We were both hungry by 10 o'clock. Now that Natu was feeling better, there was nothing for her to eat. I had a word with the Chief to organise a truck for us to go to Lenakel tomorrow. He wanted to see the wedding video from Natu's small camcorder but she didn't have the connector leads and plugs to charge it up.

We spent the morning up in the kitchen talking to the Chief, Sam and Jean about the kastom ways. The Chief told us a secret story about the volcano, which is their God, and the flying fox and how his ancestors received their powers. The Chief confirmed Donald's story regarding how the chiefs at Sulphur Bay had sold their volcano to the government without his grandfather's knowledge. It was too late to do anything now.

The Chief said he would take me up to Yasur on Saturday, the kastom route directly from Itabu, not the tourist route. The Chief spoke about how he contacts the spirit of nabanga, which is the banyan tree, to get answers to his questions.

Jean gave us a coconut each so we could drink the milk by using the inner portions of a grass stem as a straw. We were also given some roasted taro on leaf plates. We enjoyed both as we were hungry. Nahu brought us our lunch – rice and beef stew. The men were still cooking the beef today, the hooves in the fire. Natu was now eating well thankfully.

In the first two or three days, we had many small ants in our hut, which always seemed to find any trace of food. After a week, there were very few ants at all in the hut, which was unusual. When I mentioned this to Natu, she looked a little ashamed and confessed to me that she had politely asked them to go – or die!

At 4:30 I went to the nakamal. The Chief was late as he had gone to get some more kava. After our meal, we went to bed early. I had a nightmare. I saw clear images before my face, especially the face of the flying fox, which changed into a black man with the face of a snarling bat. Then other surreal, unconnected images came and went very clearly. At one point, I saw the face of a native Ni-Van chief, his face painted in what appeared to be white clay, but in the style of the human skull. He was clearly in distress. The nightmare became brutal and violent in tribal warfare. I woke perspiring and alarmed. It was very real to me.

19th September 2008
Retail Therapy   Washing entrails in sea

The truck arrived at 6:30 am to take us to Lenakel to shop. Natu was excited, as she was looking forward to doing some "retail therapy". After a quick breakfast at 7:30, the Chief, Donald and his son Wai Wai, Nikwei, Chief Naknow, Sam and the others piled into the back of the truck. The journey took over two hours, since one of the rear wheels came loose, so the men banged on the cab roof to get the driver to stop. He tightened the loose wheel nuts and we carried on.

We got to Lenakel, which is known locally as "black man's town" and Port Vila is known locally as "white man's town". Natu was in her element going round the simple shops, buying different food and a large frying pan, lava-lava and clothes for the women in the village. I bought some bush knives for the men. We then went to the open air market held near the beach. Natu bought fresh vegetables and fruit, plus a hand-woven bag to carry it in. Sam accompanied her and helped her.

The Chief was "itching" to go to the small fresh fish restaurant on the beach, which we went to on one of my last visits. I suggested that we go there for a meal and everybody was excited. We left Chief Naknow near the market as he lived in Lenakel. As we parted, I pressed a good quality penknife into his hand and smiled. We walked away and I turned to see him examining the penknife carefully, his eyes full of wonder and excitement at such a rare gift.

We crossed the road to the white coral beach, where the Pacific Ocean looked so blue and inviting. We left our food and bush knives on the grass outside and piled into the restaurant. The men were buzzing with excitement, as I was paying, of course. Whilst we ate our fish and rice, two girls dragged the stomach and entrails of a cow across the road and down the beach to wash it in the sea. They cut away the intestines carefully, not noticing that, as they were knee deep in the sea, a stray dog was chewing the end of the intestine and pulling it up the beach. The Chief and men laughed so hard. The Chief shouted to them to tell them. When the girls eventually saw the dog, they laughed and almost fell into the water chasing the dog away.

Everyone, on the whole, seemed to be laughing most of the time. When I asked the Chief what the girls would do with the entrails, he just said that they would eat them. We left the restaurant and waited at the store for the truck to arrive at 1:30 pm. We also met Kenneth from Erromango, whom I had met on my second visit. He wrote the letters to me on behalf of the Chief regarding the wedding preparations and requirements.

I joined the men and one woman in the back of the truck. Natu sat in the front with the driver. Fortunately, the truck had a tarpaulin cage so we could stand as the truck bounced along the dirt roads. On our way back to Itabu village, we saw villagers planting yams on the slopes of the mountains. For some reason, this caused great excitement to the men in the back of the truck. We stopped at the roadside markets for more fresh food.

As we crossed the ash plain, the high winds created a sand storm and caused the volcanic smoke and sharp dust from Yasur to create a sea of silver mica and black sand. Many people who lived on the lee side of the volcano had bad respiratory disease due to the high levels of airborne dust, which contains minute particles of glass.

When we arrived at Itabu, we unloaded everything and then the Chief, Kenneth and I went to the nakamal at Kenneth's village nearby for kava. Donald and the others came later. The kava was very strong.

On my arrival back at Itabu, Natu had cooked some soup on the family fire in the new pan, along with some fresh bread. We also had fresh salad and fried onions which we shared with the family. Natu showed them how to cook the food and how to dip their bread in the soup. They all thought it was great fun!

20th September 2008
Natu threatens to kill Challen   Spirit Highway

We had a wonderful breakfast enjoying the fresh bread, tomato, cucumber, banana and marmalade from our shopping trip. We returned to our leaf hut and sat on the plank outside just taking in the sounds, sights and smells of the village. Suddenly a harrier (or eagle, as the Chief refers to it) flew slowly over the village square, which is a tribal indication of confirming a spiritual or sacred insight, knowledge, wisdom or ceremony. It is the totem bird of this tribe and it lives on the volcano slopes so, when it flies over the village, it is seen as a good omen and that something important will happen.

Tourists arrived for the men's nambas kastom dance so we were invited to watch, since Natu had not seen this process before. A young man strolled past where I sat and smiled and said, 'Hello.' I didn't recognise him at first; then, when he accompanied the two Canadian tourists to the nakamal, I recognised him as Challen from the Hosea camp. He was very articulate and knowledgeable but, even so, I still would never trust anyone from the SDA camp. I asked Challen to ask the Chief what was the name of the principal Goddess in the kastom culture. The nearest they could understand was "what was the name of Majikjiki's wife?" which in essence I suppose is the same thing. As Majikjiki is the principal deity, then understandably his wife would be the feminine equivalent. Majikjiki's wife is called Karapanuman. Challen also said that Yasur's two wives are known as Monga and Sapai. I became confused with these names, since they were different from the names that were previously given to me when I asked the same question.

One of the French Canadian tourists wanted a boar's tusk armband that was on display, along with a few carvings, all made by Nikwei. She said she did not have any money with her but could she bring it later. The Chief was confused and clearly didn't know what to do. Natu, sensing his discomfort, spoke up and said, 'The artifacts here have to be paid for before they are taken. What I will do is to pay on your behalf and you can give me the money later.'

Natu gave the Chief the money. The tourist said that she would give the money to Challen, who promised faithfully that he would bring it to Natu, but, as he was employed by the Hoseas, we assumed the money would be stolen, but the tourists trusted Seventh Day Adventist natives, thinking them to have the simple high morals and ethics of the kastom people, which they did not. Natu knew this also, so she went up to Challen in front of the Chief and everyone else and grabbed him by his shirt collar, threatening to kill him if he did not bring the money to her! This went down exceedingly well with the Chief and the other men. Natu had passed another test!

The Chief, Donald, Sam and I then set off to go to the volcano, the kastom way, directly from Itabu village. This is a little-used path and the Chief got lost, much to his embarrassment, so Donald took over. We passed through the rain forest, dwarfed by the huge banyan trees, up to a high ridge where the views were spectacular. Around the banyan trees were deep holes, possibly 20 feet or more, exposing a tangle of roots, caused by recent earthquakes. Smaller holes about a foot deep pitted the ground so we had to be careful where we walked. Many landslides occurred regularly and the paths often disappeared and had to be rebuilt further in.

We passed through a group of dwellings and the son of the family came onwards with us. The path dropped away sharply on our left to a deep ravine below. I could not see the bottom and it was very dangerous underfoot. We climbed and slid on our hands and knees until we reached the top of the ridge which looked down to a lava plain, then across to the volcano crater. The local people were constructing a leaf hut at the summit for tourists to stay. I did not know how they expected them to come.

From the top of the ridge, we could see clearly the horizon of the Pacific Ocean and the distant island of Futuna. We rested at the top; I felt cold. Two men arrived out of the forest, carrying bush knives, and spoke to the Chief and others. The Chief told them what Natu had said and done to Challen. The men were delighted; a new legend was born! She had earned some serious street credibility with the tribe! The Chief turned to me and pointed out a phenomenon I found fascinating. From the volcano crater, via the bat roosts in the banyan trees below, to the upper nakamal was the path of the "spirit men", which he called Kassosu. I recognised this phenomenon as a spirit highway and I expected that it connected with the sacred pool of Itabu, since this is where the Chief told me about how he called back the souls of the dead, helping them travel to the volcano to the Well of Souls, to God or where they believe God resides.

On our way back to Itabu, we stopped at the village we passed through initially, as the father wanted to catch a pig with his dogs. Eventually a small pig was caught and bound. Chief Wai Wai turned to me and said, 'Iarueri, this is our kastom. As we have faced danger, the pig is an offering to Tamaffa with kava for your visit.'

The pig, bound and silent, was carried back with us by Donald. We stopped at the side of an amazing banyan tree, two in fact, opposite each other, where earthquake activity had created deep holes exposing their roots. I couldn't see the bottom of these holes. Seeing my interest, Donald climbed into the hole and down the roots with the pig, wanting his photo taken.

When we arrived at the nakamal, the pig was dispatched then prepared for the evening kava ritual. I was too late back so missed out on my lunch. This was upsetting, as Natu told me that she and the women would cook an omelette for me. They rarely cooked eggs simply because the dogs or the pigs found them first. Natu showed them how to tell if an egg was bad or good by floating it in water. They were fascinated.

The Chief said I was not to eat, as it was too near kava ritual time. This was not good news for me, as my stomach was empty. I had plenty of water to drink in the hope this would help me tolerate the kava better. For our evening meal, we had the cold omelette with salad that Natu had cooked for lunch.

The dogs were very noisy in the evening again and both Natu and I sensed that the dogs were barking at energetic phenomena in some way.

21st September 2008

Banyan Portal   Reposition crystal   Petrified child

We had a good breakfast of bread, sliced tomato, cucumber, pawpaw and banana. Natu showed Jean how to use the medical pack she had bought for the tribe in Brisbane and explained about the "use by" dates on jars and tins in the kitchen and pantry, something they had no awareness of.

Donald, Jean, Natu and I, with a retinue of children, went into the forest to visit a particular banyan tree which touched my heart in some way on the last walk. When we arrived, Natu was spellbound by the majesty of the tree but, not only that, the other one nearby of a similar size and spread had between them created an energetic portal into another dimension. The herbage on the ground between these two trees was sparse but around them it was much more lush. Natu connected with the spirits of the trees and received a spiritual experience. Donald climbed down into the large hole caused by the earthquake again until he virtually disappeared into the darkness. The long slender roots bounced like rubber as he climbed down them.

Natu wanted her photo taken between the banyan trees at the entrance of the energetic portal, then sat in meditation for a brief time. When Natu had finished, I sat by one of the banyan trees and did my dreaming.

In the shamanic journey I sat quietly with my back to one of the huge aerial roots, being aware of Donald looking at me, not fully understanding what I was doing. I felt myself descend down between the long slender roots deep into the earth until I reached a cavern and, in the centre, a round flat raised stone, like an altar stone. This stone was covered in soil and forest floor debris, roots and leaves. I could see an oblong crystal lying on its side with a banyan root growing around it, encapsulating it as part of its form.

I asked the ancestors for instructions and was told to clear the debris and free the crystal. This I did, also clearing an open channel through the roots to the light and sky above. The crystal was about 9 inches long, not an obelisk or a pyramid but something in between. It had many narrow, fine grooves or ridges upon each face and, when cleaned, they appeared to have a function of creating or holding extra energy in some way. I was then told to hold it firmly and to place it upright upon the centre of the flat round altar stone and to rotate it slowly until I became aware of a change of energy frequency. This I did and the effect, when it occurred, was absolutely spectacular. A bolt of light ascended through the opening in the roots of the banyan tree into the sky and, in a split second, another descended into the crystal, irradiating the cavern with intense red, blue and white light. It felt as if the crystal had been reconnected to a light grid around the planet. Instantly I saw the same process of cleansing and realignment taking place within the root system of the banyan tree opposite the portal.

The portal was reactivated, with a humming sound which soon became inaudible. The power was indescribable, exciting and a little frightening. I then felt myself ascending through the roots to the surface, where I sat and reintegrated within my physical body and here I clearly saw the ancestral tribesmen coming through the portal. The warriors had their faces painted with white paint. They told me they were the guardians of the portal and they would now take over, thanking Natu and me for reactivating the spirit gateway that connected with them.

We returned to the village for an omelette lunch, which was prepared and cooked for us by Nahu, the first omelette she had ever done. It was very good. We complimented her and she blushed.

After lunch, the Chief wanted me to visit another village some distance away to speak to the men and take some photos. They also wanted to try to encourage tourists but, like most of the locals, didn't have any idea or concept of what was involved. The Chief and I, with a posse of men, drove off in the truck hired from the Hoseas to the village of Iamrawaing overlooking the volcano from the top of the opposite ridge.

It was a great 4 x 4 drive up steep tracks, the truck grounding often, probably because of the weight of the men in the back. I could never go anywhere with just the Chief alone, his men always accompanied him, which may be a tradition from the feudal times – or they just loved a good day out!

The village was not well situated for tourists. It was high on the mountain ridge and downwind from the volcano, so it was very windy, cold and dusty. The villagers wanted to build a tourist leaf hut but they had no idea of what the average tourist would expect. These people were relations of Nikwei so he brought a large basket of taro for them as a gift. The women of the village had never had a white man visit them before, so they produced lap lap for me to eat which I shared with the others.

Sam took me for a walk around the village, which seemed divided into two with a large open field between the dwellings for some reason. Here upon a narrow path, we encountered a very small boy, a toddler. When he saw me, his eyes opened wide and bulged out of his head and he screamed as if he were being murdered. He kept bending over to look at the ground in the hope that this white, hairy, ugly devil would be gone when he straightened up again. But no, the strange alien was still before him. He screamed again. The locals laughed, explaining to me that he had never seen a white man before.

When it was time to leave, they gave me a live chicken as an offering in a similar way to the small pig caught by the other villagers. I had to hold this bird. The chickens were peculiar in this part of the world, since they seemed to have a phenomenon that their feathers looked as though they were back to front, almost as if they had put their coat on the wrong way round. I mentioned this to the truck driver, who said I could have one and take it home to England.

I explained this was not possible for quarantine reasons but I thanked him very much anyway.

We returned to Itabu by 4:00 pm. Natu gave Nikwei the tambourine and penny whistles she had brought with her for the children. He was seriously impressed. The penny whistles were brought from home and the small tambourine Natu bought in a market in Lenakel. As is their kastom, Nikwei soon returned with a boar's tusk arm bracelet in exchange – a gift for a gift. This type of boar's tusk bracelet is worn above the elbow.

The Chief had arranged that the truck remained so Natu and Jean could go up to the volcano at night, as Natu had not seen this before. I stayed behind to go to the nakamal with the men. When Natu left, they went to Jungle Oasis Lodge to collect some tourists en route who also wanted to see the volcano by night. By chance, Natu saw Challen and, unfortunately for him, he saw Natu! Immediately he started to panic and shouted to her that he had the money and pulled out of his pocket the American dollars to give to her so there was no need for her to follow through with her threat!

At the nakamal tonight, the Chief was very emotional. He sat next to me at the fire and we sat silently together in the wood smoke and darkness. I could feel his heart pain. He spoke softly to me so that the men wouldn't hear, 'Iarueri. When I die, will you take care of my family?' pointing with his thumb to Donald, who sat chewing kava root.

I assured him I would do my best. He then said he wanted to do a ceremony tomorrow, when Natu, Namu and Nahu would have ear sticks pushed through their ears, the ear opened by the three needles by Sam. I felt concern, as I thought Natu had reached her limit, so asked the Chief what size the ear sticks would be. He didn't really understand my question. We were meant to have our earlobes pierced to receive the grading sticks of the High Chief the next time we met after my third initiation but, because of Martha's death, he is not permitted to do certain sacred ceremony for at least a year. He had told me the ear sticks we would wear were pencil sized, so I asked him if the three women would have pencil sized sticks pushed through their ears. He said, 'Yes.' I knew Natu would not permit this and was worried as to what to say to her and to him.

The kava was very strong and gritty tonight. I returned to our leaf hut and we had our evening meal of rice and tuna. I told Natu of the Chief's plans. She said, 'No way!' I told her I could not understand why a beautiful woman would not want such an incredible offering and privilege to adorn her face. I was lucky to escape with a slap!

22nd September 2008
Kastom ear sticks   Plank collapses

After breakfast, I spoke to the Chief and said Natu would not agree to the ear sticks. He looked disappointed. I then asked him to show me the exact size by breaking one from a nearby bush and they were actually very small, in fact the size of a matchstick. I felt elated and relieved, as Natu already had pierced ears, so these sticks would go through anyway. I called Natu over and the Chief gave her the small stick, which she managed to get through her ear. The Chief was delighted and Natu agreed to the ceremony. As Natu already had her ears pierced, there was no longer a need to do the full ceremony. The Chief explained that his three top women, Natu, Namu and Nahu, would get their ear sticks today and all represented the position of the High Woman. I asked the Chief what the ear sticks represented and he said it showed that these women were high graded kastom women, not Christians. It was a great honour.

When the Chief was ready, he called Natu. Outside Jean and Nahu waited to receive their ear sticks. Namu, who was meant to receive them, was nowhere to be seen! Jean explained to Natu that she had her moon time (which is her period) so was not allowed to cook or take part in any ceremony. This explained why Namu could not participate in the grading ceremony as planned.

Natu had sharpened sticks about one inch long pushed through both ear lobes by Sam, fortunately, through the holes that already existed. Jean replaced Namu. Both Jean and Nahu had sticks put into one ear only. Nahu had an ear stick pushed through her right ear and Jean had one pushed through her left ear. I could not find out why this was the case. I believed, however, that Natu was given the principal role as High Woman.   After the ceremony, we both sat on the plank outside our leaf hut, which duly broke in half sending me tumbling to the ground, much to Natu's delight! Donald who was standing nearby talking to us was horrified and worried that I had hurt myself. Natu was virtually bent double with laughter. Donald saw the funny side after he realised I was fine and called over the boys to carry away the broken pieces.

As we walked to the hut, we saw a huge, green caterpillar on the stem of a bush. Then a honeybee landed between our feet on the ground and remained there motionless. As we entered the doorway of our hut, a butterfly flew past. In shamanic terms, this is spirit communication. It is the language of the soul of the earth, the language of the heart. Let me explain. The seat represented the past. It was old and damaged; it broke. The caterpillar, which was the green colour of the heart centre, represented the metamorphosis which was change. The honeybee between our feet represented sweetness from the heavens which was brought to the ground and the butterfly represented spiritual awakening.

We were in the hut a very short time. When we emerged, the caterpillar had been eaten, the bee had died and was being dragged off by the ants and two new chairs replaced the old plank. Everything is an illusion; nothing lasts, so enjoy the moment – now. Natu and I were content to remain at Itabu today to read and meditate, to prepare for our departure tomorrow. The local barber arrived and shaved the heads of all the children because of the constant lice infestation.

At about 3:00 pm, Nikwei and his little band arrived and played songs for us, while most danced. A grass skirt was put on Natu and she was shown the John Frum Cargo dance by Jean and Namu. The Chief and I then left for the nakamal with the other men. The Chief had got fresh kava for our last night together. He said that it was very strong kava as, when the root is cut, it should be yellow – the deeper the yellow, the stronger the kava. It was sulphur yellow and I prayed I would not disgrace myself on my last night by vomiting.

Donald asked me the name of my nephew. I was impressed that he had remembered this, also remembering no doubt that I had no children, especially sons, of my own. I told Donald about Aaron. He tried several times to pronounce his name but could not manage it. Then he spoke quietly to me as we sat together under the starlight by the fire, 'Iarueri. When my father dies and you die, will Aaron be my brother?'

My heart was moved by the simplicity and innocence of the question and how he relayed it to me. It was a poignant and emotional request. I said I felt sure he would love to be his brother. Donald smiled and nodded. A tear glistened in his eye.

After taking the kava with the High Chief, I returned to my log beside the fire. I was called for a second cup in the ritual. The Chief had four cups of kava, which I had never seen him take before. We all knew this was our last kava ritual together. The first kava that was drunk was for the ceremony of the women who had received their kastom ear sticks. We drank to Majikjiki and Tamaffa to honour their process and to give thanks.

I returned for my evening meal. Natu distributed gifts to the women tonight that she had bought for them in Lenakel. She gave Namu a large, sharp diving knife in a sheath which we had brought from the Isle of Man. This unusual gift was to honour her as the future Big Woman.

23rd September 2008
Boar's tusk bracelet

We were up early. I distributed the final gifts of bush knives to the men and Natu had a few more gifts for the women. The truck was ordered for an early departure. We left Itabu at 8:30 am, leaving our Vanuatu family behind. Some wept as we left; many piled into the truck to go to the airport with us, including Jean and Nahu. The Chief wept as we embraced. Others looked away, clearly upset, especially Donald.

We arrived at Port Vila at lunchtime and booked into our hotel. We had a good feed of fish and chips! We did some shopping. I wanted to buy Natu a boar's tusk bracelet as a gift from the High Chief to the High Woman. We walked to all of the stores and markets until at last we found the exact thing we were looking for. A woman, upon the request for a tusk bracelet, brought out from under the counter a brown paper bag containing two new tusk bracelets, which she had just received – one a near perfect circle in growth. The tusk had grown back into the jaw of the pig and back in on itself to the root. It was extremely rare and unusual and extremely expensive. Natu loved it! I went to change some traveller's cheques to pay for it while Natu put it on and waited for my return. On my arrival, Natu was sitting behind the counter with the local woman, both laughing and talking together.

We had a good meal in the evening and returned to the hotel. Natu was covered in red bites from the bed bugs in Itabu. We each had an excellent long soak in a hot bath. The silt and grit left in the bottom of the bath afterwards could have been used to pot up a small plant. Our feet were almost clean again. The bed was just luxurious, with clean sheets and no companions!

24th September 2008
Tattoo – cathartic reaction

We arrived in Brisbane in Australia, Maggie still wearing her kastom ear sticks. I persuaded Maggie to go to a tattoo studio to get her tribal tattoo tidied up, for cosmetic reasons, as it looked a bit ragged. The woman, who was doing this work, was rude, aggressive and clearly "on" something. I should have stopped her and gone elsewhere but she quickly tattooed over the tribal marks and pronounced, 'It's done.' Maggie was clearly affected by this woman's energy and the whole dismissiveness of the process. We walked to the Botanic Gardens and sat quietly on a bench among the trees and grass. For some two hours she was barely able to speak, feeling angry and in a deep emotional maelstrom. Maggie felt that she had defiled the tribal tattoo in some way, which had been done in a sacred ceremony in a loving, nurturing space. After her inner turmoil had eased, we strolled around the gardens to the boardwalk in the mangrove swamp and there, at our feet, was a stick in the exact shape of the tribal tokka stick! It was clearly a sign from Spirit.

Later in the day, we were browsing in a book store and, opening a book at random, saw a photo of two Papuan warriors, one holding a stick looking like a tokka stick. Maggie felt much better. Everything was perfect. Every action or thought has a corresponding reaction, which was a perfect outcome. Maybe Maggie had agreed at some level of consciousness to help the woman in the tattoo studio to ease her pain in some way as a healing response? Who knows? What is important is to remember that it is not the events that matter but how we react to them, what issues or feelings that are raised or brought to the surface to be worked through and released.

Maggie wore her kastom ear sticks for the duration of our stay in Australia, leaving them in until we arrived in Dubai to stay with her daughter and her husband. She had been pushed to her limit with the long, hot, uncomfortable hikes up to the volcano and to the bat caves, the sickness during and after the ceremonies, the wedding and the primitive living conditions. She never complained publicly except to voice her fear of letting me down before the Chief. I was very proud of her fortitude and courage and the way she interacted with the tribe. They loved her as I do.

4th November 2009
Holy feather   Kassosu myth   Amazon   Knight

I had been corresponding with the Chief over the months and some weeks ago I wrote to the Chief enclosing the feather of a guinea fowl, which has upon it black and white spots which I thought was very symbolic of the black and white serpent twins. Today, I received a letter from him calling us back to Vanuatu for the final ceremony. I presumed he meant that this was to receive our kastom ear sticks.

The letter, as written, said, 'My brother, I am writing to you to give you the secret and the last important ceremony that we have to do with Kassosu Yasur, the secret God. Now you show me the feather of the chicken. This feather is so holy in the secret of Yasur Kassosu. I am still waiting to give you this but you show the feather now. I will tell you the last secret power which you still feel that we are going to make in other ceremony. So it begins.'

The Myth

'The first person in the world was God, Kassosu Yasur. One day he went to the garden to cut the bush. When he was cutting the bush, suddenly he cut his left hand. He stopped cutting the bush and he put down his hand in the hole of a tree called nawaias but it was full of water. So the next day, he went to the garden again and, when he finished working, he went and sat down under the tree for a short break. At that moment, he saw a woman and 12 children. They were all black but amongst them was a white boy. They are going to swim in the hole where the Kassosu put his blood. Suddenly he jumped out from the bush and grabbed hold of the white child. He asked him, "Where is your father?" The child said, "I have no father, only my mother." She was working and was very thirsty and she drank from the water in the hole of the nawaias tree. She didn't know that, when Kassosu Yasur had a bleeding hand, he had plunged it into the water before she had drunk from it. Kassosu still asked questions and said, "Where is your father?" to the white boy. The child repeated again that it has no father, only a mother. "When my mother drank the water from the hole in the tree, she gave birth to me, so I am white." So Kassosu bowed his head and said, "I am your father."'

The letter continued. The Chief wrote, 'My brother, I will stop here. The last part I will give you is very secret and holy in the spirit. I will let you know about this, so what we are going to do is that you have to come out and see me again and I will give you the last power. When you are ready to come, we will sleep in the mountains for one week, so I will give you the power, which is very secret. I am now holding this secret power but, now you have shown this in the feather, the black and white. After this then, you offer your blood to Yasur and we will do this last important ceremony together.'

Over the months that followed, we continued to correspond with each other, which was a great joy to me. Maggie and I taught shamanic and dowsing workshops as fundraisers for the tribe. I decided to stop shaving and grow my beard in January so it would be impressively wild and untamed when we returned to Vanuatu later in the year, 2010.

In March 2010, Maggie and I went to Ecuador to the headwaters of the Amazon rain forest to stay with the Huaorani tribe in their community Eco Lodge on the Shiripuno River at Quehueri'ono. We wanted to see how they coped with tourists and how they organised and ran their lodge to get some ideas for the Chief in Vanuatu, since the environment is similar. The local people told us of the brutality of the missionaries, in particular the Jesuits who traded in child slave labour.

Prior to my investiture as a Knight of The Noble Order of Tara in 2010, I had to undertake an all night vigil of prayer and contemplation with my sword.

During this process, I connected with the guardians at the cave of the ancestral skulls in Vanuatu. At the close of this meditation, one of the Yeramanus said, 'May your skull grow moss.'

I replied, 'What do you mean by that?'

He said simply, 'Think about it and work it out.'

I always get irritated when Spirit says that sort of thing but, of course, as true teachers they will not "spoon feed" you with every answer. By contemplating such a statement, great spiritual insights can be gained which are your gifts for eternity. A given answer is soon forgotten!

The fire burning in the hearth all night, along with the presence of my sacred sword, comforted me during the long hours of the vigil until I had worked the riddle out. I felt rather elated, to say the least, and reconnected to the Yeramanu skull keeper to offer my insight. He nodded and smiled but remained silent.

In a culture where the skull is venerated as the receptacle of the soul, the place where the ancestral wisdom resides, this statement obviously was of great importance and I felt that it was an ancient tribal blessing lost now to the annals of time.

Only those who are great chiefs, Yeramanus, healers or warriors would have their skulls placed in the sacred caves that overlooked the villages after their death.

I remembered studying the skulls and skeletons in such a cave high in the mountains overlooking the village of Aseki in N.E. Papua, New Guinea. These skulls were covered in moss, algae and lichens because of the heat and humidity. (The role of the skull keeper is to protect and keep the skulls clean.)

The riddle became clear now. "May your skull grow moss" is a blessing to you, wishing you such greatness that your own skull would be venerated as a man of honour and placed with the others in the sacred cave for centuries to come. The ordinary person's skull would be disposed of or treated or used in a different way.

Another insight I received during this vigil was that receiving the accolade of Knight in a physical (as well as esoteric) Order grounded the consciousness into third dimensional reality of the Knights of the Golden Order of the Dragon Sword. The robes in both Orders are the same colour. The sword was made for me by a local blacksmith in a traditional forge and the sword sheath was crafted with my High Chief's grade mark along its length by a local artisan skilled in leather art and design.

Spirit instructed me specifically prior to my sword being made that it had to be the length of my spine from the base of my skull to the tip of the coccyx. This has great esoteric significance. For a Questing Knight, the sword is not a weapon but an extension of his energy body. The sword develops a level of consciousness through the focus and intent of the knight. The sword is the knight and acts as an altar and a portal to other realms through the soul, or part, extended into it by the knight. If a knight's sword is lost or broken in battle, he experiences soul loss or soul fragmentation. The surrender of a sword to a victor is not merely the handing over of a war souvenir, but rather the soul of the knight (army or nation) unless you withdraw that aspect of yourself back into your being or land. Take great care in the acquisition of old, used swords. They carry energy that could make you sick, especially if they are still carrying an active curse or battle programme. The same principle applies with a chief's staff or any object of power, including sacred stones and skulls.

PART 5

KASSOSU

Decision

The Chief had invited me back for the final ceremony, a blood ritual of some sort, where I would receive the final secret.

I wrote to Chief Wai Wai in January 2010 to ask if it were possible for us to arrive in August, since we had other commitments in June and July which would have been the best time to travel, so avoiding the mosquito season.

By mid June I still had not received a reply. I was getting anxious, as flights had to be booked. I didn't want to spend a fortune travelling to the South Pacific to find that the Chief had gone on "walkabout". I was forced to make a decision, as Barbara Meiklejohn-Free, a gifted "seer" and shamanka, had invited me to join her small group going to participate in Sun Dance at Wounded Knee in America, which takes place in the first two weeks of August. Whilst in America, I would be half way to Vanuatu, so it made sense to continue on from there, meeting up with Maggie later in Los Angeles so we could travel together.

Maggie suggested maybe I had to make a choice between the two. I badly wanted to experience the first part of Sun Dance, a rare opportunity, and complete my final initiation with the Chief. I struggled for many days with the dilemma, especially the finances, finally deciding to do both and trusting in Spirit that everything would work out as hoped. The very next day I received a letter from Chief Wai Wai confirming our visit in August. Another test from Spirit!

Because of planned strikes by British Airways crews, the travel agent couldn't book flights from America to Australia, so we had to go via New Zealand. We therefore decided to return via Hawai'i, enabling me to connect with the volcanoes there.

5th August 2010
Sun Dance

After meeting up with Barbara's group in the USA, we eventually arrived at Wounded Knee in the Pine Ridge Reservation, South Dakota, for the Lakota/Sioux Blue Star Woman Sun Dance.

During the next two weeks, we participated in many sacred ceremonies and rituals, including the erection of a new World Tree, where, over the course of the next few days, flesh offerings were given by the Sun Dancers, supporters and onlookers. I didn't realise it at the time, but this connection to the Lakota World Tree was significant to what took place later in Vanuatu.

19th August 2010

After returning to Los Angeles from Sun Dance, I met Maggie, who came out from London for our onward journey together to New Zealand, then on to Vanuatu.

24th August 2010

We arrived in Port Vila, Vanuatu. The taxi driver who picked us up was a cousin of High Chief Wai Wai Rawi and came from Itabu. Now that we were back in the tribal lands, it felt wrong to call each other by our western names, so we reverted to our tribal names. Natu bought two island dresses from the market and we changed some money into Vatu. We tried several times to ring the Chief on his mobile phone and other contacts, but there was no reply, so we hoped that he would be at the airport on Tanna to meet us the following day.

25ᵗʰ August 2010
Tourist road kill   Big Woman arrives

We were up at 4:30 am for the early flight to Tanna Island. Natu found some sticks from the bushes at the airport and put them in her ears for kastom sticks and wore one of the island dresses. She wanted to make sure she arrived at Tanna Island and Itabu dressed the same as the local women. As always, she looked gorgeous in everything she wore.

After checking in our bags and ourselves being weighed, we walked across the tarmac to the plane and were told there was a weight problem with our aircraft. Our bags were to be flown out on the next flight leaving Vila at 2:00 pm. We were directed to a small plane that looked like a pregnant locust.

After a very noisy flight, we landed at Tanna, but the Chief was not there to meet us. This had never happened before. I had written to him several months ago telling him of our arrival and departure times and the relevant dates, knowing he would then organise a truck to pick us up.

We got a lift into Lenakel to have a look around and wait until 3:00 pm for the arrival of the next flight to retrieve our bags. We had a fried fish meal at the seaside restaurant and learnt from a local man of a tokka dance taking place in the southwest of Tanna. This was really good news. We had a drink at a coffee house, explaining to the woman our predicament and she kindly telephoned a man who had a truck. He came and collected us and took us back to the airport to collect two tourists and our bags. We then went on to Itabu.

Natu had bought two melons, some bread and eggs to take back with us. The roads were in a terrible state after recent flooding and erosion. She sat in the front with the driver and I sat in the back with the two tourists. The driver was a bull-faced local man wearing orange and blue shorts and a yellow and black T-shirt. He whistled nervously when the truck's suspension "bottomed out" over the ruts, causing the layer of red dust inside the truck to cover the immaculately over-dressed Italian tourists, making them cough and sneeze. Natu bounced like a storm-tossed cork in a raging sea, every so often exclaiming 'Wow!' as we negotiated a dangerous part of the road.

Another vehicle carrying tourists overtook us. Our driver tried several times to regain the lead, but the other driver kept forcing him off the road. At one point, we were racing parallel to each other, each vehicle creating choking red dust clouds, neither giving way to the other. I was expecting an accident at any moment with impressive tourist road kill. Fortunately, the other driver gave way and we passed until we were overtaken again. We had lost the lead but our driver seemed to be content now with being second.

The dried out river bed running through the volcanic ash plain was deeply eroded and careful 4 x 4 driving was essential. I prayed I wouldn't have an omelette in my bag after being thrown about so much for two hours over the rough dirt roads.

We eventually arrived at Itabu at 5:30 pm. Nahu and the children spotted Natu in the truck and squealed and shouted with delight, running alongside the vehicle until it stopped in the centre of the village. Big Woman had arrived! A young man ran up, introducing himself as Michael. He spoke very good English.

He explained that he was Absalom's (Nakuhu) son. I remembered him as my guide in 2005. He apologised to us after we had explained our story, saying there was no telephone network working in the region and there was a shortage of road fuel on the island, so he was intrigued as to how we had managed to get a lift. We were not expected. It seemed the Chief had not received my letter. Michael explained that the Chief, Donald and the other men were at the Iaqurimano nakamal tonight doing a kastom ceremony because two chiefs had just ended a violent land ownership dispute through Chief Wai Wai's mediation, so kava and a pig were being used to formally accept the deal on both sides.

It was now dark. Yasur volcano was roaring, filling the clear, starlit sky with a red glow. The moon was full, the flying foxes silhouetted against her, with the cicadas calling out their night prayers to Majikjiki. There was a deep peace in this place; it seemed to touch my very soul. I was back home.

Namu and Nahu had prepared a meal for us after we had been shown to our leaf hut to unpack. The same hut we had used for our marriage celebrations. Fond memories returned. There had been many changes along the route from Lenakel, as well as Itabu, since our last visit. The Seventh Day Adventist Church was in ruins and a new one was being built across the road. A new primary school had been constructed at Iaqurimano with funding from the Australian government. In Itabu, the old ruined restaurant and several leaf huts had finally been demolished and removed. New family huts and a new "restaurant" were being built. The restaurant we were using would survive until the end of the year, we were told, and then it would be demolished before it fell down. Nothing lasts long in the rain forest.   Nikwei had carved a 10 ft black-palm statue of a chief in nambas, which stood outside our hut.

No oil lamps were brought out in the evenings, only candles on this visit. We were both tired and, after our meal, fell into our marital bed. The legs were still uneven, causing the bed to slope to one side. I kept rolling on to Natu in the night, using the bed as an excuse!

26th August 2010
Tank overflow   Black spear in heart   Church – hack off arms
During the early hours of the morning, we heard water running. Initially, I thought it was a rain deluge, but Natu said that the sound came from the restaurant up the hill. Losing water was a serious matter, especially in the dry season, so at 4:00 am we decided to investigate by torchlight, Natu, in her silk pyjamas, and I, in my underpants. We must have looked bizarre as we walked through the tropical undergrowth to the storage tanks. We hoped nothing that would bite or sting would be interested in white flesh. One of the tanks was overflowing causing a rivulet to flow down the hill. We searched in the bushes for a gate valve or tap to turn off the supply from the pipe from the mains tank in the mountains, but found none. Defeated, we returned to bed. The water had stopped flowing at 6:00 am when people were moving about and using the water supply. (We later found out this happened on a regular basis, as the engineer who installed the tank didn't fit a gate valve or tap to control the water levels.)

Scarlet and emerald green parakeets squabbled in the forest canopy above our hut at dawn each day, along with the usual crescendo of roosters. We stepped out into the dawn to see Yasur belching out plumes of thick, white sulphured smoke, highlighted by a rose red blush from the fire deep within his heart.

At 7:00 am we went up to the restaurant for breakfast, fresh bread and fried eggs. The two melons that Natu had brought from Lenakel turned out to be giant grapefruits.

High Chief Wai Wai Rawi arrived to greet and welcome us. We embraced our old friend with love. He had come from an all night ceremony and vigil with the two warring chiefs, still dressed in kastom attire. He wore a palm leaf headband containing two eagle feathers, the black line across his brow indicating his grade, a band containing Majikjiki leaves on his left upper arm and a nambas covered by a lava-lava. Natu showed him her circular boar's tusk bracelet, which I had bought for her as a wedding gift on our last visit. The Chief said that it came from a particular pig found on Malakula Island in the north of Vanuatu.

The Chief asked us if we would accompany him to Sameria village to pray and give healing to his sister, Naswei. He also said that Namu and Nahu wanted to present gifts to Natu before we left. After about one hour, the two women arrived and gave Natu two beautifully made pandanus leaf bags and two red and yellow feather sticks. Natu was delighted with her gifts and asked how long it had taken to weave the bags. Namu replied, 'One year.' Natu carried one with her every day for the rest of our stay. Namu and Nahu then left.

Nikwei arrived out of the bushes. He had heard of our arrival and we embraced. Natu asked him how long it had taken him to carve the "black boy" statue of the Chief and he replied, 'One day.' Natu was surprised. He added in halting English, 'The bigger the chief, the bigger the nambas,' winking at me, laughing. Natu saw his glance towards me and passed a derogatory comment not fit to print.

After some time, the Chief arrived with Donald and Namu, who was holding Kipson, their newest child, along with their other children. Natu asked the Chief a question, referring to me as David. I quickly corrected her, saying, 'Iarueri.'

The Chief laughed and pointed to Donald's third son, then to me, and said, 'This boy is named David after you.' It was a great honour and privilege. Donald smiled and nodded. The boy buried his face into his mother's skirts.

We had to delay our departure to the village, since a small group of tourists arrived to see the kastom nambas dance. As this is the only means by which the Chief can earn money, it's important that, if and when tourists arrive, he takes every opportunity to earn some cash.

Afterwards the Chief, Natu, myself and Donald's two sons, Wai Wai and David, hiked to Sameria village up into the mountains. Natu struggled at times up the steep, slippery tracks, arriving at the village somewhat dishevelled. The Chief introduced us first to his sister's husband, Harry. He then called over Naswei for healing. She had been in great pain for about six years after a back injury, which caused breathlessness and a heart condition. Natu, a chartered physiotherapist, examined Naswei finding a misaligned vertebra and muscles in deep spasm up the centre of her spine. We called for a pandanus mat to be laid out on a flat piece of grass in the village and laid Naswei upon it. Natu worked her magic and I did the metaphysical stuff and reflexology for the relevant reflex points. As I scanned Naswei's energy body, I found a black spear in her back at the heart area. It took me some time to remove it safely, since it was embedded and was ancestral in origin. I explained my find to the Chief and to Harry. As we both worked, it began to rain, so a woman from the village stood over us with a tattered umbrella.

On the return journey to Itabu, the Chief explained many things about kastom plant medicine. Before any fruit in season can be harvested, the Chief, who holds the appropriate spirit stone for that particular plant, does a ceremony. He rubs coffee leaves in his hands to create a small ball, then places this on the appropriate kastom stone as he calls the guardian spirits of the trees or plants for permission to eat the fruits.

After returning to Itabu, we had lunch. The Chief told me to have a very small amount to eat so it would not interfere with the effects of the kava ritual. Natu wanted to revisit the two huge banyan trees that guarded a spirit portal, so she went off with Donald and a party of excited children. I stayed behind with the Chief and asked him many questions about the tokka dance and the ceremonies that lay ahead of us both over the next few days.

The Chief explained that the chief who was in charge of the main tokka dance had postponed it yet again, so we would miss the spectacle, but a smaller tokka dance was taking place in the southwest of the island that we would be able to go and see. The Chief said he and all of the southern chiefs would get together to organise a tokka dance at Itabu, or at a nearby host nakamal, for 2013. He said we couldn't participate in the tokka dance in a different region but would be expected to do so when it was hosted by chiefs under his charge. He added that, when this occurred and I had participated in the tokka dance, I would gain my eagle feathers and a permanent leaf house would be built just for Natu and I in the village. I felt excited at this prospect.

The Chief and I strolled to the nakamal; I carried the kava root to my heart, as usual. We lit a fire and prepared the kava. My job was to scrub the cut root clean of soil with coconut fibre prior to the men chewing it. Harry arrived, carrying a length of fresh sugar cane as a gift for Natu and I for the healing we did for his wife.

After preparations for the kava were underway by other men, the Chief sat next to me on a banyan root next to the fire. He said the next few days would be very important, since we were to open a spirit gate (portal) to the Kassosu, Yasur, Majikjiki and the ancestral Yeramanus.

A small pig was carried in by a man and given to the High Chief, who laid it in the centre of the nakamal after it had been swept clean of falling banyan leaves by a young boy. He instructed me to place the kava root next to the pig and then to place my hands upon both of them. The Chief called for the club that was kept in the banyan tree. Donald brought it over, handing it to me. I placed the club upon the pig's skull, handing the club back to Donald, who dispatched the pig instantly, blood gushing from its ears into the black volcanic earth. Men hung the pig from a tree at the edge of the nakamal and singed off its hair with burning dried palm leaves, rolled together like a torch, then scraped off the burnt hair with a bush knife prior to butchering it. As usual the flesh and offal was cooked over the fire on pointed sticks, predictably raw and bloody on the inside and burnt black on the outside.

The Chief and I drank the kava together first, calling for the portal to be opened to the Kassosu. I had forgotten how awful kava was, shuddering at the effect it had upon my body and mind again. I was given some pig flesh and rice to eat, which helped to take away the nausea and headache. My brain became hot and I began to drift in meditation between worlds. In the darkness, the Chief came to the fire where I sat in silent prayer with the other men, offering me a second shell of kava to drink. I politely refused.

After the Chief had taken his second shell, he came to sit alongside me and the other men. Whispering, he said, 'Iarueri, I want to ask you a question which is really troubling me. The Seventh Day Adventist Christians are telling me that, in 2012, all the kastom men will have their arms hacked off by the church men and those Christians who go to church on a Sunday will be thrown into hell's fires. Only the Seventh Day Adventist Christians, who worship on a Saturday, will be saved. Is this true?'

I laughed out loud, forgetting to be silent at prayer time. I replied, 'Chief, this is all lies as usual. A true religion teaches that all men are equal and to love and respect each other and all life.'

The Chief and the other men said, 'Thank you,' and, in unison, they all laughed, whispering amongst themselves. An evening discussing the kastom ways and Christian lies ensued, as usual, but in whispered tones beneath the starlight and the banyan tree to honour Tamaffa, the spirit of the nakamal. The Chief whispered to me that we were to sleep in the jungle from tomorrow night, one night at a time, to meet the Kassosu, not a full week as I had previously understood.

Donald escorted me back to our leaf hut, where I collapsed on to the bed, feeling very sick. Natu had organised a flask of hot water and some tea, ready for my arrival from the nakamal, remembering the state I was in on our last visit. I was too ill to eat dinner. I prayed to the kava spirit for grace, and what was it that she needed from me so that I would no longer get sick?

27th August 2010
Foreskin forest   Kassosu manifestation

After breakfast, I went for a wash to discover that a rat had eaten part of my bar of soap. I wondered if he would leave a trail of rainbow-coloured bubbles through the forest when he passed wind.

When the Chief arrived, I asked him what the new building was that was being constructed on the roadside at the end of the track to the village. He said a church. I looked at him in total disbelief! He saw my startled look and explained that a missionary had asked him for permission to build the church for the local community on the understanding he would not interfere with the kastom ways. The Chief said that, as he was Chief he had to provide places of worship for all of his community members. I asked him what he would do if the church lied to him and tried to turn the Christian community against the kastom way. He replied that they understood he would take the building back from them if this happened.

During our conversations, the Chief explained that, when a new leaf house was being built for a particular man and his wife, a ceremony was done, always involving a pig and kava, and his beard was shaved off. The hair was then pushed up inside the thatch. The Chief said I was to undertake the beard shaving ceremony in a few days time, with a bamboo knife. Because of the protocol of offering tobacco at the nakamal, I asked the Chief the correct way to do this, since I had brought some more loose tobacco, pipes, papers and lighters for the men. He said to give it all to him and he would distribute it throughout the community, which I knew would be good for him. This he did, for wherever we went, I always saw the tobacco and lighters which I had bought.

The Chief also explained that he had now passed full power of Big Woman (High Woman) to Namu. This may now explain why Donald's beard is much thicker than last time. I felt that the Chief was beginning to relinquish his authority and delegate more responsibility to Donald, now that Martha, his wife, walked at his side as an ancestor.

The Chief asked me to go with him to Selgae village to do some healing on a girl called Janet. Again the young woman had neck and back problems. We met Chief Tukuriary as we waited for the young woman to come from the fields. This gave me the opportunity to ask the Chief some more questions about the kastom ways.

I asked him to explain in more detail about the circumcision ceremonies, which were very important in their culture. Again, he verified information I had gleaned in the past, including that the man who performed the ritual had to be of the correct kastom lineage trained in this art. The foreskin was cut off with a bamboo knife, then wrapped in a small leaf and pushed through a hole in a newly sprouted coconut. The coconut was then planted and would grow into a full size tree, but these trees were marked in some way so people knew not to eat the coconuts from them (isn't that a wonderful and respectful way to dispose of a boy's foreskin, again a blood ritual, rather than dumping it into a rubbish bin in a hospital). I mused at the prospect of having a selected area of sacred trees kept for this ceremony – a foreskin forest. I asked the Chief why circumcision was so important to his culture. The Chief held out a crooked, downward-pointing finger, clearly indicating a flaccid penis. 'After circumcision, it makes a man strong to please his wife.' He then held out a stiff finger, pointing up at 45 degrees.

The Chief then spoke more about the ensuing ceremonies that would take place for us both. After spending the night in the jungle to meet the Kassosu, we would have our right earlobes pierced to take a kastom ear stick. Another tattoo would be done on the left upper arm and Natu, Namu and Nahu would be expected to receive the female equivalent. I wondered with trepidation how Natu would take this exciting news!

After the healing, Janet gave me a pandanus mat and two feather sticks, as an exchange. This gifting is part of their kastom culture to prevent loss of face and future obligation.

As we left Selgae village, we diverted off to Iaqurimano school. The Chief wanted to speak to a particular woman who lived behind the school about the napen-napen dance, which is performed by the women. This dance would take place in a few days time, he explained, and the Chief wanted Natu to take part. This was important in some way. We got permission from the woman, so the Chief was delighted about this.

We were not far from the nearby bat cave that I was expecting to visit with Natu on our last visit, so I asked the Chief if it was possible to do this. He agreed.

On our return to Itabu, we met Chief Kabari. Both he and Chief Tukuriary were principal guests at our wedding. When we arrived at Itabu, Natu was sitting in the sunshine outside our hut, reading. I wondered how she would react to a jungle hike in the mountains and the tattoo ceremony. After I had told her the wonderful news, she looked at me with a look of pity for a stupid person. 'Tell me, please, and the good bit is?' …….

I now knew how an imbecile felt. I feebly replied, 'Well, darling, last time we were here, you said you were sorry to have missed the experience of wading through bat guano. You now have this fantastic opportunity.'

Natu gave me a look that confirmed I was indeed an imbecile. 'You still don't understand women!' she replied. She laughed.

In the afternoon, the Chief, Donald and I went to a secret place in the jungle, where we were to encounter the Kassosu. On the way, the Chief asked me if I had had any dreams after the kava ritual to ask for the spirit gate to be opened. I said I had not had one but told him of a dream that Natu had had which was relevant. He was very pleased. He said that he had dreamt of one of the Kassosu (spirit men) shooting a flying fox with a bow and arrow. This was a good sign, he added.

When we arrived at the secret location, I was informed that only the three of us were permitted at this place, the place where, before him, his father and grandfather had actually shaken hands with the spirit men to receive their power. We began to build a shelter for the Chief and me from poles and palm leaves cut from the rain forest in the traditional Melanesian style. As we worked, the Chief explained more, saying that on no account was I permitted to reveal anything about the location or what took place in or around it, especially to the other men at the nakamal. I gave my word.

After completing the bush shelter, we returned to the nakamal for the kava ritual at dusk. Another small pig had been obtained, as before. Again, it was laid in the centre of the nakamal and I was to lay the kava root against the pig and place my hands upon both. The Chief instructed me to fetch the club from its place in the banyan tree and to "kill it strong". I offered my prayers to the spirit of the pig, to the kava and the Kassosu and killed the pig outright with one blow. I felt no emotional anguish this time, which I didn't understand. I just did what was expected.

When I told Natu about how I felt later, she said, 'You have finally learnt how to truly honour the spirit of the pig.'

I didn't really understand what she meant, but I recognised that inwardly I had passed another test, for when I had killed the pig I automatically knew to open a portal to the spirit world for the spirit of the pig to travel through it to its correct destination and dimension. When there was an emotional charge involved, this often diverted the spirit highway away from the animal, so its spirit could get lost in the Astral World. For those who condemn this ritual, they need to look at the brutality of an average abattoir.

The pig was duly dehaired and butchered in the usual manner whilst we prepared the kava. After the ritual, I returned to our leaf hut to await the arrival of the Chief and go into the forest for the night.

The Chief and I walked quickly through the darkness into the rain forest by torchlight; I tripped several times. I had been instructed to wear clothing of a certain colour, as he did. We carried our pandanus mats and blankets, placing them on a bed of ferns on the earth floor inside the shelter. We fell asleep, soon wakening to the sounds of the Kassosu, the wild spirit men approaching. As I explained previously, I am not permitted to say what happened, except to say that a third dimensional manifestation took place from out of the spirit portal. It was awesome!

The Kassosu came right up to our shelter, then suddenly they left, disappearing into the forest. The Chief explained that they were frightened by my smell because they weren't used to it. We decided to go back to sleep in the hope they may return later in the night. Unfortunately, in the early hours of the morning, I really wanted to urinate. I couldn't hold it any longer, so I tried to creep out of the shelter, in the darkness, over the Chief where he slept by the doorway, touching him as I did. He jumped and shouted loudly because he thought that the Kassosu had actually gripped him in the night and were trying to kill him. I had a job to stifle my laughter, but he was truly very frightened. The physical encounter we had prayed for did not materialise fully.

28th August 2010

Napen-Napen dance   Bat cave   "Strong Eye"

After returning to sleep in the hope that the Kassosu would return again, we awoke at dawn and began walking to the vicinity of a flying fox roost in a huge banyan tree. It was an uncomfortable night, for I had ants in my underpants and the ground was very hard. It rained during the night but at least we were perfectly dry. We had made camp at a known portal on a spirit highway, the Chief had explained. We would return again tonight after kava.

The Chief said that, when he first met me in 2003, he had had a dream where the Kassosu had come to him, showing him the two of us participating in this secret ceremony and the years of preparation leading up to it. He said that this was the final stage of my receiving the full lineage of the Yeramanu and the power that went with it, as his father and grandfather had done before him.

As we walked back to Itabu, the Chief explained who the Kassosu were and what they looked like, how they sounded and what they did. It was important, he said, that we were both to touch them physically for the transference of power from spirit to human, including their knowledge, but that they were easily frightened, so patience was essential.

We left the rain forest and entered Donald's encampment at the edge of Itabu. Kipson, his youngest son, who was about 18 months old, came toddling out of a leaf hut brandishing a large sharp knife, waving it dangerously close to the front of my trousers. I said to the Chief, 'This boy needs to be careful or he will circumcise somebody!'

The Chief laughed, taking the knife from the child and returning it to Donald.

After breakfast, the Chief, myself, Natu, Nahu and a squad of giggling children walked to the Iaqurimano nakamal to watch the napen-napen dance by the local women. All the women wore grass skirts and leaves in their hair and all had their faces brightly painted. Samson was gatekeeper, also attired in a grass skirt, with red body paint. His leg was fine now and he walked normally, as the last time I saw him at our wedding, he was walking like a cripple with the aid of a large staff.

After the first round of dancing, the Chief instructed Natu to go with the women to prepare for the next performance. She and the other dancers came back, looking exotic and beautiful. The Chief and Samson virtually rolled about laughing at the enthusiasm that Natu put into her dancing, especially when it came to the fighting sequences and beating a pandanus pad. I said to the Chief that Natu must be thinking that the pad was my head. He laughed and nodded, tears running down his face. After the dancing, Natu was breathless and glowing. The Chief said we would go to the bat cave now. Natu put her hand on her hip, raising her eyebrows. I smiled at her.

We hiked up a mountain ridge, eventually reaching the bat cave after negotiating overgrown paths and rotten wooden steps. I had been here in 2004; it was now hidden by the jungle. Natu and I sat on a stone at the cave entrance to remove our boots and socks, since we now had to walk through a stream into the darkness of the cave. A water spider, the size of a man's hand, glided on the water surface out of the blackness, floating towards us. Natu thought it was really cute! The Chief touched the spider with a stick and it scurried back into the darkness, lurking somewhere. I wondered how big the colony of spiders was.

I had remembered to bring a torch, so, bending at 45 degrees to get into the cave, Natu followed the boys and I followed her. Well, somebody had to protect her rear! The water soon changed to thick, oozing, sticky, smelly guano, which we waded through calf deep, seeing cockroaches, centipedes and other unidentifiable insects crawling around our legs by torchlight. Between our toes, we felt creepy crawlies. At this point, we could stand upright in the cave and, with the aid of the torch, stood in absolute awe, watching hundreds of small bats wheel and dive around us, dropping guano on our heads. Natu was delighted, thankfully.

We then waded back through the bat guano, emerging into the daylight, washing our legs in the murky stream, then, putting on our footwear, returned to Itabu. By the time we had arrived back at the village, the face paint Natu wore from the dancing had streaked with sweat, creating rivulets that ran down her face and into her clothes, giving her a decidedly wild appearance!

The Chief then took me to one side, explaining that he had changed his mind about returning to the jungle shelter that night. The Kassosu were not used to my smell, he said, as it was unfamiliar to them. We would try the following evening. I felt disappointed. The Chief saw my expression, and said the blankets and items of clothing that we had left at the shelter would remain, as the Kassosu would come into the shelter during the night and check it all out, hopefully, getting used to my energy. This explanation made sense. He then added that Harold at Sameria village had invited men to his meeting place to drink kava and to eat lap lap, to say farewell to an American anthropologist, who had been staying in their village for several years on and off and who even spoke the local dialect. The Chief couldn't refuse, basically, which meant, by the time we returned to Itabu, it would be too late to go to the jungle shelter.

We arrived, as promised, and were introduced to the other men. The Chief explained that, as the men were drinking kava in a place where there was no banyan tree, it was not a nakamal, but simply a meeting place. This meant there was no ritual protocol and no calling in Tamaffa. There were about 35 men present, all of whom brought bits of food to share and kava root. I managed to avoid the lap lap, after drinking my shell full of kava, but was given some burnt wild pigeon, which still had feathers attached to the flesh in places. The anthropologist and I talked together for a while.

'The local men say you worked in a hospital opening skulls,' he said.

I replied, 'That's right. It was a bit gruesome at times.'

'The people in these parts call you "Strong Eye".'

That was news to me! Unfortunately, the Chief asked me to have a second shell of kava, which, stupidly, I accepted. I felt very ill. As my brain began to go dead, I asked the Chief why women were not allowed to drink kava. He replied that kava is seen as being female. Women are not permitted to take on more power, basically, probably because the men would feel inadequate. I dare say that there are various reasons for this.

Others from Itabu arrived. As the light was beginning to fade, we decided to hike down the mountainside in near darkness. This was very risky, especially when I felt ill and uncoordinated. I wanted to vomit several times but managed to hold it back. My head felt as if it was in a vice. We got back to Itabu after dark. The Chief said we were going to the nakamal to drink more kava. I politely refused, explaining that I felt really ill.

I went to bed, feeling sick and dizzy. I didn't sleep all night. Natu had received several bites, which had become red and swollen. One bite in particular on her ring finger knuckle caused her finger to swell around her rings, which she was, therefore, unable to take off.

29th August 2010
Route march   Hot springs   Rotten scaffold   Chicken sacrifice

I itched all over, as if I had multiple bites during the night. The barking dogs, that normally plagued the village, were seldom seen and generally quiet at night times. When Natu made enquiries about the packs of dogs we had seen last visit, she was told that they had been "moved on" and that occasionally the dogs were eaten.

After breakfast, the Chief arrived, calling out 'Ramasan Nap Nappan' – good morning in his language. We asked him to draw the tattoos he and I would wear and those that the women would wear. He explained the kastom word for tattoo in his language was natadao. I gave the Chief a pen and paper. After several attempts, he was clearly struggling. Natu loaned him her reading glasses, which seemed to help, but he was getting very frustrated. He eventually put the pen and paper down and exclaimed that he couldn't do it, but then went to the earth and drew the designs in the soil, explaining what each part meant. Basically, the designs represent what the women do and what the men do in kastom society.

I asked the Chief if we could walk to Port Resolution to see the hot springs. The Chief agreed and asked hopefully if we could have a fish dinner there. He rang somebody on his mobile phone straight away, smiling at the thought. We left immediately. I loved this spontaneity. En route, I asked the Chief about Chief Noar and he said he had just died.

The walk to Port Resolution usually took about two hours. We got to the hot springs, which are in the same area, in just over one hour. The Chief had assigned his youngest daughter, Tuna, as Natu's chaperone. It was a particularly sweltering day; by the time we got to the hot springs, Natu looked like a grease spot. Sweat dripped from the end of her nose, her face was red from the heat and her island dress clung to her, as if she had just emerged fully clothed, siren-like from the sea.

'You're glowing, sweetheart,' I whispered into her ear.

'Don't you dare say anything else after that route march,' she replied.

After paying the kastom owner of the springs, two local boys acted as our guides, while the Chief and Tuna sat in the shade under a tree at the edge of the beach. We were guided along the black sand beach to a water hole in the rocks, where the surf broke. The water was gushing out at over 100 degrees. My glasses steamed up. Locals still use these water holes to cook and wash clothes in, or I should say, at a point where the water is manageable. This water hole was boiling, bananas were being cooked in it.

We then climbed up a steep cliff path into the rain forest, where the boulders contained coral and shell fossils. We climbed above the tree line to open scrub land; the ground was hot to the touch because of volcanic activity and the sun was fierce. Natu was really suffering. We were shown hot clay deposits that the locals traditionally use for body painting, different colours of reds, yellows, blues and greens.

We began our descent, taking a different route, which led to a chasm venting out steam. From here, we descended to the cliff edge to see a boiling blow hole, or geyser, on the rocks. Wooden scaffolding and a steep ladder had been built, leading from the cliff top to the rocks. One of the boys went down first, followed by me. Natu sensibly refused to even entertain the idea. By the time I got halfway down the structure, it began to sway. I looked down at my choices should it all collapse. It was very unsafe and rotten. A hole full of boiling water, giving off copious amounts of steam, sharp rocks or the pounding surf, equally boiling from volcanic vents – basically, the choices came down to being boiled, steamed, poached or scrambled. I was glad to get back to the cliff top. All the wooden steps and handrails leading up to the coloured clay areas were equally rotten.

We began our descent back to the shore. The lead guide decided to stop and point out something of interest at the very point where the track had collapsed, falling away to the rocks below. I hung on to Natu until we moved on. She was clearly ill at ease as she doesn't like heights. The boys knocked a couple of pawpaw out of a tree and gave us a slice each, which was very welcome.

As we began our final descent to the beach, Natu said to me, 'If there is no fried fish dinner, somebody is going to die.' I often wondered why she looked at me when she came out with such statements.

We eventually arrived back to the Chief and Tuna at 2:00 pm. The Chief looked sad. He told us that the restaurant was closed. No meal of any description was available anywhere. We were both very hungry and tired, as all we had eaten for breakfast was dog biscuits, or what the locals call crackers. Natu was not a happy person. She looked at me in such a way that I felt like the condemned man.

A local man came up to us, carrying a bible, and then sat with us. This was the last straw, I thought! The Chief introduced him to us as Karapaban. He said he was the kastom owner of the part of Yasur volcano that came down to the sea. The bible, which he showed us, was translated into Bislama. He had been taking part in a Christian beach mission. The Chief asked me if I would give him some healing – again, another back injury.

Two coconuts were obtained and we drank the milk from them, which was very refreshing. We left the beach, feeling hot, thirsty and hungry, ready for a two hour uphill walk back to Itabu. I was really worrying now about Natu because, at some point on our climb to the hot springs, she had hurt her ankle. Other girls had gathered around Natu, as usual, and joined our little group as we returned to Itabu.

En route, we called at a new encampment where Nikwei, his mother and other villagers were preparing for their singing and dancing, John Frum style. The Chief pointed out a stern-looking man sitting alone under the shade of a tree. I didn't like his energy at all. This, the Chief said, was Fred! I questioned the Chief about this as, during the tribal warfare in 2004, I was told by Moses that Fred had been killed. The Chief said that he wasn't killed but others were, explaining that he was led away to be executed but, because the Chief had intervened, the warring tribe had spared his life, including the life of Nikwei. This man clearly had a charismatic hold over Nikwei and his band of followers. I felt concerned for my friend.

We left for Itabu. Natu was getting the local girls, who accompanied her, to sing songs. Traditionally, the womenfolk always walk behind the men; this is the kastom way. Natu took the lead with the giggling girls, overtaking the Chief and me. The Chief thought this was hilarious. We then tried to overtake the women, but they then barged us off the road. Only Natu could get away with this. The girls had placed scarlet coral in Natu's hair. Natu was a magnet for children and young people everywhere she went. Everybody loved her. Two of the girls gathered wild oranges for us, which were delicious, and the Chief broke open some coconuts for us to eat by smashing them against some rocks. I found a small, squashed lizard on the road, so I picked it up by its tail, pretending to drop it into my open mouth.

'Iarueri, don't eat it; don't eat it,' the Chief exclaimed.

Natu looked at me, disowning this sad person, shaking her head, sighing with exaggerated embarrassment.

When we arrived back at Itabu, Natu was exhausted. She hadn't eaten all day and was dehydrated. She went to lie on our bed. Glenda, the Chief's third youngest daughter, arrived, presenting me with a live chicken for us both as a gift from Chief Kabari for the healing I had done. I knew that, as a gift to us both, it was important that Natu was also present to hold the bird. I took the chicken under my arm, excusing myself from the Chief and Glenda, and dropped the bound bird on to the bed, on to Natu's belly. The bird squawked; Natu squawked. The chicken then pecked her. Natu, realising immediately the situation, offered the beautiful creature her blessing for its sacrifice. The three of us emerged from the hut. Natu thanked Glenda, inviting her to accompany Namu, Nahu and herself to Lenakel for a women's shopping spree. No men were allowed. The women were really excited about this trip the next day.

The Chief called Nahu and gave her the chicken, and she left with a long carving knife. Natu returned to bed to get some rest; the Chief and I went to the nakamal. I helped prepared the kava and, thankfully, the Chief allowed me to abstain tonight. Again, for some reason, the Chief decided that we were not going to sleep in the jungle to meet the Kassosu, but we would do so the following evening. I was very disappointed. I returned to Natu and a welcomed chicken dinner.

30th August 2010
Yeramanu myth   Kassosu can kill

Shopping day for the women today! All were dressed in their finest clothes. Namu wore the island dress Natu had given to her on our last visit. Predictably, the Chief would not allow the women to go to Lenakel unescorted, so poor Donald was given the job of minder. Natu, Namu, Nahu, Glenda and Tuna, with an assortment of children, drove off, waving. I felt sorry for Namu, as all of her family was with her, including Donald, her husband, and their children, so she was unable to relax. Natu said she hoped to get the girls a fried fish dinner on the beach in Lenakel before they left. I reminded Donald not to lose Natu. He could hardly look at Natu without laughing, giving the thumbs-up sign and grinning.

I stayed behind with the Chief. I asked him more questions about the Kassosu. He told me a story that his father had passed down to him.
The Myth

Long ago, two women decided to go into the jungle to the nakamal (banyan tree) of the flying fox. When they got there, they climbed up into the tree with the invitation of the flying fox. The bat said that, if they were to hang upside-down, like the other bats, they would receive the spiritual gifts of the Kassosu. One of the women became frightened that she would fall, so she climbed back down the tree and ran away. The other woman remained and hung by her legs, as the flying fox had directed. The flying fox then had sex with her. She soon gave birth and the offspring was the first Yeramanu. These are known as the bat men or, as the Chief said, 'in your culture, they will be known as the dragon men.'

The Chief admitted that he was afraid of the encounter between the Kassosu and us. He knew all about what would take place, as his father had described it all in detail to him, but this, like for myself, was his first contact experience. I said I was really excited about it. The Chief looked at me in the same way Natu does, saying, 'Iarueri, Iarueri. Contact with the Kassosu can kill a man if the right preparation and safeguards are not adhered to.'

I realised then that the seven years of preparation for this moment were crucial for the process, especially for our safety. The phrase "fools walk in where angels fear to tread" came into my mind. If physical contact was made, then the rest of the ceremonies could go ahead, he explained. The Chief wanted us to walk to Loanengo village to go to Jungle Oasis to speak with Kelson, for some reason. I was never able to work this one out. He was hoping to find Chief Nakweran, one of the organisers for the tokka dance, to see if Natu and I could attend and to find out time, date and location.

On the road, we passed a small boy, carrying a plastic can. He was obviously in distress. The Chief stopped, asking him what the trouble was. The boy explained he was sent out by his father to find fuel for the truck, but the boy couldn't find anyone at a particular village where there was meant to be fuel. The Chief told the boy to walk with us until we reached that village. Once there, the Chief stood at the boundary, calling out until somebody arrived. After a brief discussion, the man told the boy where to get his fuel from.

We returned to the road, where we met a local man who had Down's Syndrome, and who was deaf and dumb. I remembered him clearly playing in the string band at our wedding ceremony. The Chief told me that his name was Trahee. He too was in a state of distress, wandering aimlessly. He had lost his way. The Chief told him, through sign language, directions where to go. This is the mark of a great man. The man is the chief; the chief is not the man.

We passed the Apostolic Church, which had a Christian women's convention. One of the women glared and scowled at the Chief as we passed, simply because he was kastom. I was quite shocked, since I had never seen this ignorance before.

When we arrived at Jungle Oasis, I met Kelson. We embraced; it felt like a Judas embrace. As usual, he was the same – smiles on the outside, but a twisted heart on the inside. The meeting between us was very strained. Kelson had organised lunch for the two of us, at a price of course, cooked by Jerry. Jerry and his family had moved from Port Resolution to Loanengo village, so he had work at the Jungle Oasis.

The Chief, Kelson and I sat together to talk. Kelson said he was standing as a member of parliament for Tanna Island again, after failing in his last attempt. He had somehow managed to persuade the Chief to help him. Apparently, the authorities had heard that Kelson was stealing from the Chief and tourists, so threatened to revoke his licence. He now pays the Chief for the kastom dancing for his guests. I warned the Chief not to trust him. However, I was pleased to see everybody getting on and communicating with each other.

Kelson and Jerry invited the Chief, Natu and I to a Seventh Day Adventist wedding in a couple of day's time. The Chief and I looked at each other and raised our eyebrows. As we left Jungle Oasis, I asked the Chief if we could go with our faces painted and wearing nambas. The Chief was bent over in the middle of the road, laughing, tears running down his cheeks, saying that they would all be frightened of us and run away.

We met Chief Nakweran at the Apostolic Church, sitting on the grass, talking to another man. He said Natu and I could have permission to attend the tokka dance and gave the Chief the relevant details.

When we arrived at Itabu, the Chief told me to rest in preparation for the night in the jungle. I was just dozing off when a truck arrived with Natu and her party, much earlier than expected. The driver had to pick up tourists from the airport, so had to return for a specific time. Natu didn't get her fish dinner again, but had got a good amount of food to share.

Donald handed the Chief a letter he had collected from their post office box in Lenakel. It was the letter I had written in June giving the Chief the details of our arrival and departure. Natu had bought a reasonably priced guitar for Nikwei and his group, as music is so very important to him.

The Chief and I went to the nakamal to prepare the kava and to light the fire. It had rained heavily each night since our first jungle camp. The Chief said we would not camp tonight either. I felt bitterly disappointed. He admitted somewhat sheepishly that he didn't want to get soaked. I felt he was really frightened and was procrastinating. He added that it gave the Kassosu more time to become familiar with the camp and my smell. We were running out of time!

I drank one shell of kava, alongside the Chief, praying aloud that we may encounter the Kassosu. I returned to our hut, where Natu and I went for our evening meal.

31ˢᵗ August 2010
Kabbable

During the night, the Chief's two flee-bitten, mongrel puppies howled outside our hut. It was strangely haunting. It was a very wet night and continued to rain well into the morning. Natu told me at the breakfast table she had dreamt of us meeting the Kassosu at the very time that the dogs howled. We both looked forward to the fresh bread and fruit, along with the fried eggs bought in Lenakel but were disappointed. Nahu had fried the fresh bread and the eggs were burnt and greasy. We couldn't eat it, so we decided to poison the puppies, who begged for food under the table. Even they refused most of it.

After breakfast, the Chief asked me for 30,000 Vatu (approximately £200) for a large pig for the feast for the ceremonies. The cost of pigs in Vanuatu is very high and gives grade and status to the host, especially if the pig is large. I felt anxious, as we hadn't budgeted for this substantial cash outlay.

The Chief and Michael arrived at the breakfast table to ask the perennial question of "how can they get more tourists?". I had gone over the same questions and answers on each visit in the past, so I let Natu do the explaining. She was forthright and honest, telling the Chief he was not ready yet to provide for the creature comforts of the average tourist, but should be acceptable to eco-friendly backpackers. He accepted Natu's words with grace and respected her wisdom. Natu also gave him some ideas we had collected from visiting the Huaorani tribe in the Amazon.

Natu and Tuna then went off to Loanengo village, invited by Jerry, so Natu could undertake a physiotherapy assessment of Ealise at Jerry's house. The Chief and I went off to Sanback village for me to give healing to an old man. On the way, the Chief told me that his name was Kabbable and that he lived in the hut on which the roof and one side had collapsed. When we arrived, he came out of this hovel into the rain on his hands and feet, as though he was walking like a crab. I recognised him straight away from our wedding feast. Apparently, he had got drunk on kava two years ago and had fallen off a bridge, hurting his back. They thought his back was broken, although he had sensation and movement in his legs.

The Chief took me to one side in the village to show me the wild chicken traps made out of bamboo pieces, explaining in detail how they were used. Wild pigs were also caught in a noose tied to a branch under tension, lured by coconuts.

On our return to Itabu, the Chief gave me demonstrations of various kastom dances. He also added that the tattoo which I had received in 2005 had a much deeper meaning than he had previously explained. The mark I wore was the mark of the Kassosu. It was their grade mark, he said. This now made more sense to me, remembering that after I had been created a chief, the first guardianship given to me was that of the flying fox. It seemed now that tribal tattoos have multi-layered levels of meaning and awareness as you travel up through the grades.

1st September 2010
Doubt   Tokka dance   Search for tattooist

During the night, Natu voiced her misgivings of receiving another tattoo. The tokka tattoo she had received at her grading ceremony prior to our wedding meant something significant and spiritual to her. She was really looking forward to the tokka dance because of this connection. I encouraged her to follow her heart and refuse it if it felt right.

I had abdominal cramps and diarrhoea today. We went to see the tokka dance, leaving early in the truck as the drive we were told was very long. The road was washed out along the coast, so we had to drive into Lenakel, then back down the coast road to the southwest of the island. The coastal track ran alongside black sand-dunes, kissed by rolling white surf from a deep blue ocean. The beaches were deserted. The track was rough, especially once we had left the main road, crossing rivers and deep ruts in four-wheel drive. Natu was in the cab with the driver; I was in the back of the truck with the Chief, Nikwei, Donald, Jack and other men and boys from the village.

For some reason, during the entire day, I felt anxious. I prayed for help, strength and the courage I needed. My mind was full of doubt and anxiety. It had taken me seven years to reach this point of the journey and in the final days I doubted everything. Why was I here? What was I supposed to be doing? Was it an ego trip? What was it all for, anyway? I felt very emotional and wanted to be held by my wife, to hear her words of comfort and wisdom, encouragement and support, to reassure me what I was about to accomplish was worth it all. Personal intimate touch was not the kastom way and was seen as taboo. I needed Natu. I felt vulnerable, alone and frightened. I suppressed my feelings as we arrived at Infitanna village for the tokka dance, after a three hour, rough drive.

The dancers had finished their first round and were resting before the second round of seven dances. One of the men travelling with us gifted me with an eagle's feather. We stopped at the edge of a huge nakamal, surrounded by four large banyan trees, some of which contained tree houses. It was important for Natu to see and connect with the dancers and the tokka spirit. The men and boys resumed their singing and dancing, using the tokka sticks, as the Chief had previously described.

A local man invited me to sit with some elders at the edge of the nakamal and explained in simple English what each of the dances meant. The dances represented life in the kastom community. The main body of dancers, approximately thirty in all, wore grass skirts, foliage armbands and headdresses, sang and stamped their feet, while boys and other men broke free to enact typical kastom scenarios to the cheers from the crowd. Then the tokka dance began, the men wielding their sticks with force against each other in a breathtaking performance resembling a mixture of martial arts and Morris Dance. Many had come to see the dancing from all over the island. It was an authentic Melanesian festival. Natu and I were the only non-locals present.

After the performance, the dancers left to walk to another remote village to repeat the dancing and celebrations. We returned to Lenakel. Natu was dreaming of a fried fish dinner again. We bought two large bags of rice for our feast but returned to Itabu by a different route to Lowin village, where Sam and his family lived, so Natu missed out yet again on a decent meal! The plan was that we would collect Sam and return with him to Itabu for the natadao, or tattoo, ceremony, since only he or his family had the kastom lineage to do this. The Chief explained that nobody at Itabu did. (Other families on the island also hold this privilege and lineage.) The Chief sent out boy runners to try to find Sam, as he was nowhere to be found. The Chief found Sam's father at the local nakamal. We learnt that Sam and his wife, Nellie, who is the Chief's eldest daughter, were in a remote valley at another nakamal, attending the circumcision ceremony and festival of 29 boys. The festivities would last all night, we were told. Once this was established, the Chief sent out other boy runners to find Sam's younger brother, Graham. The Chief looked frustrated. He decided that, as time was getting late, he needed to be back at our nakamal for dusk, so decided to abandon the search and leave. However, after we had driven a couple of miles out of the village, we met Graham and another brother walking on the road. The truck pulled up and the Chief told them to get in the back.

By the time we had arrived back at Itau, the other men had prepared the kava. Again, for some reason, the Chief decided that we would not go and sleep in the jungle that night. I felt very frustrated at his decision and rather annoyed. Maybe he knew something I didn't. Was this another test of some sort from Spirit, I wondered?

2nd September 2010
Pig's heart   Dance challenge   Beard shaving   Tattoo

The Chief came to our leaf hut and asked us to have an early breakfast so we could be at Donald's camp to begin the ritual of killing the pig. When we arrived, we found the pig was a very large, fat sow. She was bound and laid on the ground and the kava root laid next to her. The Chief handed to me a very heavy club after we had pulled the pig into the centre of the encampment, where he said I was to symbolically hold it to her skull. This I did, passing the club back to him. He then did the same, passing the club to Graham, who had been chosen for the privilege and the honour to kill it. After several heavy blows, the skull split open, blood gushing from the ears which, as usual, the dogs greedily lapped up. We then had to carry the pig to a low branch, where a large hook was put through its jaw enabling it to be hung for the hair-burning and scraping part. I had to start this process off by firing the pig, followed by the Chief and other men. Graham then butchered the pig as the women, including Natu, began preparing lap lap at the side of the fire, heating the volcanic stones ready for the earth oven.

The heart was the first thing to be cut out of the pig. The Chief handed the hot, bloody organ to me to carry to the fire. He cut a pointed stick and, in usual fashion, pierced the heart at one end and stuck the other in the ground. The flames were so fierce that the heart soon turned black, the fat dripping and spitting, running in rivulets from it, causing flash-burning. Donald came to the rescue and moved it, turning it occasionally. Graham's prize was the tongue.

We returned to the carcass, the Chief handing to me large, heavy, bloody and slippery portions of meat, which were still very hot. We were told that the reason that the pig was so fat was because of the coconuts, and the oils that they contained, which it ate. The Chief and I both carried these large portions of meat to the women, where we dumped them on to a pile of freshly cut leaves. The women then cut the flesh into small strips for lap lap. Other portions were left whole for the larger cooking pots or the earth ovens. The Chief then cut bits from the heart after it had been partially cooked. Again, as usual, it was black on the outside, raw and running with blood in the middle. He placed these portions into a leaf and sprinkled salt upon them. The Chief said it was very important that Natu and I had some of the heart to eat. I managed to eat my portions, gulping the meat down quickly. The Chief offered some to Natu, which she refused (wisely, in my opinion). The Chief accepted her decision and ate some heart also. Natu said later, had she fully understood the importance of eating the fresh heart, she would have done so. She thought she was being offered kidney.

I excused myself, returning to our leaf hut to go to the toilet. By the time I got there, I became suddenly ill, without warning. I had severe abdominal cramps, nausea, sweating and diarrhoea, all at the same time. I sat on the toilet not knowing which end was going to explode first. Sweat dripped off the end of my nose. I became saturated all over and began to feel dizzy and then faint. I could feel myself drifting into a state of unconsciousness. Natu came to my aid, as she knew something was wrong. She took a look at me and said it was "a spirit sickness". Apparently, she had experienced a similar thing prior to receiving a spiritual shift while she was in Tibet some years ago.

Natu made sure that I was all right before she left me, returning to Donald's camp, as she knew that Nikwei and his musical troupe were arriving to begin the celebrations and feast. She took the guitar with her that she had bought in Lenakel. After a short time, the sickness left as quickly as it had arrived. It seems that I had had a major energetic detox prior to connecting with the Kassosu. It felt as though the process was actually taking place in one of my energy bodies, but reacting in the physical.

I returned to Donald's camp, feeling fine but a little weak and shaken. When I arrived, the Chief was standing in front of the people, in full flow giving a speech. The Chief was explaining to all gathered about how Natu and I had come to Itabu and the completion of the myth of the return of the white serpent, the return of the white twin. Other men spoke also, taking it in turns, the Chief responding to their questions. All looked at Natu and I, smiled and nodded. We felt very welcomed amongst these people as part of their family. The Chief then nodded to Natu, she stood and he beckoned Nikwei to come over to her. Natu presented his new guitar to him. He was absolutely delighted.

Singing and dancing then took place. The Chief, Donald and I wore grass skirts, much to Natu's delight. Natu recognised the large woman in the crowd who had danced seductively at our wedding feast. The two women held each other's gaze, nodding to each other "across the arena". The large woman smiled; there was a twinkle in her eye. This was going to be interesting. The large woman then began to dance very seductively and slowly, holding Natu's gaze. It was clearly a challenge to Natu.

Natu recognised that the gauntlet had been thrown down to her and she held the other woman's gaze as she danced back. The two women began to dance, moving ever nearer and closer to each other. Some of the men in the crowd sat mesmerised, staring at Natu in particular. They had never seen a white woman dance this way. The local woman danced in typical Melanesian style. Natu, who used to be an Arabic dance teacher, did the belly dance. The two women kept gazing at each other, except for when they turned and spun, their hips moving, gyrating seductively, all their wobbly bits bouncing amazingly. The men sat open-mouthed; the other women cheered and laughed and egged each other on. It was really hilarious and very erotic; some of the men were clearly embarrassed and crossed their legs. The Chief stood, his eyes as wide as saucers, his chin dropped, looking at both women. He didn't know whether to laugh or cry.

The two women closed in the middle of the arena. This was truly a bout and I wondered what the outcome would be. All of a sudden, the big woman just exploded into laughter and bent over double, hitting the ground with her hands, tears running down her face. She just couldn't contain herself any longer. She came over to Natu and held her face tightly in both hands and kissed her on both cheeks. This was the first time I had ever seen such tactile affection. I turned to look at the Chief. He thought it was seriously funny. Tears were streaming down his face and he was bent double. Natu later told me that this was Namu's sister. We never knew what her name was.

By this time, the pig had been cooked in a variety of ways and some of the pork and rice were brought to us on a plate to eat. The band had a break soon afterwards and had their meal, followed by everybody else. I estimated that there were about 60 people present. The Chief came up to us and told us that, when Nikwei's band had finished the final songs, the ceremonies would begin. He whispered to me that he had decided to do the ceremonies now, because he had thought that, if we do the different rituals, then that might make the connection between the Kassosu easier. I saw the logic in this. It was time! I felt a little nervous but, after seven years of preparation, I was now ready.

The Chief, Nikwei, myself, Natu, Nahu and Donald's eldest son, Niai Paian, went to the lower nakamal for the secret ceremonies to take place. It seemed the Chief was starting to bring in Donald's eldest son to train him in ceremony and ritual, because he will continue the lineage on Donald's death. Again, strangely, Namu did not come, which she was meant to do.

We left Natu and Nahu in the nakamal and we walked through the passageway through the banyan tree to the preparation site behind. The hut we had changed in previously was no longer standing. We stood naked in the rain forest and changed into our nambas. A leaf necklace was placed around my neck, followed by a boar's tusk necklace that Nikwei had made for me, for this ceremony.

The Chief looked at me, his eyes softened and he spoke quietly, 'Iarueri, remember who you are and what your name means. Your name means God.'

At that very moment, another man and a small boy appeared, who were fully clothed, to speak urgently with the Chief. The small child disappeared somewhere behind me in the bushes. Suddenly, I felt a sharp prod into my anus. Spinning quickly around, I saw the little boy triumphantly holding up a digit.

'You do not stick your finger up God's ass,' I shouted in a staccato voice.

The men bend over double laughing. The boy wailed as though he had been savaged by a demon. I felt embarrassed and couldn't help but laugh also. The little brat had scored a complete bull's-eye. He was clearly a master in his art. It was a shock; I simply wasn't expecting something like that to take place. I wondered afterwards how many other innocent men had succumbed to the deadly finger of death.

The lesson I learnt from this experience is that it is our birthright to remember the potential of who we are all becoming. Instantly I had this realisation that I was "brought down to earth" by a probe into my base chakra, therefore grounding this process to avoid ego contamination.

Even the smallest person can change the evolution of our world by such flashes of enlightenment that automatically affect the collective Quantum Field of human consciousness wherever we are on the planet.

This child was my teacher.

After we had composed ourselves and the man and child had left, the Chief led the way back through the banyan tree, followed by myself, Nikwei and Niai. I was instructed to sit at the southern end of the nakamal on a bamboo seat. Nahu tried desperately to suppress her giggles at seeing my white, hairy ass. Graham and his brother sat nearby, watching and waiting for the Chief's instructions to begin their art of tattooing.

The Chief magically pulled from his nambas a razor. Why he kept it in there, to this day, I've often wondered, but thankfully it was not a bamboo knife. The Chief explained, as he began to dry shave me, that a bamboo knife would not be sharp enough, as my beard was too coarse. The process was very uncomfortable. The Chief kept commenting several times through the ceremony, 'Very strong, very strong. Good, good.' He usually said this when he snagged the beard in the razor blade, bringing tears to my eyes and nicking my skin, causing wet patches, which I assumed was blood. I classed the beard-scraping ceremony as another blood ritual.

As handfuls of hair fell from my face, Nikwei gathered it carefully from my nambas and the ground around my feet. The Chief said that, on this occasion, my beard hair would be pushed into a hole in a young coconut, so a tree will grow with my hair as part of it. He added that, even though I may return to the Isle of Man (UK), part of me will always remain in my homeland.

After the Chief had scraped the hair and flesh from my face, he left a small, Hitler-like moustache, beneath my nose. I think the reason why he left this was because he was frightened of ripping my lip apart. (The following morning, I cut it off with a pair of nail scissors, hoping that there was no spiritual significance about leaving it. Natu said I looked silly with it.)

Nikwei then had his beard shaved off, followed by the Chief, but the trouble was that the blade was now so blunt that the Chief was in too much pain, so it was left. Surprisingly, the Chief said after the beard-shaving ceremony that there was no need for me to have a beard any longer. Once I had reached this particular grade level, I could choose whether I wanted a beard or not. I could never understand the logic behind this, because previously I was told by several people that on no occasion was the beard to be removed. I never found out the reason for this statement.

It was now time for the natadao (tattoo) ceremony. I asked the Chief what Graham's kastom name was, and he replied Tarro, the same as the vegetable. It is always good to use the kastom name when sacred ceremony is taking place. A long discussion between the Chief, Tarro and Nikwei then ensued. Each compared the drawing the Chief had made in the earth (now copied on a scrap of paper) and the tattoo I had received in 2005 by Graham's brother. I had no idea what they were talking about, for they were speaking in their native tongue. It seemed that a compromise had been reached between the tattooist and the

Chief, and that the tattoo design was to be changed. The same discussion happened for Nahu's tattoo.

Tarro began his art on my arm and his brother started to do the tattoo on Nahu's arm. Donald suddenly arrived at this time, having overseen the procedures of the feast. When he saw my shaven face, he burst into tears, wiping them away with his T-shirt. Tarro, using three needles, as Sam had done previously, dipping them into a mixture of black plant dye, charcoal and lamp soot, contained within a small clam shell from the beach. His work was skilful and precise; it was also very painful. As he worked, he wiped the blood away with a dirty rag, checking to see that he hadn't missed a line, then going over it time and time again. The light was beginning to fade. The Chief stopped Tarro and his brother and said that the tattoos were to be completed tomorrow, as we had to get to the nakamal for the kava ritual. He whispered to me that we were going to meet the Kassosu tonight. At last, I felt that things were beginning to move.

As we entered the nakamal, the other men had prepared the kava. They stared long and hard at us. We must have looked so different without our beards.

After the kava ritual, I returned to our hut to prepare and wait for the Chief. I felt so excited. I waited and waited. Natu went to sleep. Eventually, I went to bed at midnight. I was so disappointed. There were over 30 men at the nakamal that night. I expected he had difficulty in leaving early.

Natu now had abdominal cramps and diarrhoea and didn't look very well.

3rd September 2010
Bloody tattoo   Ear piercing   Tourist shot   Police   Kassosu

I had a bad night; Natu did too. I couldn't sleep because of the pain of the tattoo. When we saw the Chief after breakfast, he apologised to me for not coming as planned, but he had become very sick suddenly and had to go to bed. Natu and I looked at each other, raising our eyebrows. Natu said that she saw Graham and his brother leave in a truck late last night. I hoped they would return today, but they didn't.

As Natu and I sat in the sunshine, resting and enjoying each other's company, two men and a woman came up to us and told us that they would complete the tattoos on myself and Nahu. The Chief had told them to do this. It turned out that they were from a different tribe, who also held the natadao lineage. I had never seriously thought of a tattoo as being a blood ritual before, until what took place this day.

Nahu was already waiting on the bench near our hut. Again, there was no sign of Namu. The principal tattooist was a man called Nase. He worked on Nahu. The other man's name was Alfred. I never found out what his kastom name was, but he worked on me. Their female assistant prepared the clam shells for both, with the charcoal, plant juices and lamp soot. They mixed this on a regular basis, constantly keeping it working, so that it wouldn't dry out in the sun. I noticed that Alfred used three needles, one of which was slightly longer than the other two. Natu told me afterwards that she had found out the reason for this was that the first needle penetrated the skin into the blood supply, the other needles held the charcoal, plant dyes and lamp soot. The needles were never cleaned between people.

Nase redrew the top part of my tattoo for Alfred to copy. I had thought Tarro's work was very painful but Alfred's work was nothing more than brutal and sadistic. I felt blood run down my arm, feeling it dripping from my elbow on to the earth. It was wiped away with a filthy rag. This bloody assault lasted for over an hour. We were all sitting in full sunshine. It was hot, sweaty, uncomfortable and at times I felt weak. The pain in my arm was excruciating. I kept eye contact with Natu. She was sending love, strength, courage and support to me. She wanted to hold me, I wanted to hold her, but I knew that this was not the kastom way. I knew that she was holding me energetically in her arms. I could tell by Natu's expression that it was not good. Occasionally, she came up to me and whispered, 'Do you want to stop?' I said, 'No.' I straightened my spine and sat upright, as a High Chief should do.

The Chief then suddenly arrived, carrying a large bunch of bananas. He'd been on walkabout somewhere. He watched the natadao ceremony that Nahu and I were going through. He clearly looked shocked, knowing that it was his turn next. Eventually, Alfred finished the blood ritual on me and called for the Chief to change places. Nase continued to work on Nahu. I watched as the blood ran down her arm. She winced, she turned away, she was very brave, very strong. He was being much more gentle with her but, even so, the blood still flowed down her arm. She was biting her lip several times. We looked at each other and smiled. I nodded to honour her bravery. She nodded back to honour mine.

Most indigenous peoples work with blood rituals such as tattoos and piercings because they understand that blood is a sacred, vital force that is energetically alive with the codes of your lineage. The skin or surface of the body is a barrier between the inner and outer worlds. When you bleed in sacred ceremony, you are offering your blood lineage and, therefore, releasing the secret codes of your true identity to the Earth Mother and Cosmos. There is the potential of receiving great insights through this process, providing it is done correctly.

The Chief clearly was not happy about the savagery of Alfred's work and complained. Each time Alfred tried to start the tattoo on the Chief, he stopped him, clearly losing face before all of us. This was now a public ceremony. Initially, the ceremony last night was held in the nakamal and it was secret. Now that it had started, it was held in a public place, so a crowd had gathered. Natu had a quiet word with the Chief, giving him a breathing exercise to focus on, and I placed my hands upon his knees, smiling to him, encouraging him to go through with this tattoo experience. Others then arrived and they attempted to hold him down and force his arm. I felt sorry for him.

Eventually, Alfred began his brutal work on the Chief's arm. Once he had started and the Chief had got over the initial shock, he was able to let him continue, although he was clearly suffering and in great pain. Alfred completed a smaller outline of the tattoo than mine, but did not complete the inner design, since the Chief had had enough and stopped him.

The Chief refused to have his ears pierced, but encouraged Nahu and I to do so. Nahu had had enough, but still went through with the ear-piercing ceremony after I had done so. Alfred picked up a grubby orange spine and, after massaging my right earlobe for a while, pushed the thorn through my ear. It felt as if I had been burnt. The thorn was withdrawn and another piece of wood from the spine of a palm leaf was pushed through and left in position. Tarro had made a good grade mark; Alfred had made a mess. I decided to have the tattoo redone when I got back home to the Isle of Man, but, after the localised trauma, I would have to allow a minimum of one month for the wound to heal. As I ran my fingers over the wound, I could feel lumps of charcoal in my flesh. I wondered if they would work themselves in or work themselves out. Only time would tell.

The Chief told me that the left ear would be done on our next visit, which he kept reminding us about, which would be 2013. I had had enough anyway. The ear sticks should be the width and size of a short pencil, he explained. He had already explained this to me in the past and he cut a piece of wood, showing me the size and the width. I tried to encourage him to have his ears pierced, but he wouldn't have it. He said Alfred was too rough.

I had a sense of completion now. I had given my word to Spirit that I would complete the tests and ceremonies. I now had done that. I was really impressed with the strength and courage of Nahu. The Chief paid tribute to us both for our courage, some would say stupidity perhaps, to endure the ordeal of these blood rituals. He admitted that he couldn't do it. He said that his father was also tattooed across his right cheekbone, but he would not spoil his face. He said his father's generation was the first to wear western clothing. His grandparents were naked, except for grass skirts and nambas. He also went on to explain that, when he was a child, if kastom parents pierced their children's ears, the church would get the police involved. The church managed to get the practice outlawed. Until this interference, everybody on Tanna Island had kastom ear sticks.

As we finished the natadao ceremony, two strange men arrived, wanting to speak to the Chief urgently. It turned out they were police officers, making enquiries about two boys from the Itabu region who had shot and injured a female tourist with a catapult when she was travelling in the back of a truck. The driver had made a complaint to the police, reporting the incident. The police, the Chief and Donald were in conversation about this situation for some time. The Chief told them to bring the boys to the nakamal tonight.

The Chief wanted me to visit the volcano crater after lunch to give my thanks and prayers to Yasur. Nase was my guide on this occasion. He kept addressing Natu and I as Apu, meaning elder. Nase kept a blistering pace. I was sore after the tattoo and ear-piercing ceremony, so struggled in the heat of the day. Yasur was as impressive and somewhat frightening as ever. I offered my prayers to him. On our return, Nase made us both fern headdresses to act as hats for shade.

On our arrival back at Itabu, we went to the nakamal. The two police officers and a third man arrived, accompanied by four boys of different ages. The police had confirmed that the culprits had come from Itabu. They wanted the Chief to speak to them. Discussions began by various other men also, one suggesting that the boys did community service. Nase whispered to me that the boys had also stolen some cooked pork and some rice from a house. The two youngest boys were made to apologise to the man, so I assumed that it was from his house the food was stolen. The two older boys had their photographs taken on a mobile phone by the police. None of the boys took it very seriously, all sniggered and laughed throughout the whole proceedings. I wondered what the outcome would be.

The Chief whispered to me that we were going to the jungle this night! I returned buoyant to our hut after the kava ritual, looking forward to this at long last. As I waited, Natu and I stood outside in the darkness, watching the fireflies playing tag around our leaf hut. Bizarrely small fires started around the village, with no explanation! Natu later asked the Chief what the fires were about and he said it was the Kassosu.

At 8:30 pm, the Chief arrived at our leaf hut. He was drunk with kava, swaying from side to side. His speech was slurred. I felt devastated. On our last night together, he was always this way, very emotional at our parting and would drink several shells of kava, praying for my safe return. He was also not wearing the right coloured clothing that previously he said was essential and important.

We gathered our sleeping gear, stumbling off into the jungle by torchlight, accompanied by the Chief's two flea-ridden pups. Eventually, after reaching our jungle camp, we settled down and fell asleep, waking soon afterwards to the sound of the Kassosu approaching our shelter. It was so exciting. It was the most bizarre sound you would imagine. The Chief crawled out of the shelter, standing in the darkness, facing the Kassosu. I was behind him in a few seconds. I was excited and exhilarated at the prospect of physical contact from the Dragon Men. I couldn't tell if there was just one, or more, but, for some reason, I suddenly heard them leaving, moving away through the undergrowth. They had gone. I felt devastated. The Chief said they wouldn't return now, so we packed up our gear and returned through the darkness to the village. I felt angry we had not connected each and every night, as originally planned. The lessons I learnt from this experience were: (a) because my expectations were so high and focused only on one outcome, I had closed off all other avenues and possibilities; and (b) if you search for enlightenment from "outside", it will always elude you. Truth is found within. It is always there, if we are prepared to look.

During our return to the village, the Chief picked several types of leaves, explaining they were kastom leaves, leaves to connect with the Kassosu. When we arrived at our leaf hut, he instructed me to go inside and lay the leaves he had given me under my pillow to help me connect with the Dragon Men in my dreams. I wondered why he hadn't given me these before? He then told me to go inside and close the wooden door, whilst he chewed different kastom leaves. He then sprayed and spat the juice on to the door to mark our hut for the Kassosu to visit during the night. He also said that Natu may dream about the Kassosu now.

I couldn't sleep because of the pain of my tattoo and ear piercing. I managed to reconnect with the jungle camp and had a sense and a feeling of flying on a Dragon. I had been aware of them watching me for several days. As I flew on my Dragon, along with the other Dragon Riders, we arrived at a huge banyan tree, which they called the "World Tree". We flew through and around its branches. Many life forms lived within, upon and around this tree. They told me that this tree was a multi-dimensional portal to different realms, including other worlds in our solar system and beyond.

4th September 2010
Tattoo meaning

The Chief came and sat with us at breakfast. He told Natu that his father had shaken hands and communicated with the Kassosu on many occasions.

The reason why you kill a pig and drink kava, he explained, was as offerings to the Kassosu as a gift. When they ate and drank the food (the energetic counterpart), their energy was reduced so, therefore, it was less dangerous for human interaction, so you wouldn't be killed. Somehow, the energy of the pig and the kava reduced the Kassosu energy so they couldn't harm you.

I was pleased that the Chief had taken Natu into his confidence and explained a few brief things about the Kassosu to her. She understood that what we went through was secret.

The Chief was very quiet and looked sad. Today, we were leaving Itabu for Lenakel and home. At 8:30, we left Itabu, arriving at Lenakel about two hours later. The Chief wanted a football to help the youths to keep occupied after the incidents of the last few days, but, because it was Saturday, few shops were open, so we couldn't find one. We then went on to the airport to wait some time for our return flight to Vila. During this time, I asked the Chief to explain in more detail about the different tattoo I had received and to explain what it actually meant.

He explained to me again how each segment represented a spirit stone of a particular fruit, vegetable or animal which was native to the island, and the whole design was contained within the banyan tree, as the spirit stones were always beneath this tree. The banyan tree is the World Tree and it's beneath this tree that the Chief always stands to receive his power. The Chief said I was to continue to sleep with the Kassosu leaves under my pillow until the energy of the leaves had left. He would take kava and call Tamaffa and ask the Kassosu at the nakamal to strengthen the connection between us. I was to let him know if this connection had been made when I got home. If not, he would do another ceremony. He also said that the Kassosu were frightened of modern technology, such as generators, chain saws and even people wearing glasses. The energy of these things made them sick, he said.

The Chief reminded me that he would be hosting the next tokka dance and that it was important for Natu and I to return then. He said we would continue and make another attempt at touching the Kassosu over a period of one week. He added that the second ear stick will be prepared and the left ear will be pierced on our arrival in 2013; he said, 'On no account are you to wear an earring. Only a kastom stick.'

After waiting for an hour, the Chief decided to leave with his party back to Itabu. We embraced and said our farewells, and soon boarded our flight to Vila.

After checking in to the hotel, we went to the local market, before having some local fish and chips back at the hotel. Most of the local staff had been trained by Europeans for the tourist industry, so it was good to eat palatable food again. We were both very tired; Natu was still not well, she looked tired and was unable to eat her food properly. I could tell she was losing weight and that something was wrong. We decided to have an early night and looked forward to a soak in a hot, steaming bath to try to get clean again. Natu was the first one in the bath. After she had had her soak, she got out, the water was drained away and what was left behind was the equivalent of the mud flats of a tidal estuary in a mangrove swamp. Of course, when I got out of the bath after my soak, the bath was perfectly clean! When I mentioned this fact to Natu, I ducked just in time! It felt so good to sleep again in a proper bed with clean sheets.

5th September 2010
Feathers confiscated – New Zealand

We couldn't sleep because of the local drunks and immature boy racers driving up and down outside the hotel, with loud music blaring, all night. Natu was not well.

After checking in for our flight to Aeotorea (New Zealand), Natu tried to get some sleep, arriving in Auckland about three hours later. The New Zealand bio-security and quarantine officials confiscated my Kassosu leaves, eagle feather and Maggie's feather sticks. They were destroyed. Our boots were removed from our bags and disinfected. By the time we got to our hotel, Maggie was exhausted and clearly very ill. Bruising began to appear on my arm around the tattoo.

6th September 2010

Maggie had a high temperature, with a fever and diarrhoea. I was starting to worry about her now.

7th September 2010

Maggie had a bad night. We left Auckland, New Zealand, on 7th September, arriving in Honolulu, Hawai'i on 6th September. This was very confusing. Because we had crossed the International Date Line, we had gained an extra day. Maggie asked an air hostess on the Air New Zealand flight if there was a possibility of any vacant seats so that she could stretch out on and sleep. Fortunately, there were some at the back of the aircraft, so at least she was able to have some rest.

7th September 2010 (again)

I lost my ear stick at some point and my ear was now inflamed and swollen. Maggie lost her voice and could no longer eat. I was getting very concerned about her health, all she wanted to do was sleep.

9th September 2010
Pneumonia

Maggie was too weak to get out of bed, except for running to the toilet with diarrhoea and the sensation of nausea. During the early hours of the morning, she started to have malaria-like symptoms. She was shivering, yet was burning up and she finally asked me to get a doctor. Fortunately, there was a 24-hour medical centre at the hotel we were staying at, so I helped her dress at 4:00 am and we went down to the clinic for 5:00 am to see the on call doctor. After doing the paperwork and paying the fee, Maggie was then examined by the doctor, who diagnosed her as having pneumonia and also some unspecified organism. He told her that she was very ill. He prescribed strong antibiotics and nausea medication. Maggie was to spend the entire time in Honolulu in bed ill.

I wondered that, had this situation occurred on Tanna Island, the outcome may have been quite different.

10th September 2010
Kilauea Volcano – Hawai'i   World Tree

Maggie encouraged me to visit the volcano on the Big Island in Hawai'i. She said that it was important for me to do this and, since all she wanted to do was sleep and rest, she insisted that I go. Once I knew that she was safe, comfortable and resting, I was able to relax my guard, for I had been nursing her for the last four days.

Because of the time restrictions, I was only able to book on a tourist trip, which flew to Big Island, where we were met by a tour guide from a local company. I needed to connect with Pele, the Goddess of the volcano, at Hawai'i. I knew that, because Hawai'i is part of the Pacific Ring of Fire, I would be able to connect with Yasur, the Kassosu and Yeramanu lineage at the World Tree.

We arrived at K'lauea Volcano. In the centre of this volcanic caldera was the active crater of Halema'uma'u. According to local legend and tradition, this was the place where the Goddess Pele lived. Because of the time restrictions of the tour, I was not able to sit and connect deeply with Pele, as I normally would have done, but I did make a connection with her. I felt really good about it because, whilst I was with the tribe in Vanuatu, no matter how much I tried to meditate and connect with the ancestors and spirits, I didn't receive any insights of any significance and I was unable to dream and have visions, as I normally did. This concerned me, for I wasn't really sure what was happening. Now that I had connected to Pele, I felt much better, because I knew that the magma which flowed beneath the earth connected me back to Yasur and all of the other volcanoes and their guardians on the Pacific Ring of Fire which I had visited in Papua, New Guinea, New Britain Island, New Zealand and Ecuador.

We also visited a site at the coast where the lava was spilling into the sea, causing copious quantities of steam and where a local town had been totally destroyed some time ago, buried under 60 feet of lava.

Somehow the guardians of these volcanoes became my family and I became one with them. Everything seemed to be interconnected with each other; all were our relations.

On the way back to the airport, our group was tired after hiking and, in the darkness and the silence of our journey, the movement of the vehicle rocked me and gently swayed me into a meditative state, where at last I could connect with Spirit, finding myself again at the jungle meeting place at the portal of the Kassosu. Before me I saw the rain forest illuminated in an eerie glow of blue-white light and beyond a vague image of Dragon Men and the World Tree. I connected to this amazing structure. This connection was very emotional, as though I had found my lost family, my true race, which was not of this world. I was instructed by the Dragon Men to reactivate the Yeramanu tattoo and given instructions on how to do this. This made following spirit connections with them more profound and intimate.

In and around this huge banyan tree lived a myriad of creatures not of this realm. Those in the canopy, upper and lower branches, trunk and roots were all living in their own worlds, their own dimensions and each stretched out further and further into timeless space. Deep beneath the World Tree was a volcanic lava lake and, within the magma, was Pele. I then received an insight: Pele was the Goddess of magma, she was deep within the earth; Yasur was the God of lava which was thrown up in explosive power into the air. I had never had this realisation before; a place of perfect balance. Pele seemed to manifest in different forms: the maiden, the woman and the crone. Yasur and Majikjiki seemed to be one and the same. Majikjiki rose from the lava and he wore a cloak of black and scarlet fire. He invited me into his realm, where I became eternal flame.

During the flight back to Honolulu, it was very quiet, people were subdued, there were very few passengers, and the drone of the aircraft engines and the movement through the element of air allowed me to drift off again into a meditative state.

Once more I connected to the portal, to the realms of the Kassosu and found myself within the shadow, the shelter of the World Tree and the myriad creatures and beings that were connected with it. As I looked into the lava lake, I saw that it was full of water and yet there was no physical interaction that you would expect in third dimensional consciousness, but then I kept reminding myself that I wasn't in third dimensional consciousness, so these laws did not exist.

It reminded me of a previous experience, when I connected to the Golden Order of the Dragon Sword. It all started to make sense, it all started to come together, the pieces of the jigsaw started to make a picture in my mind.

When I looked up into the World Tree, I saw waterfalls of different coloured light. I saw things that I could not explain, things that are not of this world. I saw portals that led out into a timeless universe to more portals and then even more portals. I realised that the Kassosu, even though they may well be at the lower end of spirit manifestation in physical reality, were guardians to the portal which led to things beyond my comprehension. I thought about the flying fox myth the Chief told me about. There is always a foundation of truth that a myth is built upon. I began to wonder, with this new insight of the union between the flying fox (fruit bat) and that woman who was brave enough to climb the banyan tree. The offspring of that union was half bat and half human. The Chief said that this was the first Yeramanu and he referred to the Kassosu as the Wild Spirit Men, the Bat Men or the Dragon Men.

With this knowledge, it sheds a new light on to the deity beings of ancient Egypt and other cultures, such as Hinduism. Egyptologists assume that the beings, such as Horus (who was part human, part falcon), Anubis (part human and part jackal), Thoth (part human and part ibis) and Bastet (part human and part cat) for example, were all symbolic. What of European beings, centaur (part human and part horse), mermaid (part human and part fish), satyr (part human and part goat), and what about vampires, werewolves and the Green Man? What if these beings were the offspring of the mating between other life forms and human beings? This brings a totally different understanding to deity consciousness. The other things which I began to understand was that, as I watched some of these beings, which were half human, half other level of consciousness, move, speak and dance, I suddenly received the insight that the snake dancers copied the movement of a particular being. The insight from this experience is that ancient tribal dance, song and music, perhaps ceremony also, is a reflection or a copy of non-human materialisation, whose arrival became our deity to be worshipped. It has been known in esoteric circles for generations that we are constantly visited by intra and extraterrestrial alien humanoid life forms. I believe we are about to witness physical materialisation now through different portals. I think that the average human being is almost ready to accept and take responsibility for this phenomenon, even though the governments of the worlds are trying to suppress it and stop it.

On my arrival back at the hotel late at night, I found Maggie sitting up in bed, watching TV. She looked much better and brighter, but she was still very poorly and very weak. The antibiotics had had a miraculous effect upon her thankfully. I knew instinctively that she needed a special type of female "medicine", which was retail therapy. The following day, which was our last day in Honolulu, I was able to help her out on to the street and into the sunlight for the first time, where, in a short distance, she was able to do some shopping and have a look at some of the markets. She had to sit on a regular basis, but we took our time and we sat beneath a huge ficus, a banyan-like tree, to have a drink and something to eat.

12th September 2010

Maggie was getting stronger daily. We left Honolulu, checking our bags in for Los Angeles, where we were to stay overnight. Unbeknown to us, the ticket clerk had checked our baggage in all the way to London, which meant that we were both in flimsy clothing for a hot climate. Maggie had no warm clothing to change into for the return leg of our flight back to the UK and the Isle of Man. We left brilliant blue skies and warm sunshine, arriving in the UK to a cold, windy, rainy day. Fortunately, as a surprise for Maggie, I had arranged for a car and driver to collect us from Heathrow airport to drive us the long distance to Gatwick airport for an overnight stay at a hotel. We were glad to get home the following day.

21st September 2010 – Autumn Equinox
Dragon Man

Early in the morning, I was lying with my arms wrapped around Maggie, dreaming about the connection to the Kassosu. Ordinarily, this would be potentially risky, since when you journey into other realms and dimensions, if you are in physical contact with another person, you can draw a soul part of theirs into the dream space. If they are not prepared for this, then there is a possibility that a soul fragment may be left behind, causing some level of soul loss or stress until it is returned. However, Maggie had connected with the Kassosu on several occasions, with the Chief's approval and knowledge, so I knew that, by holding her, she would be safe as an experienced dreamer. In other words: her soul was already familiar with the energy of the Kassosu and had already integrated with it, or been initiated into that level of awareness.

I saw and met a Dragon Man clearly (I am not permitted to disclose any information about him/her). After what seemed like half an hour of interaction, the Dragon Man spoke, 'There are two levels of consciousness of the Yeramanu. After the union between the kiri (flying fox) and the woman, twins were born. One twin was black and was more bat than human. The other twin was white and more human than bat. It is the white twin aspect that you need to connect with. Your brother's role (the Chief) is to connect with the other aspect, hence his fear. It is important that each of you connect with each aspect to enable a state of balance to occur for re-unification. This is why you were unable to fully connect with the black twin aspect. What you perceived as your brother's procrastination was, in fact, spirit intervention for your own safety. Neither of you were fully prepared and ready this time, but, should there be another opportunity, you will have a different experience. The twin aspects of the kiri and human hold different levels of consciousness. You hold the level of the upper realms, your brother the lower realms. Neither is more advanced or important than the other. Both are equal. Without one aspect, the other cannot function. Your role is to bring the higher level of the Yeramanu to your brother, so that he can ground it into the lower level. Everything is perfect. Be patient. You have been trying too hard to make contact with the Kassosu. This creates a tighter thought/mind pattern, closing the inner portals. Relax, allow, do not try to force or rush. You have been asking the wrong questions and have placed your focus and intent in the wrong place. The key to spirit communication is having the awareness to know what to ask for, otherwise you may draw to you that which you are not able to deal with. Your brother holds part of the secret of the Kassosu. You hold the other part, which you now need to reveal to him. Neither of you hold the full truth, but together you hold both halves.'

Maggie stirred and smiled. This realisation about the Kassosu came at one of the very times of perfect balance within the year, that of the Autumn Equinox, when day and night are equal times. Now is the time that the human race is ready and prepared for the coming of the enlightened children, the children who have perfect balance. No longer is there going to be duality as we understand it, but from this point there is the possibility of unity within the human race and all life.

22nd September 2010
Birth

At about seven minutes past midnight, the phone rang and it was Katrina, Maggie's daughter, who lives in Dubai, telling her that her waters had broken and her baby was on its way. She was in hospital and wanted her mother to be at her side. Maggie had already planned to be at her daughter's baby's birth, but the baby appeared to be coming about two weeks early, so we frantically packed and she was able to get standby flights from the Isle of Man to London and London to Dubai. Meanwhile, as she was flying to Dubai, word came through that Katrina had given birth to a baby girl, local time not long after midday, choosing her time to arrive at the Equinox, at the time of the full moon. Children like these are special and there are many of them now. These children will bring enlightenment, peace, love and truth. It is our job now to care for them, to respect and to honour them. They are our future. Our earth depends on them. We now have to prepare them for their roles as leaders in the community in the next few years.

May your skull grow moss.

The End

WARNING

Do not allow others to take your flesh, blood, body fluids, hair or nail parings, especially in a tribal culture, unless you know and trust those who are doing the ritual or ceremony. Those who wish to manipulate or devitalise your energy body can use these substances in sorcery to create soul loss.

Take care of disposing of such substances if someone is observing you, especially in Africa. Wash your own underwear and handkerchiefs, and dispose of sanitary wear sensibly if you are in areas known for their black magic.

Also, it is inadvisable to meditate when on public transport, or similar, unless precautions have been taken to create a safe dreaming space. Scanning your seat and the localised environment is essential to clear toxic psychic imprints and thoughtforms of previous travellers and their Astral attachments. There are occasions when you would NOT open yourself on any occasion. Use common sense and make sure you close down correctly and ground.

AFTERWORD

22nd October 2010

As I sat in meditation, I asked to be connected to the lineage keepers of the White Yeramanu. I found myself entering the great banyan tree at the upper nakamel at Itabu and, from within its interior, began to ascend quickly, until my awareness was just above the tree canopy. I began to feel as if I were expanding, and what the tree felt. I realised that I had shapeshifted. I was the tree!

I felt huge, powerful, strong and wise. A flock of flying foxes settled within my upper branches. I could feel the heaviness of their combined weight, hear their gossip. The banyan and flying foxes had initially been separate entities; now, in the stillness of their roost, the tree and flying foxes were one soul. We breathed and sighed at the same time.

I was aware that my energy was no longer restricted to this one tree. My roots extended through the dark earth to touch the roots of the other banyan trees, hundreds of yards apart. My ethereal branches reached through a myriad of portals into unknown levels of consciousness along with the other trees. We were not individual, separate trees, but rather one organism, parts of a whole, like the neural pathways of the brain. What was remarkable for me was that I FELT it!

I looked down at the earth and saw Chief Wai Wai looking up at me as he performed the Kassosu portal opening rite. My attention was then drawn across the tree canopies where, through a mist of sparkling Chi, a portal opened and, from within its mysterious depths, exploded two Dragons, one black, the other white. The Black Dragon spiralled downwards to the Chief. He ran for his life! The White Dragon skimmed the tree canopy, cascading Chi like a bow wave, landing in "my" branches. I felt his/her weight in my "arms".

The Chief had instructed me previously on how to recognise the Kassosu through a peculiar manifestation in their eyes. The White Dragon displayed this phenomenon. As an energetic resonance and entrainment took place, I became the Dragon Man, merging together as one. I was aware of the discomfort he/she endured through this process. I felt invincible, as though I had merged with an Archangel. Do the Kassosu belong to the hierarchy of Beings known sometimes as Earth Angels or Soul Shepherds, I wondered?

Then a different energetic entrainment took place. I now felt the Dragon Man was male. He also displayed markings similar to my tribal tattoos. He conveyed to me that both of our marks, or energetic signatures, had to realign for the completion of the lineage attunement. After some time, the markings on both of our right arms adjusted and the signature stabilised as the same. The problem was with the tattoo on my left arm. The bottom part was fine, but the top part was not holding the energetic charge and was leaking. This was because the tattooist did not hold the correct intent and focus whilst performing the work. I now have to have this mark redone to hold its energetic integrity, then try to realign later.

At this point, I saw the Black Dragon and the Chief merge as one successfully. I pondered upon this, as his tattoos were not complete; mine were. I received the reply that he already held the blood lineage, so it wasn't necessary. I did not.

What does the future hold? Will I take my place as an Earth Keeper through the lineage of the White Yeramanu or will I join the ranks of The Dragon Riders that patrol the portals of consciousness? Only time will tell as I prepare myself to return to Vanuatu to meet the Dragon Men in 2013.

High Chief Iarueri Rawi

APPENDIX A

CANNIBALISM

We are all descended from cannibals.

The last officially recorded cannibal feast in Vanuatu was in 1969 by the "Big Nambus" tribe at South West Bay, Malekula Island. There are unconfirmed reports of cannibalism as late as the early 1970s on Malekula and also in 1987 on Efate Island.

According to reports, only on Tanna Island were dead people eaten as part of their mortuary practices, providing they were not diseased. It goes without saying that they also participated in the traditional cannibalistic feasts.

In Malekula, the ritual of cooking a person was described thus – "We dig a hole in the ground and put in hot stones. The long pig (human) is cut into pieces and laid on the top. Yams and taro are added, then more hot rocks, which are covered by banana leaves and soil to keep the steam in. Standard baking time in the earth oven is three to five hours. The chief of the village always gets the head to eat. We killed people who stole our women or who came to fight us."

Most cannibalism was a result of tribal warfare or cruel slave traders and missionaries from Europe, who were eaten as revenge killings for stealing boys and young men. White people were considered too salty and tough, because of their diet. Some reports favour Orientals, as their diet made their flesh sweet. Many captives were hung in trees and their limbs hacked off as needed to eat or for trade.

Apart from the head, the choice cuts were from the inner upper arms, forearms, thighs, buttocks, palms of the hands and women's breasts. Everything was eaten, except the hair, teeth and nails.

Contrary to popular belief, cannibalism was a sacred, ritualistic practice, where the spirit of the deceased was honoured and revered.

Medicinal cannibalism was commonplace in Europe, especially Germany, up to the end of the 18th century, where doctors prescribed the consumption of human blood, brains, bone (powdered) and flesh in a variety of remedies, usually from cadavers.

APPENDIX B
HIGH CHIEF WAI WAI RAWI'S
FAMILY TREE

Systemic destruction of the tribal lineage keepers
by the Christian Church

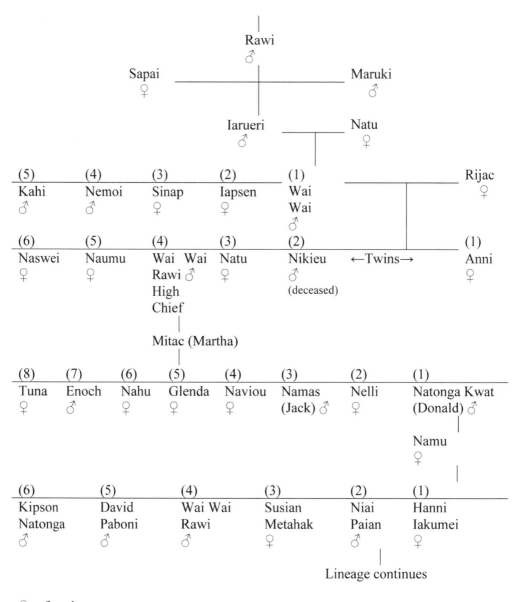

Rawi ♂

Sapai ♀ ———————————— Maruki ♂

Iarueri ♂ ——————— Natu ♀

(5)	(4)	(3)	(2)	(1)		Rijac
Kahi ♂	Nemoi ♂	Sinap ♀	Iapsen ♀	Wai Wai ♂		♀

(6)	(5)	(4)	(3)	(2)	←Twins→	(1)
Naswei ♀	Naumu ♀	Wai Wai Rawi ♂ High Chief	Natu ♀	Nikieu ♂ (deceased)		Anni ♀

Mitac (Martha)

(8)	(7)	(6)	(5)	(4)	(3)	(2)	(1)
Tuna ♀	Enoch ♂	Nahu ♀	Glenda ♀	Naviou ♀	Namas (Jack) ♂	Nelli ♀	Natonga Kwat (Donald) ♂

Namu ♀

(6)	(5)	(4)	(3)	(2)	(1)
Kipson Natonga ♂	David Paboni ♂	Wai Wai Rawi ♂	Susian Metahak ♀	Niai Paian ♂	Hanni Iakumei ♀

Lineage continues

♀ = female

♂ = male

228

APPENDIX C

CRYSTAL SKULL

The amethyst skull given to the High Chief was sent to me from the current caretaker of an ancient life-size, clear quartz skull, now in the U.S.A. The small amethyst skull was placed next to the large crystal skull, now known as "Synergy", for several days to be energised specifically for this rare ceremony in Vanuatu. It is suggested that "Synergy", although found in South America, actually originated from Melanesia (Vanuatu?).

"Synergy" can be traced back several thousand years with some reliability, making it one of the oldest crystal skulls known at this time. It is the size of a human skull. I have worked with "Synergy" in Avalon and I am informed that I was a previous skull keeper in a past life.

It is widely acknowledged in esoteric circles that there are supposed to be thirteen crystal skulls, each representing, amongst other things, a particular frequency or resonance of the strands of our ancient DNA, which was deactivated to prevent our species from reaching its full potential. When the twelve skulls are located and in position, the thirteenth will manifest to aid our collective spiritual ascension.

Each crystal skull usually has a nominated caretaker and, depending upon the energetic "mission" of the skull, a suitable name given which often denotes what the skull does. When the "mission" is completed, the skull frequency alters for the next phase, thereby changing its name and caretaker. The skull must be gifted freely to the next caretaker chosen.

Crystal skulls carry primordial memory of the collective consciousness of our race. They are programmed to hold and resonate specific imprints and codes. They are the ancient record keepers.

Maggie has also worked with an ancient crystal skull in Scotland.

APPENDIX D

SACRED CIRCLE OF ITABU (Masculine)

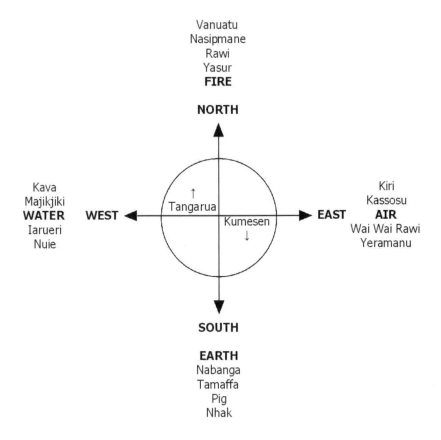

Key: Tangarua (above) – The original God man from the Stars.

          Kumesen (below) – The black twin that perpetuated the blood lineage who remained on Nhak.

East: The element of Air, the place from where the cyclones come.

          Wai Wai Rawi – Direct descendant of Kumesen, the black serpent and lineage holder of High Chief.

          Kassosu – Spirit bat men who emerge from the smoke of Yasur.

          Yeramanu – The original medicine man, the offspring between the mating of flying fox and humans. From the realms of Spirit.

          Kiri – Tribal name for the flying fox (fruit bats).

South: The element of Earth, towards the South Pole and Southern Cross, towards the moon.

Nabanga – Banyan tree. The World Tree connecting all of the spiritual realms, its branches reaching through portals inter-dimensionally, yet roots deep in the earth.

Tamaffa – Guardian spirit of the nakamal, the sacred earth/rain forest temple.

Pig – Principal tribal and cultural totem of primal power and courage. Digs in the ground. Sacrifical blood offered back to the earth.

Nhak – Tribal name for Tanna Island. The place where their ancestors' bones are buried.

West: The element of Water, towards the sacred mountains where most of the rains fall, feeding the waterfalls.

Iarueri – According to tribal myth, the descendant from the firstborn son of Tangarua, swept to the west on a tidal wave. The White Serpent. The White Twin.

Majikjiki – The firstborn son of Tangarua, Guardian of the Sacred Pool of Itabu. God of Nature.

Kava – Medicinal/teacher plant to aid communication with the ancestors; it is mixed and drunk in water.

Nuie – The Spirit Guardian of the Sacred Pool of Itabu.

North: The element of Fire, the place of the volcano and ash plains. Towards the equator and midday sun.

Yasur – "The Old Man", volcano, magma and lava. God, the Well of Souls where the dead depart to the ancestral realms.

Rawi – Last confirmed ancestor surviving the Christian genocide. Lineage of volcano guardianship.

Nasipmane – Name of the tribe, from the ancestors of Maruki and Rawi.

Vanuatu – The nation of many islands north of Tanna island.

GLOSSARY

AKASHA

Akasha is a place in the Angelic Realms where the records are deposited for planet Earth. It is a location. Akashic Records are a recording of all activities, thoughts and emotions of each individual soul who has experienced Earth conditions in any form. The records are deposited by the soul itself and it is an automatic process at each death.

ANCESTORS

The Ancestors are our predecessors, including the possibility of our own soul parts from past incarnations. We have ancestral blood line lineages and spiritual lineages. The connection to the Nasipmane tribe is part of my spiritual lineage with a high probability of a blood line lineage as an ancestor of that culture. Ancestral lineage is also held within the energetic genes and DNA as cellular memory.

BISLAMA

The English-based pidgin used through the archipelago. Originally evolved from the "business" English that was used by Europeans trading throughout the Pacific from about 1830 onwards. For the first time it allowed isolated communities speaking different languages to communicate with each other. Certain letters can be interchanged (for example: p and b, k and g, e and i) so Itabu can also be written as Itapu, or Etapu. Kipson (Donald's youngest son) can also be Gibson.

CEREMONY AND RITUAL

There is much confusion between the two and it is hard to distinguish clearly where the boundaries lie, if in fact there are any.

Ceremony and ritual are forms of acts, prayers and offerings. Tribal ceremony tends to be more intuitive and spontaneous under Spirit guidance, working in harmony with Nature.

Ritualistic practices are usually performed before, during or after ceremony. Ritual, therefore, is usually adherence to particular practices, following strict protocol, etiquette and cultural rules.

DREAMING

In the context of this book, dreaming is a term often used by shamans or meditators when they pass through the veil of illusion and enter the Other Worlds to communicate with Spirit through visions, auditory or kinaesthetic experiences.

EARTH OVEN

A traditional way of steaming and cooking food throughout the South Pacific Islands.

In Tanna, a platform of timber is placed on the earth, sometimes over a pit, with kindling, which can be very large for an important feast. Volcanic rocks are placed on this platform and smaller timbers cover these. The wood is lit, causing the stones to become red hot as they are eventually buried in the glowing embers.

The stones are raked out of the fire with sticks and rolled to a clean earth site or pit nearby. Banana and fern leaves are placed over the rocks and then the food, wrapped in banana leaves, placed on top of them. These packages are then covered by more banana and fern leaves and, with sticks, the earth is dug and thrown by hand on to the contents until a conical mound about three to four feet has been created. A kava leaf is placed in the top. When the kava leaf changes colour and wilts (steamed) the food is cooked. The mound is broken down and the hot food removed and unwrapped to eat.

JOHN FRUM CARGO CULT

No one knows for sure where or how the cult started, sometimes called Jon Frum. The main explanation is that the name stands for "John from America". During World War II, there was a huge influx of American troops in the islands, including black personnel. It is said that a black medical corps member, called John, handed out free medicine and "cargo" to the local people. He wore the red cross insignia, which is the symbol used for the cult today. Many cult members still wait for him to return with a plane full of free cargo for them. Their dances are military. All John Frum villages have red crosses at their boundary.

KASSOSU AND YERAMANU

The Chief also used the word Kassoso. To avoid confusion, I have used the same word throughout the book.

The Gods Yasur and Majikjiki have Kassosu aspects and, at times, seem to merge together as one. The Kassosu are the Wild Spirit Men, also referred to as Bat Men and Dragon Men. They are part flying fox (bat) and part human, in various forms, and began the lineages of the first Yeramanus (shamans). They have the ability to manifest and materialise through energetic portals into the physical world, with the aid of specific ritual.

Yeramanus were traditionally venerated and sometimes feared, as they were magicians. In modern times, they fulfil the role of priest and healer.

KAVA (Piper methysticum)

40 different subspecies. It is drunk throughout the Pacific Islands. Kava is an amalgam of up to 14 analgesics and anaesthetics with natural pain suppressant properties. It is also antibacterial and has diuretic and decongestant qualities. Locals use it against malaria and find it aids relaxation to communicate with the ancestors.

LAP LAP
Vanuatu's national dish. It is made by grating manioc, taro or yams into a glutinous paste, mixed with coconut milk. Pieces of meat may be added. The mixture is wrapped in leaves and tied with fine vines. The packages are then cooked in an earth oven.

LEGEND
An unverified popular story handed down through recent generations. Fact and fiction are usually woven into these stories, which tend to change with each narrator.

MAGMA AND LAVA
There are three types of magma: (a) liquid magma, usually a mixture consisting mostly of silicates; (b) magma containing gas, deep in the earth, where it is under great pressure (as the magma reaches the surface, pressure is reduced, forming bubbles and explosive activity); and (c) magma containing crystal solids in suspension.

How magma is formed is dependent on local tectonic activity and conditions, where the rock becomes molten and is forced under extreme pressure through cracks and fissures. Some reach the surface through different types of volcanoes, others form into huge magma chambers beneath the ground.

When the magma reaches the surface, it is called lava.

MYTH
A traditional, pictorial story, usually originating in an ancient pre-literate society, dealing with Gods, supernatural beings, ancestors and heroes that serve as primordial types in a primitive view of the world. Myths are stories containing a veiled message or teaching, which tend to be kept in their original form, so often have a foundation of truth.

NAMBAS
Penis sheaths worn by most kastom men, especially during ceremonies or at kava rituals at the nakamals. These are made of a variety of plant fibres or leaves, such as hibiscus, pandanus or banana. The penis is either tied tightly between the rolled fibres and the belly or tied inside the roll and is a symbol of phallic fertility and virility. Some of the tribes in the Northern Islands and Papua, New Guinea wear bamboo or wooden nambas. They are often dyed different colours, depending on the plant material used.

PANDANUS
Sometimes called "screw pine" because of the coiled shape of its slender stems. It is palm-like. The leaves are used for weaving into mats and other items.

STORY TELLERS

The story tellers and song writers held a venerated position in tribal life and came from a select lineage, similar to the Druidic Bards of our ancestors.

The story tellers kept a mental record of the lineages of the chiefs and their ancestors for centuries, plus the myths and legends of their culture which, when told in the correct way, enabled the listeners to become part of the living story through shamanic dreaming at some level. Stories are, therefore, spiritual food which feeds the souls of the listeners as well as the teller for, during these sessions, portals are opened to the ancestors to enable them to communicate directly to those assembled. In modern language, these story tellers were gifted seers and mediums. For this reason, as with all indigenous tribal peoples worldwide, the Establishment, ie Church and Governments would actively target these souls for assassination, torture, incarceration or slave labour. If a people no longer know who they are, they become leaderless, fragmented and vulnerable, so open to exploitation, humiliation and degradation.

TAFEA
This province gets its name from Vanuatu's five most southerly populated islands – Tanna, Aniwa, Futuna, Erromango and Aneityum.

TAM TAM
Very large carved wooden slit-drums, set into the earth at a particular angle to aid playing. Originally used to send coded messages to nearby villages. The drum is beaten with a heavy stick causing the sound to travel long distances. Ordinary skin drums cannot be used in hot, humid conditions as the skin becomes slack, moist and mouldy.

TRISKELE
The ancient sun symbol in the form of the three legs (Triskele) being the national badge of the Kingdom of Mann. It is unclear how the Isle of Man obtained this powerful symbol – some suggest either via the Vikings from Scandinavia or from Sicily via Alexander III when the island was part of Scotland. Occultists believe the symbol came from Atlantis. In the northern hemisphere it spins clockwise; in the southern hemisphere anticlockwise, following the motion of the sun. It is the symbol of Manannan, God of the Isle of Man. It is also the secret symbol of the tribal creation myth.

THE WHITE HEADHUNTER
>by Nigel Randell. Constable. ISBN 1-84119-601-0.
>Highly recommended.

SANGOMA
>by James Hall. Tarcher/Putnam. ISBN 0-87477-780-1.

INITIATION
>by Elizabeth B Jenkins. Piatkus. ISBN 0-7499-1798-9.

ZULU SHAMAN
>by Vusamasulu Credo Mutwa. Destiny Books. ISBN 0-89281-129-3.

FOUNDATION FOR INSPIRATIONAL AND ORACULAR STUDIES (FIOS)
Co-founded by John and Caitlin Matthews and Felicity Wombwell, offers a progressive shamanic practicioner training programme.
For details of curriculum and current courses, see:

www.hallowquest.org.uk or BCM Hallowquest, London, WC1N 3XX, U.K.

SPIRIT VISIONS
>Training courses, drums, music, etc on Celtic Shamanism
>Founded by Barbara Meiklejohn-Free.

>www.spiritvisions.co.uk or www.barbarameiklejohnfree.com

THE BRITISH SOCIETY OF DOWSERS
>Training courses, books and dowsing equipment.

>www.britishdowsers.org or info@britishdowsers.org

>Tel: 01684 576969

THE FELLOWSHIP OF ISIS (FOI)
An international organisation dedicated to honouring the Goddess in Her many forms. Founded by the Baron Strathloc and Olivia Robertson.
Iseums, Lyceums, Groves and Priories.
Training and books.

www.fellowshipofisis.com

PATHWAY TEACHING
    Shamanic training courses in Ireland. Founded by Paul O'Halloran.

    www.pathwayteaching.com or paul@pathwayteaching.com

    Tel: ROI: + 353 (0)86 8525529

HIGH CHIEF WAI WAI RAWI
    (Itabu Village)
    P O Box 85
    Lenakel
    Tanna
    Vanuatu
    Please enclose a self-addressed envelope and International Reply Coupon.

DAVID LEESLEY
For those who wish to contact the author, please direct all enquiries via the publisher.

AUTHOR'S PROFILE

David was born on the Isle of Man (British Isles) and, after gaining horticultural qualifications, emigrated to Australia in 1974. Whilst on a Trans African Expedition in 1976, he had an "out of body" experience at Nyiragongo Volcano, Zaire (Congo). This led him to realise his future path as a healer.

David trained at the Royal Melbourne Hospital in the Department of Anatomical Pathology in 1979 and undertook several ornithological expeditions to remote areas of the world to study with indigenous tribes. He was elected as a Fellow of the Royal Geographical Society in 1983.

In 1984, David received an official government citation for creating the first registered private Bird Sanctuary and Nature Reserve on the Isle of Man.

In 1988, he began professional training as a healer in various disciplines of complementary medicine, especially shamanism and dowsing, in both the UK and Australia.

In 2007, David was elected as a Fellow of the Royal Anthropological Institute and, in 2008, ordained as a priest in the Fellowship of Isis.

David is a registered tutor with the British Society of Dowsers and is a Knight of The Noble Order of Tara.